American Dreamer

American Dreamer

How I Escaped Communist Vietnam and Built a
Successful Life in America

**Tim Tran
(Tran Manh Khiem)**

with **Tom Fields-Meyer**

PACIFIC
UNIVERSITY
PRESS

FOREST GROVE, OREGON

PACIFIC UNIVERSITY PRESS
2043 College Way
Forest Grove, Oregon 97116

Cover design by Alex Bell

Cover image inspired by a photograph of Vietnamese refugees from the Jesuit Refugee Service (The Legacy of Jesuit Father Pedro Arrupe, 13 November 2013)

ISBN 978-1-945398-02-5 (pbk)
ISBN 978-1-945398-03-2 (ePub)
ISBN 978-1-945398-04-9 (mobi)

While this book recounts actual events and describes real people, some names and identifying details have been changed to protect the privacy, identity, and safety of individuals. It is also important to note that memories are subject to the passage of time and the limitations of the human mind, and we apologize for any inadvertent inaccuracies.

Published in the United States of America

First Edition

To the memory of my parents, who instilled in me the ethics of hard work, patience, and perseverance.

To the memory of John M. Shank, founder and president of Johnstone Supply, Inc. — my tough boss, kind mentor, and good friend.

Table of Contents

Preface

I have had an interesting and eventful life. Over the years, many friends have encouraged me to write my story, but the arduous work of composing a lengthy, complex memoir and the difficult task of publishing it discouraged me. Recently, though, I realized that I had an important story to tell.

I dedicate my story to my adopted country, the United States of America, which provided refuge and support to me, a once-penniless refugee, a "man without a country."

I also dedicate this book to my American countrymen and the memory of the more than fifty-eight thousand men and women who made the ultimate sacrifice and whose names are inscribed on the Vietnam Veterans Memorial in Washington DC; to the more than one million South Vietnamese soldiers who died in the war; to the millions of civilians—in both North and South Vietnam—killed in the conflict; and to the approximately half-million South Vietnamese and ethnic Chinese who lost their lives while trying to escape communism.

I also feel that I owe it to my fellow Vietnamese Americans—to the next and future generations—to share my story.

I always had a love for America from my early childhood. Since I returned to the US as a refugee after spending time here as a student and became a naturalized citizen, my love for this country and its people has deepened. As one who has received so much from this country, I owe it an enormous debt. And as a relatively new citizen of this great nation, I want to give back as much as I can. What I can give, in truth, is just a small token compared to what I owe.

Despite the many challenges that our country faces (there are always challenges), I always look forward with optimism and believe that America's best days lie ahead.

I wanted to share my life story: my experiences, my successes, and my failures. This is my personal story, the story of an underprivileged third-world kid whose life was shaped by a proxy war between superpowers. I became a toddler refugee from Communism at the tender age of four, navigated through a treacherous and tough life, and ultimately survived to live the American dream in the greatest country on earth.

It is a story of hard work, of valuing education as the means of pulling yourself up by the bootstraps. It is a story of sheer perseverance and good luck. It is a story of preparation meeting once-in-a-lifetime opportunity and producing success. My story could only happen in our beloved America.

I must thank all of the people who have touched my life in beneficial ways. Some are mentioned in this book, but there simply wasn't enough room for everyone or every detail. They know who they are and how they helped me. I owe each of them a debt of gratitude, and I hope they accept my apology for not including them. I have one promise: if this book is well received and a sequel is warranted, I will include more of my benefactors' names and teachable stories next time around.

As I write these words, I feel glad that the relationship between Communist Vietnam and the United States has vastly improved in recent years. The two former adversaries have reconciled and are building closer and warmer ties. I hope that the Communist victors will reconcile with their fraternal, vanquished brothers, the former soldiers of the Army of the Republic of Vietnam, giving them the honor and dignity they deserve.

Acknowledgments

I thank Lesley Hallick, president of Pacific University, and her staff for setting in motion the work of writing my memoir. I thank Isaac Gilman, Dean of University Libraries, for managing this project and introducing me to my co-author, Tom Fields-Meyer. I thank Tom for his guidance, encouragement, and patience in working with me on this book. Tom has been a writer, a collaborator, and a friend. I thank my wife, Cathy, for her support during the course of writing this book as well as the support she has given me throughout our marriage of forty-five years.

A Note about Vietnamese Names

This book follows the traditional style for Vietnamese personal names: a family name, followed by a middle name, followed by a given name. Thus, my full name, in Vietnamese style, is written as Tran Manh Khiem: Tran is my family name, Manh my middle name, and Khiem my given name.

Prologue

May 1979

This was not how my life was supposed to end. And yet it was difficult to imagine any other outcome.

The boat was a flimsy wooden fishing vessel that might have safely carried forty passengers. More than three hundred of us were packed aboard, on the deck and down below, our bodies pressed together so tightly that it was difficult for anyone to move. We had set out six days earlier for what should have been a voyage of three days—four, tops.

Then came the sea pirates, one band after another of Thai fishermen who had discovered that robbing desperate refugees at knifepoint was easier and more profitable than reeling in mackerel all day. The bandits seized our valuables first—gold, jewelry, cash in various currencies—and then, later, stripped from our bodies anything of even marginal value.

Worst of all, the scoundrels went after our meager food and water supply, slashing bags of rice and puncturing countless water jugs in their search for loot, leaving us in the intense May heat with virtually no fresh water. And then they sabotaged the fuel reserves, rendering one engine useless and the other barely functional.

There, somewhere in the endless waters of the Gulf of Thailand, our boat simply floated, directionless.

Just a few years earlier, my future had looked promising and limitless. I had earned a degree from a prestigious American university. I had landed an executive position at a large international petroleum company that assured me a rapid path to promotion. I had planned to marry the love of my life.

Then everything changed. For four painful years, I had done everything in my power to escape Communist Vietnam. All of those efforts had culminated in this voyage: finally, I had managed to board this boat, feeling, for the first time in years, a sense of hope.

Now that hope was fading. With no water or food, nearly everyone onboard sat in silence, trying to conserve what little energy we had left.

The only sounds I could hear were the water lapping against the boat's hull and the low roar of the lone working engine. From near the center of the deck, I gazed out at the mass of bodies—still, silent, weak.

This was not how I was supposed to die.

And then, precisely at the moment when my last trace of hope vanished, just when I was resigned to meet my death at sea on this floating ghost village, I heard a man's weak voice piercing the deadly silence.

"I see a mountain!" he was saying. "I see land!"

Part One

The Early Years

Four-Year-Old Refugee

My earliest memory is of standing on a boat, feeling terribly seasick and throwing up. The year was 1954. I was four years old. The boat was heading from the port of Haiphong, on the northern coast of Vietnam, toward Saigon. I was with my mother and father, bound for a new life.

Before then, I had known only Ho Doi, the small coastal village where I was born in the Thai Binh province's Thuy An district, situated on the Red River delta on the Gulf of Tonkin, a region known for its rice, silk, and seafood. Like almost everyone else in the village, my family lived in a house with a thatched roof and mud walls. Every few years, typhoons would sweep through and level most of the village's structures, and then people would rebuild.

My father's father, Nguyen Dinh Giang, was among the wealthiest people in the village. With my grandmother, Thi Hot, he owned a spread of a few acres where they farmed rice and mulberries. The family also tended to a herd of several dozen water buffalo.

My father was born Nguyen Dinh Muu in 1928, the second of four children. (He had an older brother and two younger sisters.) He was quiet and studious, though like most boys in the village, he went to school only through fifth or sixth grade.

At eighteen, he married my mother, Nguyen Thi Noi, who was two years his senior and the third of four children. Her parents were less affluent than his, working the land like most of their neighbors.

Weddings in Vietnam weren't romantic affairs. The bride's and groom's parents simply came to an agreement about marrying off their children, who often barely knew each other before the marriage. Once married, the wife was considered part of the husband's family, which had gained a laborer.

With no desire to fulfill his destiny of working the land and running the family rice farm, my father soon left the village to join thousands of other young people in the Viet Minh, the nationalist movement led by Ho Chi Minh, which was fighting for Vietnam's independence from France.

He saw it purely as a nationalist struggle, employing guerilla tactics to attack French installations. With only meager supplies of ammunition, the group used surprise attacks and overwhelming numbers to cause as many casualties as possible and then quickly withdrew before the French could send in reinforcements.

My father fought for the cause for a couple of years before coming to the realization that, while pushing for independence, the movement was hiding its Communist ideology. Like thousands of other patriotic youths who had joined the Viet Minh, he wanted no part of Communism, so he left the movement and, not wanting to return to work the family farm, fled to Hanoi. Fearing the Communists might track him down and punish him for going AWOL, my father, like many others fighting for independence from France, changed his name—from Nguyen Dinh Muu to Tran Duy Tinh. (Tran is the second most common Vietnamese surname, after Nguyen.) To further conceal his identity, he even changed his birthday. In Hanoi, he worked as a manual laborer and later as a tutor for the children of wealthy families. He returned to the village occasionally to visit my mother.

I was born in 1950. Since it was a home birth in a rural village, there was no birth certificate and my birth date was never recorded. In Vietnamese culture, we don't celebrate birthdays and the date of one's birth is considered inconsequential. We do commemorate the anniversary of a person's death, however.

The year 1954 turned out to be a watershed year for Vietnam. After eight years of fighting the French, Viet Minh forces emerged victorious in the battle of Dien Bien Phu. That led to the Geneva Conference, a meeting of representatives from Vietnam, Cambodia, the United States, the USSR, China, France, and several other countries to settle outstanding issues following the First Indochina War. That July, the Geneva Accords called for the French to withdraw their troops from northern Vietnam. They also established a provisional military demarcation line, dividing North Vietnam from South Vietnam at approximately the 17th parallel. The North would be controlled by the Communists, backed by the Soviet Union and China, while the South would be controlled by the nationalists, supported by the French and Americans. The agreements allowed a three-hundred-day grace period, ending on May 18, 1955, during which people could move freely between the two Vietnams before the border was sealed. The partition between North and South was intended to be temporary, pending elections in 1956 to reunify the country under a nationally elected government.

That meant people in both the North and the South had to decide: Should they stay in place? Should they move? What were the risks? What were the dangers? Was it worth leaving all that they knew—their homes, their loved ones, their ancestral graves, and their lifestyles—for an unknown future in the other half of the country?

What made the decision even more difficult was that both sides engaged in propaganda. The US Navy supplied most of the boats transporting northerners from the port of Haiphong to the South. The boats were flat-bottomed landing crafts equipped with flat ramps in the bow to load and unload passengers and cargo. (Some wealthy people were able to make the trip by air, flying from Gia Lam Airport in Hanoi to Saigon, but for most, the only option was traveling by sea.) The Communists put out propaganda to scare people out of fleeing the North with ominous warnings that boarding the "open-mouthed" boats posed significant risk: the Americans would rob refugees of their possessions, then dump them out into the sea. At the same time, the French waged their own campaign to encourage Catholics from the North to move south. Their slogan: "Christ has gone south."

At the time, my father was working in Hanoi. He sent word to my mother to bring me and meet him at the port of Haiphong, about fifty kilometers from our village. He was eager to leave. He had chosen to abandon the Communist cause, and now that the Communists were gaining power in the North, he feared for his life. The choice to leave home wasn't easy for my mother, who knew she might never again see her parents, her siblings, or her village of Ho Doi. She understood she might never return to Thai Binh.

Despite that, when my father sent word, my mother did as he requested: she left the village, carrying me, and made her way to Haiphong. There, the three of us boarded a landing craft along with dozens of other families, all of us leaving the only lives we knew for the new and unknown. We were part of a massive migration: in all, some one million northerners would move south, while one hundred thousand southerners relocated to the North.

Our boat was bound for Saigon, my father's intended destination, with some stops along the way. The landing craft moved through the water at a very low speed and being overloaded with refugees made it even slower. It was particularly uncomfortable in high seas, and at four years old I simply wasn't accustomed to that kind of motion. Not surprisingly, I suffered terrible seasickness. After a journey of several days and some 1,300 kilometers, the boat docked at Nha Trang, then a relatively small fishing village in the central part of Vietnam. Tired of contending with a retching toddler, my father decided that we should disembark there.

Nha Trang

In Nha Trang, we found ourselves among a significant contingent of other refugees. From the very beginning, the government of the American- and French-backed State of Vietnam was welcoming and accommodating. President Ngo Dinh Diem was aware that the refugees had made the choice to leave the Communist North and cast our lots with the South, so he made great efforts to take care of us—with considerable help from the United States.

Our first home in Nha Trang was a tent in a refugee camp, provided by the government as part of South Vietnam's refugee-resettlement program. The government also gave us a daily food ration and some money to cover basic needs. For the first time, I tasted cheese, which came in cylindrical metal tins bearing the insignia of USAID, the United States Agency for International Development. Dairy products weren't a typical part of the Vietnamese diet, except among French-educated people who ate haute cuisine. Cows and water buffalo were used not for milk but for labor. (As the joke went, in rural Vietnam, we didn't butcher a cow until the odometer read one hundred thousand kilometers.) The people distributing food in Nha Trang cut the large chunks of cheese into smaller pieces and made sure the children got to eat first. It was an unfamiliar taste, but I found it filling and delicious.

My parents were industrious people who had no intention of depending on government aid for survival. Not long after we arrived in Nha Trang, my mother took it upon herself to start earning money as a food vendor, preparing che, a sweet dessert soup, and xoi, a sweet rice dish, and selling the foods in nearby neighborhoods. She would rise at 2 or 3 a.m. to prepare the food, then leave the house around 5 a.m. balancing a don ganh, a bamboo pole, on one shoulder with a basket of her prepared foods hanging from each end. She carried the freshly cooked foods through residential areas, calling out to announce her arrival just as families were waking up, ready for breakfast. Her efforts brought in money to support our family. Meanwhile, my father worked odd jobs—any work he could find.

After about a year, my parents had accumulated enough savings to move out of the refugee camp and rent a more permanent home, a small thatched-roof hut that was situated behind a large pagoda, in the shade of a towering banyan tree. In the mornings, the Buddhist monks who lived at the pagoda would walk the streets carrying bowls into which people would place food donations. Sometimes when the monks had extra, they would share it with me.

We lived that way for two years, from 1954 to 1956. In 1955, my mother gave birth to my oldest sister. They named her Thanh Binh, which means "calm and peaceful." The name reflected my parents' feelings about that time in our family's life. After my father's years as a Viet Minh guerilla and the upheaval of leaving our home, in Nha Trang we had found, at least for a time, a respite from violence and danger.

Not long after Binh's birth, we got more good news. My father landed a job as a civil servant in Tay Ninh, an inland province adjacent to the Cambodian border. It was a promising opportunity, a clerical position with the provincial bureau of the South Vietnamese Treasury Department. In 1956, our family of four relocated to Tay Ninh, traveling first by rail and then on provincial buses.

It was my first time on a train, and at age six, I still wasn't accustomed to moving vehicles. Again I experienced motion sickness, and my poor father had to apologize to the unfortunate fellow passenger whose trousers bore the brunt of my nausea.

Tay Ninh

The terrain in Tay Ninh was a marked contrast from the coastal town from which we had come. The small town was surrounded by dense jungle full of wild animals. Many of the residents earned a living by gathering wood in the forest, then selling it as firewood. These gatherers would depart the village early in the morning and return in the afternoon carrying loads of wood on their backs. Sometimes they also returned with monkeys they had hunted as game. Not long after we arrived, news spread through town that one of the wood collectors had fallen victim to a vicious tiger. Haunted by that story, I avoided venturing into the jungle on my own, though I did hear adults share advice about what you should do if a tiger grabbed you: squeeze it by the testicles until it let you go!

Our living quarters were also a step up from the tent and hut we had shared in Nha Trang. In Tay Ninh our family lived in an apartment in the Treasury Department's compound. It was a French colonial building with a brick facade and tile roof. Originally it had probably housed French nationals, but our neighbors were other Vietnamese people, all families of Treasury Department employees. Though this new home was certainly an improvement over anywhere I had lived, the buildings lacked central plumbing. Our water came from outdoor wells, and we used outhouses.

I quickly made friends with the other children living in our building and the adjacent structures. My mother did caution me to steer clear of one particular girl, the young daughter of the provincial Treasury Department's top official, my father's ultimate boss, who lived in the large villa in the compound. Perhaps my mother worried that I might get into a conflict that could escalate from children to adults and cause my father trouble at work.

Tay Ninh was also where my father started tutoring me in reading, writing, and mathematics. Though his own education had gone only through fifth grade, he loved reading and greatly valued education. Although he grew up in a farming family, my father was physically weak and preferred to use his brain rather than his hands and muscles, and he must have seen great potential in me. He didn't use books to teach me, just pieces of paper and pencils or pens, except for a multiplication table he had torn from the back of a textbook, which he used to drill me on multiplication. Before I ever set foot in a classroom, I could read and write, add, subtract, multiply, and divide. Most importantly, my father instilled in me at that early age proper study habits, constantly reminding me to finish all of my daily homework before I did anything else.

My father also taught me by example. In his job as a clerk, he mostly copied documents by hand for his boss at the Treasury Department. But when he realized that being able to type might help him to advance, he took it upon himself to learn to type, eventually becoming so proficient that it qualified him for a higher salary. He was a self-made man, having advanced from common laborer to clerk to typist. He was happy in his work and earned enough that my mother was able to stop selling food at the market and focus on our growing family, which now included my second sister, born in Tay Ninh, whom they named Xuan Thao. The name—literally, "springtime shoot of grass"—reflected my parents' feelings of renewed optimism and hope.

By the time I formally started school, at age seven, I was already a grade or so ahead of my peers at Tay Ninh's elementary school, which was housed in a modest structure with a handful of rooms. Since my father had prepared me so well, I found school to be easy and enjoyable. He would not allow me to go out and play with my friends until I had completed the assignments that he had created for me. Sometimes I wasn't finished until seven o'clock in the evening. Why only me? I sometimes wondered. Why don't my playmates' parents give them homework?

Our years in Tay Ninh were peaceful, calm, and happy. The country's economy was growing. Our neighbors all had jobs that paid adequately. I didn't think about the past, and I didn't dream of much beyond finishing elementary school and passing the fifth-grade exam.

There was even time for road trips. My father's boss at the treasury once took my father and me along with his family on a drive to visit Angkor Wat, the famous temple in Cambodia. We were able to cross the Cambodian border with ease. It was such a peaceful and conflict-free time that we made the round trip of some seven hundred kilometers without incident.

Back in Tay Ninh, we children could wander and run free and use the open fields for barefoot soccer games. I wasn't much of a player, but I liked to watch the local team compete against teams from neighboring provinces. Once a month, the local municipality would use the same fields to screen movies about current events on an improvised outdoor screen while the locals would spread out on bamboo mats to watch. The screening was always preceded by South Vietnam's national anthem and then the Vietnamese version of "Hail to the Chief," in honor of President Diem. Everyone had to stand at attention until the anthems ended.

Then came the feature, usually a newsreel lasting between fifteen minutes and an hour. One month it featured President Diem touring the Mekong Delta after a flood, and the footage showed how the United States had sent food and blankets to aid victims of the disaster. Another time the report was about Vietnam receiving a navy destroyer from the United States at the port of Saigon.

One film report that caught my attention was about a young elephant that had been captured in the province of Tuy Hoa in the highlands of central Vietnam. The elephant was presented as a gift to the American aid mission, which was planning to transport the animal, now named Tuy Hoa, to a zoo in the United States. I didn't know at the time that this was not the last I would hear of this animal.

Most of the movies were about the news, usually in the form of propaganda aimed at cultivating pro-government sentiment. I would sit with my father and sometimes a few of his friends, enjoying the cool evening breeze while I caught glimpses of life beyond our small town.

The movies rarely mentioned anything outside of Vietnam, except for the various ways the United States and other countries were offering aid to South Vietnam. There might have been a thirty-second mention of the opening of the United Nations General Assembly, but aside from that, it was all Vietnam. Our family couldn't afford a radio, but the family of one of the more senior treasury officials owned one, and I occasionally caught the sound of music, news, or the national anthem playing just before the station's sign-off at the end of the evening.

Our history lessons in school always emphasized President Diem's role as our country's savior, building him up as South Vietnam's founding father. Our teachers covered history dating back thousands of years, through multiple dynasties, but presented all of it as the long prelude to President Diem's heroic stand against Communism. If we learned about the United States, it was about how President Eisenhower was helping to keep South Vietnam safe from the threat of Communism.

When the Geneva Accords had called for Vietnam to be split in half, the arrangement was intended to be temporary, pending the results of elections that were to take place in 1956. But the South Vietnamese delegation to Geneva never signed the agreement because President Diem knew that he stood little chance of winning an election that would pit him against Ho Chi Minh, the popular and charismatic leader of North Vietnam, who was credited with liberating Vietnam from the French. Many Vietnamese failed to see that Ho Chi Minh was a champion of Communism and that that could have a devastating impact on the country. Furthermore, North Vietnam's population was 14.7 million compared to South Vietnam's 12.4 million, so a southerner had little chance of prevailing at the polls. So, in 1955, President Diem canceled the election and declared that South Vietnam was the independent Republic of Vietnam. President Eisenhower immediately recognized the new nation. Meanwhile, throughout South Vietnam, Communist sympathizers, known as Viet Cong, were quietly establishing sleeper cells, groups of warriors who were infiltrating the society and secretly preparing themselves for a looming civil war.

As a child, I was largely shielded from these developments, but my father was keenly aware of the situation and felt strongly that Saigon, the seat of the government, would be the safest place for our family. In 1958, when I was eight years old, he landed a job as a civilian typist for the office of the Joint General Staff of the South Vietnamese military.

That meant we had to relocate again, this time to Saigon. It wasn't a difficult move, since our family owned few significant possessions. My parents packed what little they had into two suitcases, and the five of us boarded an interprovincial bus. My parents each carried one of my sisters, and I, the eldest child, followed along. Somebody tossed the bags on the rack atop the bus, and we set off for a new life.

Moving to Saigon

It took less than four hours to travel from Tay Ninh to Saigon. Upon arriving, I felt overwhelmed by everything I saw: the multistory buildings; the streets, congested with bicycles, motorcycles, some automobiles, and countless pedestrians. My parents rented a tiny house in a modest suburb near Tan Son Nhat Airport that was populated mostly by Catholic families who had relocated from the North in the migration four years earlier.

My school experience was a marked contrast to my years in Tay Ninh's small and intimate elementary school. Saigon was a crowded, overpopulated city, and the local public elementary school, Truong Minh Giang Elementary School, which went through fifth grade, had so many students that they attended in separate shifts—there were four three-hour sessions each day. My parents enrolled me in the earliest shift, which ran from 6 a.m. to 9 a.m. That meant I had to rise around five each morning to walk the mile or so to school.

Even with the multiple shifts, the classrooms were crowded, with sixty or seventy students in a single class. We were packed in so closely that our bodies were touching. The tropical heat didn't make conditions any easier: the school's lone ceiling fan was in the principal's office. At least in the early morning the day's intense heat hadn't set in yet. No matter the conditions, my classmates and I didn't complain. It was the only life we knew.

Just as in Tay Ninh, I found school relatively easy because my father had prepared me so well. And finishing each day by 9 a.m. meant that I had the rest of the day to do the more advanced homework my father continued to assign me.

Some of my more important lessons came outside of school as I learned about the realities of the world around me. Every day I passed a private Catholic school on my walk to school. One day, I noticed that every student emerging from that school was carrying a loaf of bread. I stopped one boy to ask where all the bread was coming from.

He answered without hesitation: "Oh, our school gives us bread all the time."

It was one of my first encounters with religious discrimination. President Diem's regime favored Catholics over Buddhists. I learned later that the government had been taking flour provided by the US and channeling it exclusively to Catholic schools instead of distributing it equally to all of the schools.

That discrimination took other forms as well. My mother had a cousin who served as a first lieutenant in the South Vietnamese army. After seven years' service, he still had the same rank. Why? The military had passed him over for promotion because he was a Buddhist.

About a year after we arrived in Saigon, my father purchased a small home for our family in the Phu Nhuan district, an area on the outskirts of Saigon, again not far from Tan Son Nhat Airport. When we first moved in, it was one of five attached homes sitting on a swath of farmland owned by an absentee French national. The house was a simple, one-room structure with wooden walls, a tile roof, and a cement foundation.

My father chose the lot on the east end of the development so that we would have sunlight in the morning rather than baking under the afternoon sun. The front portion was a living area with a dining table. The middle portion had two beds. The kitchen in the back had two wood-burning stoves: one for rice, one for other foods. At first, we shared a communal outhouse, but soon, my father hired workers to build us our own toilet and to dig a well from which we drew water every day.

Here in Saigon, my family grew to include my two younger brothers—Khoi born in 1958 and Khoa in 1959—and my sister Mai, born in 1961. Our neighbors were a diverse lot. One nearby family was headed by a French man married to a Vietnamese woman. Their three children spoke both Vietnamese and—when they wanted to tell secrets—French. Another neighbor was an intercity bus driver, and others were businesspeople or laborers. A first lieutenant in the South Vietnamese army purchased the largest empty lot near ours. Watching him gave me my first lesson in corruption. For months after he acquired the land, I routinely saw American-made military GMC trucks delivering construction materials to his lot: sand, cement, brick, stone, and gravel. Uniformed soldiers would unload materials and do construction work on the home. He was only a first lieutenant, but he was utilizing government supplies and free government labor to build his own private home. Another neighbor headed the forensic division of South Vietnam's national police force. I would some-times see a high-end police Jeep-like vehicle arrive at the house and drop off the man and his mistress. A few hours later, they would emerge, get back in the automobile, and head back to his workplace.

LBJ and Me

Most school days were the same, but some were special. In May 1961, the entire city was excited about the news that Lyndon Johnson, the American vice president, would be visiting Saigon to meet with President Diem and tour the city. What I didn't understand at that early age was the reason for Johnson's visit: a war was about to begin—a conflict that would change everything. With training and equipment from the American military, President Diem's South Vietnamese army had been cracking down on the Viet Cong in rural areas. And North Vietnamese troops had begun to travel clandestinely on the Ho Chi Minh Trail to infiltrate the South and smuggle ammunition to the Viet Cong guerillas.

Without knowledge of the looming war, my classmates and I found Johnson's visit simply thrilling. Our teachers announced that we would be helping to welcome him, with the thousands of others lining the route as his motorcade made its way from the airport into town. They instructed all of us students to dress up: white shirt, navy blue trousers or shorts. They gave us each two small paper flags, one South Vietnamese, one American. Then they loaded us into a school bus. That alone was a big deal! The entire Saigon school district owned only two American-made school buses. Every student traveled to school on foot or by bicycle, with the possible exception of a few children of prominent government officials, who might have been driven in automobiles. The vice president's visit was the first time most of us had ridden in a school bus, and as it happened, this bus was so new that it still smelled of fresh paint and materials.

We left school early, and the bus delivered us to a stretch of road called Cong Ly Boulevard, just outside the gates of the airport. There I stood in the crowd lining the road, in the hot sun, feeling increasingly thirsty, sweaty, and weary—but also full of anticipation. After a long wait, suddenly I heard the rumbling of motorcycles and watched as a police escort zoomed by, followed by a few automobiles. Finally came the car with Vice President Johnson, his window lowered. I could swear, as he sped by, he looked directly at me and waved. As a fourth grader, I had never even caught sight of President Diem, so it felt worth all the waiting and sweating to have the chance to stand there in my white shirt and navy blue shorts, sharing a few seconds with the second-most-powerful man in America.

"Don't Get Involved"

After completing fifth grade, I took an entrance exam for public high school, which included junior high (sixth through ninth grade) and high school (tenth through twelfth). I scored well enough to earn a place at one of South Vietnam's two best high schools: the all-boys Chu Van An High School. It had been a prestigious school in Hanoi before Vietnam's partition in 1954, when nearly all of its faculty and students relocated to Saigon. Our rival, Petrus Truong Vinh Ky, was also all-male, but its students and faculty generally had roots in the South. Both schools had many alumni serving in prominent government positions and students who were offspring of high-ranking military officers, top government officials, and the very wealthy.

Although my family was not wealthy, I was able to attend Chu Van An in part thanks to scholarship money. Beginning in my sophomore year, I applied for and received the South Vietnamese Ministry of Education's National Scholarship. Each year I was given enough to cover my textbooks and two school uniforms (white shirt, navy blue trousers), one to wear while the other set was being laundered and hung to dry in the sun. Later, in my senior year, I applied for a scholarship from a group of Vietnamese students who were studying in Christchurch, New Zealand, and had established a fund to provide financial aid to high school students in Saigon. I was delighted to learn that I had been awarded a 3,000 piaster cash scholarship. In fact, one of the young benefactors came to my house during her annual home visit and personally presented me with the award money. I was surprised and moved by this act of kindness.

At Chu Van An, the two thousand students were split evenly between two groups. Half were well-to-do, the sons of generals, department ministers, other top government officials, or wealthy businessmen who paid for private tutors for their sons. The rest were like me: smart, hardworking, and studying without special support. We all got along well. But one interest that many students shared also got us in trouble: the school had plenty of student activists, and I experienced political protest firsthand early in my time there.

In May 1963, the Diem regime's long-standing practice of oppressing Buddhists came to a head. On the most important day on the Buddhist calendar, *Phat Dan*, the Buddha's birthday, the government banned the display of Buddhist flags in the Imperial City of Hue in the northern reaches of South Vietnam. When Buddhists demonstrated to protest the ban, government troops fired on them, killing many. That sparked a campaign of civil disobedience by Buddhist monks: demonstrations, hunger strikes, even self-immolations.

Those protests soon spread to Saigon, where many university students took part. A group of older Chu Van An students organized their own protest, and many of us joined in. We were prepared to march out into the street carrying banners with anti-government slogans. As it turned out, the riot police—known as Canh Sat Chien Dau—were prepared for us. When we began marching from the school, they forcibly pushed us back inside and locked the gate from the outside, confining us to the school building.

That only served to frustrate and anger the leaders of our protest. Instead of relenting, they persisted, unfurling the banners we had prepared. Matters escalated when one of the upperclassmen emerged on an upper balcony and unfurled his own large banner, bearing a provocative message:

TRUANT STUDENTS GROW UP TO BECOME RIOT POLICE!

As I read those words, I recognized immediately that the student had crossed a line—from protest to ad hominem insult. Vietnamese culture places a premium on personal honor, and my classmate had violated that.

Sure enough, the police reacted strongly, lobbing tear-gas grenades into the school and then storming inside to quell the protest. At that, the student protesters quickly scattered. Some managed to flee, but others—including me—weren't able to escape, and the police arrested us and forced us into a police van that transported us to police headquarters. There, an officer ordered us to march inside. As the line of students entered the large holding room, we faced an intimidating police officer who reached out and gave each student a firm slap on the face as the student passed. My good friend and classmate Chi was just ahead of me in line, and he stopped in front of the officer and looked the man in the eye. "Don't you hit me!" Chi said. "My father works at the presidential palace!" The officer seemed flummoxed. He turned to one of his superiors, who simply shook his head. At that, the slapping officer waved the rest of us through, untouched.

Once we were in the holding room, another officer pulled Chi into a small office. I assumed the police intended to interrogate him. But after a few minutes, he emerged and sat next to me.

"They're going to release us," he whispered. "Just the two of us."

"How...?" I began to ask.

Chi explained that the policeman had asked if he was telling the truth, that his father actually worked at the presidential palace. Chi had offered his father's name and telephone number. "They checked to confirm it and told me they would release me and drive me home," he said. "I told them that I wouldn't go unless they released you, too."

A few minutes later, to our classmates' surprise, an officer called our names—just Chi's and mine—and escorted the two of us from the room. Outside, an officer motioned us into the back of an unmarked police car, which delivered the two of us to Chi's house. Since my bicycle was still at the school, where I had left it, I made my way home from Chi's house on foot, worrying for the entire thirty-minute walk how I would explain the day's events to my father. I was also worried about my bicycle, so when my father arrived home from work, I told him about the protest—and how I had been caught in the middle. As I had expected, he reprimanded me strongly.

"You should be grateful to President Diem," he told me. "He was the one who helped us resettle when we had to leave the North."

I tried to explain that I had been an innocent bystander, that I had already been in school when the demonstration had broken out and had simply had no way to escape the conflict.

"If that happens again, don't get involved," he scolded me. "Just stay in your classroom."

My father gave me a ride to the school, where I was happy to discover that my bicycle was still standing exactly where I had left it. I unlocked it, hopped on, and made the forty-minute ride home.

I didn't realize how lucky I had been to escape the police station until a few days later, when one of the older students who had organized the protest finally returned to school, looking wounded and traumatized. He told us that the police had tortured him terribly, binding his feet and hands and then dunking his head in a barrel of salt water mixed with soap and crushed red pepper.

"Were you afraid of dying?" I asked him.

"No," he said. "They don't want you to die." He said he had simply gone limp as the police demanded information—the identities of Buddhist monks, Communist secret sleeper cells, or others who might have collaborated in the protest. The more I heard, the more grateful I felt to my friend Chi, whose quick thinking and kindness had spared me.

An Uncertain Future

Just six months after the Chu Van An protest, in November 1963, we heard the shocking news that President Diem and his brother had committed suicide. My father almost immediately expressed doubt about the report: Diem was Catholic, he said, and Catholics don't commit suicide. Of course, we learned later that his suspicions were correct. Diem hadn't killed himself. A group of generals had staged a coup d'état, shot Diem, and stabbed his brother Nhu to death.

Like most of my contemporaries, I was happy to hear that Diem was gone. Most of us viewed his regime as a dictatorship that had come to power by rigging elections and jailing political opponents. Diem had given power to his relatives, most prominently his brother Thuc, the archbishop; his younger brother Nhu, who had headed the secret police; and Nhu's wife, Madame Nhu. His discriminatory policies toward Buddhists—the majority in South Vietnam—added to his unpopularity.

My father felt differently. He and my mother felt strongly indebted to President Diem, even though we were Buddhists and Diem was a Catholic whose government had discriminated against Buddhists. Diem had been supportive to the hundreds of thousands of refugees like our family who had immigrated from the North in 1954, offering us food, shelter, and work. We had been able to restart our lives in Nha Trang specifically because of Diem, and my parents felt eternally grateful to him for that, no matter what disagreements they might have had with his other policies.

"Don't be ungrateful," my father scolded me. "Without President Diem, we would be either stuck in the North or still homeless in the South."

With President Diem gone, South Vietnam faced an uncertain future, and matters only got worse three weeks later when we learned still more shocking news: my father heard on the radio that President John F. Kennedy had been assassinated. Wanting more details, he asked me to run to a newsstand and grab a newspaper for him so he could read more about it. The whole world was changing so quickly that it was difficult to keep up.

What followed in South Vietnam was a series of coups as various generals jockeyed for power in the wake of Diem's overthrow. There was a darkly humorous joke about generals trying to overthrow the current military strongman: "If you win, you become leader; if you lose, you become ambassador to another country." In other words, anyone seeking power either succeeded or faced exile by whoever did succeed. One coup followed another until 1965, when Nguyen Cao Ky, commander of the air force, emerged as prime minister and Lieutenant General Nguyen Van Thieu as head of state.

During these years of internal fighting and political instability, Viet Cong activity within South Vietnam intensified, and North Vietnam seized the opportunity to send more troops and weapons to the South via the Ho Chi Minh Trail. As the war escalated and the South Vietnamese army struggled in the face of both internal and external threats, the US increased its military and economic support to South Vietnam, started bombing campaigns in North Vietnam, and sent combat troops to South Vietnam. By 1965, as the war was getting closer and closer to us, the government imposed a nighttime curfew on the entire city of Saigon, so that late at night, the streets were virtually silent. Then, amid the silence, we started hearing the rumbling sound of bombs exploding in the distance. The muffled booms would continue for thirty minutes or an hour, then subside.

My father, always quiet, kept to himself and rarely spoke to me about the situation with North Vietnam—which looked increasingly threatening. Occasionally I would hear from friends that their fathers, high-ranking military officers, had been transferred to the First Military Tactical Zone, the area immediately bordering North Vietnam. My father had a cousin we called Uncle Bac who was an officer in the South Vietnamese Airborne Division. He would visit and have long conversations with my father. I wasn't allowed to sit with them, but from across the room I would listen and hear his stories about how the Viet Cong were escalating their efforts and their speculation that war would be coming to Saigon before long.

On one visit a few years earlier, in 1963, Uncle Bac had visited with my father at our house after returning from a brutal battle at Ap Bac, a small hamlet in the Dinh Tuong province. The Army of the Republic of Vietnam (ARVN) forces, accompanied by US military advisers, had planned to attack Viet Cong soldiers, but when they arrived at Ap Bac, they were pinned down by the Viet Cong. Uncle Bac's unit was ordered to parachute onto the battlefield to reinforce the ARVN fighting forces. In the melee, the Viet Cong managed to shoot down a number of helicopters. Three Americans, including a US Army captain who was serving as a military adviser, were killed in the battle.

Uncle Bac told my father that the battle of Ap Bac was considered the first major victory of the insurgent Viet Cong. I had no idea that years later, I would have deep connections to the battle, far beyond my uncle's participation.

Now, Communist troops were seizing more and more of South Vietnam's rural areas. Uncle Bac explained to my father that the sounds we were hearing were bombs being dropped by B-52s on Viet Cong and North Vietnamese troops in an effort to destroy their bases and halt their advance toward Saigon.

While those bombs were falling relatively far away, another threat felt more imminent: many nights, Viet Cong guerillas would launch rockets aimed at Saigon from the rice fields on the city's outskirts. The rockets were launched nightly, and the guerillas weren't aiming at specific targets. Their intent was to terrorize civilians. It was our luck that the rockets never fell close to our home, but occasionally we would hear that one had hit a house, in some cases killing an entire family.

After a while, I got used to falling asleep to the rumbling sounds of bombs, but we all worried about what the future might bring.

So we were relieved when reports came in March of 1965 that the US Marines had landed at Da Nang. The report on South Vietnamese radio—which we knew was propaganda—compared it to D-Day, the landing of Allied troops at Normandy in 1944. Of course, there were significant differences. The Allied troops had come face to face with German soldiers, but the American marines at Da Nang were greeted by young women who hung colorful flower leis around their necks.

Despite our gratitude for the Americans' arrival, we realized that it reflected South Vietnam's failure to fend off the Communists on its own. Along with that came the concern that the military situation was going from bad to worse.

My Mother, the Entrepreneur

Within just a few years, the number of US troops in South Vietnam jumped from a few thousand military advisers to more than five hundred thousand fighting men. Their presence transformed Saigon in all kinds of ways. The influx of American dollars led to hyperinflation, and soon the value of Vietnamese piaster tumbled to a tiny fraction of what it had once been. By then, my father had a new job with the Ministry of Justice, as a typist for the appellate court. But his fixed salary simply wasn't worth what it once would have been. My parents explained to the family that we all needed to trim our expenses as much as possible. But when his salary could no longer cover even half our monthly costs, they decided that my mother needed to go back to work.

She hadn't had a job outside the home since our family left Nha Trang, where she'd sold prepared foods door to door. But again, her entrepreneurial streak emerged, and she created a business marketing goods from post exchanges (PX), the retail stores on US military bases. Only American military personnel were authorized to shop at a PX, so she acquired her inventory in a somewhat indirect way. Many American GIs were living with Vietnamese girlfriends. In addition to supporting these young women with military pay currency (which we called "red dollars," as opposed to "green dollars"), the American GIs also gave them PX goods—cases of Coca-Cola or Pabst Blue Ribbon beer, cartons of Pall Mall cigarettes, cans of Dole fruit cocktail, or packs of Wrigley's chewing gum. My mother would purchase the goods from the women—we affectionately called them "Mrs. Americas"—and then resell them on the "gray market" to vendors in the flea markets that dotted the city. Many of these women lived in apartments not far from us, since our home was close to Tan Son Nhut, the air base that was also headquarters for the US Military Assistance Command, Vietnam (MACV).

My mother gave me a role in the enterprise as well. My job was to collect the items from the sellers, load them on my bicycle's rear rack, and deliver them to the flea market, where my mother would circulate from one merchant to another, dropping off the products. I made my deliveries either before or after school on most days.

The job had its hazards. No matter which route I took, I had to cross a bridge with a police checkpoint. Each time, I faced the risk that a police officer might stop me and force me to explain what I was doing with so many packs of Wrigley's gum or cans of Pabst Blue Ribbon. I couldn't carry too many bottles or cartons at once, and I had to hide whatever cargo I did carry under my satchel of schoolbooks. My parents weren't worried that I would be arrested but rather that I would have to offer the police officer a bribe, thus cutting into my mother's profits.

Occasionally the police stopped me, but then, seeing that I was wearing a school uniform, they would typically ask for my identification card and my draft deferment card. Once in a while, the officer would take a closer look at my load.

"What's that you're carrying?" the officer would ask.

"Oh, that's Coca-Cola," I would say. "We're having a celebration at school and I was assigned to bring it."

Sometimes my dad helped, too, carrying a load on his motorcycle. If police stopped him, he would show his ID from his government job and explain that he was delivering goods to the chief justice of the appellate court. That was usually sufficient explanation for the officers to let him pass.

With the tens of thousands of GIs in Saigon, selling PX goods on the gray market was a booming business, and my mother had a particular knack for it. She related to people well, she had an effective distribution system, and people trusted her. Best of all, the venture didn't require capital: she would pay the GIs' girlfriends from her proceeds after she sold the goods. The entire business was based on trust between the GIs' girlfriends and my mother.

Before long, she was taking in two or three times the salary my father was earning at his government job. Their two incomes meant that our family didn't go hungry. We always had rice, although our access to other staples was more limited. We had our share of vegetables, which were relatively inexpensive. Occasionally my mother would serve chicken or cut a half pound of pork or beef into thin slices, sauté it, and split it among the entire family. We couldn't afford to visit a dentist, let alone get orthodontia—luxuries reserved for the wealthy. So we were lucky not to suffer from cavities or toothaches. I did have myopia, so my parents made an exception to their usual frugality to help me obtain eyeglasses. They took me not to an optometrist but to a vendor who had me try on spectacles of varying strength until I found one that helped me see more clearly. That made a big difference.

Lessons from Mr. Hoat

While I always excelled in math and science, I also came to enjoy studying English, mostly because of a very talented teacher, Mr. Doan Viet Hoat. Mr. Hoat was an open and enthusiastic teacher who not only taught us the English language but also offered fascinating and engaging lessons about American history and current events. Learning English from a textbook could have been less than stimulating, but Mr. Hoat made it come alive, teaching us about US politics, geography, and the latest headlines. He had spent time in the US for graduate school and was eager to point out differences between American and Vietnamese culture and government. He discussed the history of discrimination against Negroes (the preferred English term at the time for African Americans). I was particularly fascinated with his stories and commentary about the Reverend Dr. Martin Luther King Jr., who had won the Nobel Peace Prize in 1964.

Mr. Hoat loved to employ humor and irony in his teaching, sometimes to dispel our romanticized notions about the United States. "You may think America is so wealthy that its streets are paved with gold," he would say. "The truth is that some of the streets aren't paved at all—and some of the poorest people have to do the paving themselves!"

He also created extraordinary opportunities for us to learn English outside the classroom: he invited his Americans friends—volunteers with a program called International Voluntary Service—to the school on Sundays so we could practice our English with native speakers. It was the first time I had encountered Americans so closely, and my English conversational skills were limited, but I enjoyed the encounters and found the Americans to be friendly, open people.

In December, with the Christmas holidays approaching, Mr. Hoat taught us that in the Western world, almost everyone celebrated Christmas. (In South Vietnam, only Catholics celebrated Christmas, so most of us had assumed the same was true elsewhere.) Mr. Hoat wrote down the English lyrics of the song "Silent Night" on the blackboard, explained their meaning, and taught us to sing the song. We all loved it.

Mr. Hoat also introduced me to one of my favorite places in Saigon. In our English class, we were studying the state of Utah, and I was assigned to write a report about Utah's national parks. Mr. Hoat suggested that the best way to find a book on the subject was to visit an American-run facility in the heart of Saigon called the Abraham Lincoln Library.

What I discovered was a remarkable place: a French colonial building with an American flag flying out front. Walking in the front doors, I stepped into a cool, air-conditioned space and looked up to see two portraits: one of President Lincoln, and the other of a smiling President Lyndon Johnson. The staffers, mostly Vietnamese citizens who were proficient in English, were helpful and well trained. One of the librarians helped me find exactly the book I needed for my school assignment.

After that first visit, I returned to the library regularly, magnetically drawn to its atmosphere, its orderly shelves, and its connection to the United States. Of course, there was also the air-conditioning, which offered a welcome respite from the tropical heat of Saigon, where temperatures were typically in the nineties with humidity over 90 percent. The library was always chilly and comfortable and had couches that made welcoming reading spots. I also made a habit of always grabbing a cup of chilled water as soon as I stepped inside.

If I came for the central air-conditioning, I stayed for the periodicals. Mr. Hoat suggested that the best way to learn about current events in the United States was to read *Time* magazine or *US News & World Report. US News*, he told us, featured condensed news summaries that we might find easier to read, but he particularly recommended *Time* for its more literary writing style. I also enjoyed reading *Life* magazine and *National Geographic*, which featured large, beautiful photographs and short captions.

Determined to learn English, I always carried a pocket-size English-Vietnamese dictionary so that whenever I came across an unfamiliar word, I could look it up. That could be a slow, time-consuming process. Occasionally the Lincoln Library made that process much easier by supplying special versions of their publications with English text on one side of a page and the Vietnamese translation on the other. In March 1968, we were shocked to hear on Saigon radio that President Johnson would not seek reelection. A few weeks later, I read the library's publication of President Johnson's full speech, side by side with Vietnamese translation. As I read the words "I shall not seek, and I will not accept, the nomination of my party for another term as your president," the Vietnamese translation made it much easier for me to understand.

Visiting the library, which was run by the United States Information Service, was like stepping into a little piece of America. For one thing, the place ran on schedule, opening and closing just as advertised. That was a sharp contrast with Vietnamese culture's looser attitude about schedules, an approach some Vietnamese like to call "rubber time." The Abraham Lincoln Library, on the other hand, opened and closed right on schedule.

The librarians were helpful and knowledgeable. When I was working on a school project about Jack London, I didn't know where to find the information, but a librarian easily found the book I needed. And when I finished with a volume, an employee would quickly scoop it up and re-shelve it. No other place in my life was so orderly, efficient, or comfortable. No wonder I kept going back.

The War Arrives

In Vietnamese culture we didn't celebrate birthdays. But we had one big celebration every year: *Tet Nguyen Dan*, the Lunar New Year, popularly known as Tet, was celebrated as everyone's birthday. On the evening of January 30, 1968, the eve of the new year, our family gathered, as we always did, to celebrate Tet at home. My mother had prepared an elaborate feast, and neighbors were partying throughout our close-knit neighborhood. Everyone was in a festive mood: friends came in and out all evening, and, as always, the loud blasts of firecrackers filled the neighborhood. We all went to bed late, eager to spend the next day continuing the celebration.

Then came the shooting.

Around 2 a.m. I was awakened by extremely loud cracking sounds. At first, I thought I was hearing more firecrackers. Then I realized that it was not fireworks but gunfire.

Someone turned on the radio. Immediately we heard that the North Vietnamese and Viet Cong had launched a widespread surprise attack on Saigon. A few hours later, the government declared martial law and imposed a twenty-four-hour curfew. Radio bulletins listed the various targets the Communists had struck: Tan Son Nhut Air Base, the presidential palace, the military compound housing the South Vietnamese Joint General Staff, the national police headquarters, and more. The radio also reported that some sections of the city had been badly damaged in the combat and from US air and artillery strikes.

One location that had suffered devastating damage was the ethnic-Chinese district near my high school known as Cho Lon, where Communist insurgents had engaged in violent clashes with South Vietnamese troops backed by American tanks. In radio news reports, US advisers described the heavy fire, which included B-40 rockets, as "coming in like hail." The Viet Cong had also attacked the US embassy, but the American military police had managed to defend that location. The announcer cautioned all listeners to stay inside and not venture out into the streets.

Sitting in my house, I came to a realization: the war that we had been dreading for so long had finally arrived in Saigon.

As dawn broke, I could hear the thundering sound of helicopters punctuated by explosions of rocket-propelled grenades. Peeking out, I spotted smoke and smelled something burning. After some time, visitors arrived at our door, friends of my mother's—two parents, their children, and a grandmother. Their house had been caught in the cross fire between Communist fighters and South Vietnamese forces. With nowhere to hide, they had run for their lives. They told us what they had seen as they fled: homes in flames, smoke everywhere. They needed a place of refuge, so my family took them in.

My mother had prepared foods for the Tet celebration, but she wanted us to hold off feasting. She explained that we didn't know how long this situation might continue. With so many mouths to feed, we would need to make the food last, so my mother instructed us to eat small portions.

Though we could hear the helicopter, the gunfire, and the grenades, the Viet Cong hadn't targeted our neighborhood directly, perhaps because it held no particular strategic value. Still, I felt frightened and worried. In contrast, my mother, who had six children to care for, reacted calmly, packing a plastic shopping bag for each of us with food and clothing. In case we had to flee the house, she wanted us to have the necessities to take care of ourselves. My parents also devised a family contingency plan and explained it to all of us. In the event we were forced to escape from home, we were to meet at the nearby home of relatives.

Meanwhile, though we were supposed to stay at home, I occasionally slipped out of the house and dropped in on neighbors, who were all doing exactly what we were: listening to radio bulletins and getting ready to run if necessary. There was nothing else to do but sit in limbo, waiting for something to happen and hoping nothing would.

As much as my parents might have wanted to reassure us, we were all street-smart kids who had grown up in a war zone. I could read the concern on my parents' faces.

The one nearby acquaintance who was nowhere to be seen was our neighbor who was a prominent official with the forensic division of South Vietnam's national police force. Most of the other officers had taken the day off for Tet, but he had gone to work for the day.

The fighting continued for a few days. It was difficult to sleep with the thundering sound of chopper blades and the periodic bursts of gunfire. With martial law and the curfew in place, we couldn't go far, so our understanding of the situation was limited to what we could gather from the radio broadcasts.

Finally, four or five days after the fighting had started, a unit of the South Vietnamese army arrived at our door in helmets and heavy boots, guns at the ready. They were going house to house in our neighborhood in search of the enemy.

"Have you seen any Viet Cong?" the soldiers demanded. "Are you hiding any Viet Cong?"

My father told them no, not here. Still, the soldiers insisted on seeing his ID—his government employment card—and then entering the house and searching the premises.

"Is the area clear of VC?" my father asked. The officer could not say for sure, but as far as he knew, yes. And they moved on.

Within a day or two, the gunfire subsided. The sounds of helicopters still permeated the area, but I knew that only the South Vietnamese and Americans had helicopters, so I found the sound reassuring. The night curfew continued, but by day we were free to venture out. After all those days cooped up at home, I stepped out—out of the house, out of the neighborhood—to see what was left of Saigon.

After Tet

That first day, I hopped on my bicycle and headed toward Chu Van An, my high school. I had heard on the radio about the fierce fighting in Hang Xanh, the Saigon suburb where my friend Binh lived, so I rode there first to check on him. I was shocked at what I saw. I knew Hang Xanh as a working-class neighborhood dotted with small businesses and factories. Now, nearly every house there had been destroyed by fire. I couldn't believe the devastation. I kept pedaling, worried about Binh and his family. Finally, I saw his house—remarkably, still in one piece.

Binh joined me on the ride to school, and along the way I took in the destruction that dotted nearly every neighborhood. At last I arrived at Chu Van An, where I came upon a number of my classmates—most of the boys in my grade—gathered in front on their bicycles. We exchanged stories about what we had seen and heard over the previous days. Fortunately, none of my friends' homes had been destroyed in the bombing, probably because most of them lived in the more affluent areas of Saigon. The Viet Cong had targeted the poorer areas, which were less effectively protected and whose locals were more likely to be supportive of the Communist cause.

The gate was open, but no one was entering the school. The reason, it turned out, was that the building was now filled with refugees—dozens and dozens of families who had lost their homes in the fighting over the previous few days.

Some of us made our way inside to the office, where we found the principal, Mr. Quynh, trying to make sense of the situation. We asked when school would resume. He didn't know. He told us to listen for a radio announcement from the Ministry of Education.

"If some of you have some time," Mr. Quynh added, "you could volunteer to help the people here."

As I walked through the school, I discovered that every classroom was filled—with parents, children, elderly people, men, and women who hadn't been as lucky as my family and me. When the Communists had attacked, many of them had had no choice but to run for their lives, leaving behind their homes, their belongings—everything they owned. They were hungry and thirsty. Some were missing family members. Mothers were trying to comfort crying babies.

We tried to help bring some order to the chaos by gathering information from everyone who had taken refuge in the school: name, address, relatives' names, names of missing relatives. We asked each family and individual to list their needs. One mother asked for diapers, another for baby formula, another for clothing for her children. We passed on the list to representatives of the South Vietnamese Red Cross.

I spent that first week working as a volunteer, riding my bicycle to the school each morning to help the unfortunate families who had taken refuge there. The Ministry of Social Services provided canned food and rice. Unfortunately, without anyone in charge, some of the displaced families had done damage to the building, carelessly starting cooking fires in the classrooms or on balconies and breaking down desks and benches for kindling and fuel. My classmates and I did our best to put a halt to that, directing them to an outside area more conducive to fires. Someone thought to gather firewood at a local park and hauled back a load that quickly sold out. One man started boiling a large pot of water outdoors, and some of the families gathered there to cook noodles or other foods.

In addition to helping the families, I also felt that we were protecting our beloved school. It was upsetting to see the classrooms where I had learned so much now in such disarray, but at the same time I had compassion for these people who had lost their homes and belongings. I knew none of them would have been there if they could have been back in their homes.

Finally, after a few weeks, with aid from the US, the government set up camps to house the refugees. The good news was that the dozens of families occupying Chu Van An were able to move out of the school. The bad news was that they left behind an awful mess: heaps of trash, dirt, random objects strewn about. By that time, most of the students in our class were showing up every day, and the principal enlisted our help to clean up the school and return it to working condition.

The principal directed us to report to our regular classrooms for the cleanup. With many dozens of us working, it took a couple of days to haul out the garbage and sort out the furniture and supplies sufficiently for the school to function. Finally, a bulletin went out that on the following Monday, school would resume.

Dreaming of America

By then, the Communist forces had cleared out of Saigon, but the fighting continued outside the city. The government-imposed curfew meant that we all had to stay home after dark, and almost every night, I would hear the *boom-boom-boom* of bombs dropped from B-52s on Communist targets. The sounds of the explosions seemed to be getting closer and lasted much longer.

I continued to excel in school. In eleventh grade, I took the first part of the baccalaureate exam, a national assessment that measured academic prowess. I did so well that I earned the designation "highest honors" (in Vietnamese, *uu*). The following year, in the baccalaureate exam's second part, I earned "high honors" (*binh*). Reaching that level of achievement meant that I had a good chance of receiving a scholarship to study abroad.

In all, about two hundred South Vietnamese students won these scholarships each year. They were selected using a few criteria: performance on the national exam, mastery of the destination country's language, and likelihood of success in an academic program.

My goal was to attend university in the United States, so I applied for a scholarship from the United States Agency for International Development (USAID). I submitted my high school grades as well as my scores on the baccalaureate exams. I also wrote a brief essay in English explaining why I hoped to study in the United States.

Not long after that, I was invited to a series of interviews. The interviewers conducted the meetings in Vietnamese and English (to test our English proficiency), asking basic questions: Where are you from? Why do you want to study abroad? What's your best subject? What field do you want to study?

I felt I had done well. I was confident in my application—after all, I had excellent grades and had been among the top scorers in the country on the national baccalaureate exams. My English comprehension was fairly good in reading and writing, and fair in listening and speaking. Then again, my father had taught me that there would always be someone who was smarter

and better than me. And I knew that many children of high-ranking officials and wealthy people were competing for the same scholarship. The bottom line: there were no guarantees.

After waiting many weeks, in late October I learned that the office had
posted the list of students chosen for scholarships to the United States. I
scanned it from the top, quickly reading each name in alphabetical order,
until I got to... *Tran Manh Khiem*. I reviewed the list of thirty names again,
then checked once more to make sure it was indeed there. It was.

I was in! I was elated. I smiled, filled with excitement and anticipation.
America, I thought, *here I come!*

"Make Me Proud"

When I got home, I told my mother I had won the scholarship. She was thrilled. "We'll have to buy you some nice, warm clothing," she said. Later that weekend relatives and friends dropped by to help me celebrate. To mark the occasion one relative presented me with a gift: a small, zippered duffel bag bearing the Pan-Am Airlines logo.

Soon after the scholarship recipients were announced, the thirty of us who were heading to America—twenty-two men and eight women—attended a series of seminars to help us prepare for the trip. I would need to undergo a physical exam and arrange for the required vaccinations and immunizations; I'd have to apply for a South Vietnamese passport and a US student visa.

At the final seminar in Saigon, the organizers explained that our experience would start with a ten-day orientation in Honolulu for all thirty of us. After that, we would split into three groups for intensive English-language programs on US college campuses to help prepare us for campus life. Fifteen students would stay in Hawaii for the English program, ten would go to Pasadena City College in California, and five—including me—would study at Georgetown University in Washington, DC. (My understanding was that the students with the best command of English were being sent to Georgetown.) I was thrilled to learn that I would be spending time in the US capital.

Later there were more celebrations in my honor, and other relatives presented me with gifts of American dollars they had acquired by exchanging Vietnamese piasters on the black market. Another relative knit a sweater for me—not something one would ever need in Vietnam, but something I would likely need in America. And my mother started buying US currency from her "Mrs. America" friends to make sure that I would arrive in America with some cash in my pockets.

When our departure day arrived, I dressed up in a shirt and tie, as the USAID officials had suggested. Since my father had to go to work, he wasn't able to see me off at the airport. Like most fathers I knew, he expressed little emotion and rarely offered praise. If my school report card had four "excellent" grades and one "good" one, he would ignore the "excellent" and asked me to explain the "good." But that morning, before he departed for the office, he did his best. "Khiem," he said, "take care of yourself. Study hard and write home."

My mother came with me to the airport to see me off. As I prepared to board the plane, she told me to take care of my health and not drink too much beer. (She had seen how much American GIs drank.) "Make me proud," she said.

After saying goodbye, I stepped away, crossed the tarmac, and walked up the stairway into the Boeing 707. As the plane ascended, I looked out the window at the urban sprawl of Saigon and the military compounds around Tan Son Nhut Air Base and contemplated the adventure ahead.

Discovering America

A New World

When I left Saigon, I felt elated. Except for my childhood journey into Cambodia with my father's friends, it was the first time I had been outside Vietnam. I felt not even a tinge of sadness about leaving the city or the country, or about parting from my parents or my siblings. I was simply filled with excitement for the adventure ahead. (And I was grateful that I didn't experience the motion sickness I had suffered from years earlier on the boat and train.)

The first flight took us to Hong Kong, where we transferred to a flight to Tokyo, and from there we flew to Honolulu. We had taken off from Saigon around 10:30 a.m., but since we crossed the International Date Line, we landed in Honolulu at 10:00 a.m., half an hour earlier than we took off. That novel change felt like a symbol of the transition I was experiencing: I felt as if I was entering a new world.

At the airport in Honolulu, the thirty of us piled into a bus. The March weather was balmy, the highway was full of automobiles, and traffic moved smoothly. I marveled at the neat suburban houses with their two-car garages and tidy, green front lawns. A lawn was almost unheard-of in Saigon, even in the most affluent neighborhoods.

Our base for that week was the campus of the University of Hawaii, where we stayed in a dormitory. Another student and I shared a room—a clean, spacious unit just down the hall from a communal bathroom and a TV lounge. The biggest shock was the cafeteria, where our instructor told us we were free to take any food item we wished, at no cost. In my two decades, I had never experienced anything like that. None of us had. Our instructor led the way, showing us how to take a tray and then a plate and choose the dishes we wanted to eat. I was among the best English speakers in our group, so I followed him, loading my tray with food, and the others trailed behind me.

Later that night, I tried settling into bed in the dorm room. As happy and content as I was, I had a difficult time getting to sleep. Lying in the darkness of the unfamiliar room, I realized why: it was too quiet. I had grown so accustomed to falling asleep to the rumble of bombs being dropped from B-52s in the distance that here, in these peaceful and safe sur-roundings, the silence was keeping me awake.

By the second or third day I had learned my way around the university dining hall, so the other scholarship students and I started going to meals independently. I made a point of sitting at tables with American students. It wasn't easy to connect, considering the language barrier, but from the be-ginning I was eager to plunge into American culture and learn everything I could.

Spotting an empty chair next to a group of American students, I asked, "May I sit here?" The students gestured for me to join them. Then I reached back in my mind, struggling to remember the words and phrases Mr. Hoat had taught me back at Chu Van An. I explained that I was an exchange stu-dent from Vietnam. Then I asked the questions my teacher Mr. Hoat had suggested asking to start a conversation: *How are you? Where are you from? What year are you in school? What's your major?*

It was easy to ask, but when the students started answering, or asking their own questions, I was so overwhelmed that I begged them to slow down.

Still, I felt grateful to Mr. Hoat for all of those Sundays when he had brought his American friends from International Voluntary Service so we could practice our English. The other Vietnamese students tended to stick together, but I wanted to meet American students and practice my English. After a while, some of my Vietnamese peers joined us. A few days later, walking into the dining hall, I spotted one of those American students, and he gestured for me to join him.

During that week, the scholarship program brought in various teachers to give us an orientation to American culture that had a bit more depth than what we had learned in Saigon. We learned practical things: how the cur-rency worked, how to use public transportation, how to mail a letter, how to make a telephone call.

Some things caught me off guard. When I met the instructor who taught us about US geography and culture, I was surprised to see that he was Japanese but spoke English without an accent. He told us that both of his parents had immigrated to Hawaii from Japan, where he was born. Pre-viously, I had been under the impression that Americans were either white or black. That seemed to be true of the many GIs I had seen in Saigon. This was my first realization that there were also ethnic Japanese, ethnic Italians and Irish, and others who were also 100 percent American. It was an eye-opener.

Even though I had studied about America and read American periodicals at the Abraham Lincoln Library, I had plenty to learn. I knew that there were fifty states and that Hawaii was the last one admitted to the union, but I didn't know that Puerto Rico and Guam were US territories. The teachers offered a more in-depth look at the US political system and the education system than I'd ever had. For the first time, I became acquainted with the A-to-F grading system, grade point averages, and the terms *midterm* and *final*. Like all of my fellow Vietnamese students, I was surprised to learn that America didn't have national exams, just the Scholastic Aptitude Test, which was part of the college admissions process.

The instructors took care to share one important word of caution. American college students were predominantly opposed to the war in Vietnam, he told us. As visitors, we were representatives of our country, and we should not take sides in those debates. We should steer clear of heated public arguments about the war and politics.

Cornflakes and Cherry Blossoms

After the orientation, some of our group stayed in Hawaii to study English at the University of Hawaii's Hilo campus. The rest of us flew from Honolulu to Los Angeles, from which one group headed to Pasadena. The remaining five of us caught another flight to Washington, DC, arriving on March 22, 1970.

Five days a week, in a classroom on the Georgetown University campus, I studied English and learned about America's culture and institutions. Our class had students from a wide variety of developing countries—from Latin America, from Africa, from South and Southeast Asia. Our teacher, Mr. Underwood, was a friendly man and an effective teacher. The course's objectives were to give us a solid orientation in American culture and, more importantly, to help us reach a level of proficiency in English that would allow us to be successful at an American college.

I immediately fell in love with Washington, DC, with its broad boulevards, its white marble memorials, and its fascinating museums. I visited the National Mall, took an elevator to the top of the Washington Monument, and walked up the steps of the Lincoln Memorial, where Dr. King had given his famous "I Have a Dream" speech less than seven years earlier. I visited the US Capitol, where security was minimal: practically anyone could just walk in.

The five of us—the Vietnamese students on USAID scholarships—lodged at a place called Harnett Hall, a boardinghouse near Dupont Circle that provided breakfast and dinner as well as rooms. In contrast to our experience in Hawaii, here we didn't have a cafeteria line or a teacher to model for us how to order our food; we were on our own. The first morning I had no idea what to order for breakfast and was afraid to ask for help. But I heard the man at the next table ask a server for cornflakes. Then the waitress brought out something brown in a bowl with a glass of milk.

"I would like cornflakes, please," I told the waitress.

She looked at the Vietnamese student sitting with me. "I would like cornflakes, please," he said.

We all ate cornflakes for breakfast every morning for about a month. Then, fortunately, we made a new acquaintance, a man named Van, a cultural attaché at the South Vietnamese embassy, who reached out to welcome us to Washington. One morning, he joined us at Harnett Hall for breakfast.

"You're so lucky to have so many options for breakfast!" he said. He told us the various ways we could order eggs: scrambled, soft-boiled, hard-boiled, over easy, and many other variations. I took mental notes, trying to remember everything he said. Thank goodness for Mr. Van. Without him, I would have been eating cornflakes for my entire stay in Washington.

Mr. Van drove a small car, a Volkswagen Beetle with diplomatic license plates, which I understood entitled him to park anywhere without penalty. And he did. Before I was comfortable negotiating public transportation, Mr. Van took me to places too far to reach by foot. What made the greatest impression was Arlington National Cemetery, where he took me to see the changing of the guard at the Tomb of the Unknown Soldier and President Kennedy's grave. He also pointed out to me the Confederate Memorial and the graves of Confederate soldiers. I felt overwhelmed as we wandered through row upon row of white headstones spread out across the immaculate green lawns. Thinking about the war back in Vietnam, I felt a deep sense of admiration for the way America honored its soldiers on these hallowed grounds.

With Mr. Van and on my own, I took in plenty of other tourist spots: the Iwo Jima Memorial, the National Gallery of Art, the Smithsonian National Museum of Natural History. During the annual National Cherry Blossom Festival, I walked from Dupont Circle to where the parade was passing by and then took in the beautiful view of the pink blossoms around the Tidal Basin. What a sight!

In such moments, I sometimes felt a pang of guilt about being so far from home. While I enjoyed one experience after another, halfway across the world, my classmates, my friends, were fighting a war for our country. That feeling never left my mind: *Why me? Why am I so lucky, and why not them?*

Vietnam from Afar

In some ways Vietnam felt very far away, but on the other hand, the war in Vietnam was a topic of constant discussion in America. I did my best to keep up on what was going on back home in South Vietnam by regularly visiting the Georgetown library's periodical room, where most of the magazine covers had photos relating to the war in Vietnam. Of course, unlike the Abraham Lincoln Library, this library didn't supply bilingual publications, and I wasn't fluent enough in English to read and understand everything on my own. But I flipped through *Life* and *Look*, the photo magazines, and after I examined the photographs from Vietnam, I could usually make sense of the captions.

Seeing the war from the American press's point of view gave me an entirely new perspective on what had been happening in my home country. The American public felt that the administration and the Pentagon had misled them about the war, and many had lost faith in their government. Back home, the South Vietnamese government's propaganda gave the impression that we were winning every battle and the war was going quite well. Reading *Life* and *Look* and seeing the photographs from Vietnam gave me a different perspective.

With everything the media was reporting, it was no wonder that the American students I encountered were almost unanimously opposed to America's involvement in the war. And I had come to Washington at a particularly charged moment. On April 30, just five weeks after my arrival, President Richard Nixon revealed in a televised address that the US had been conducting a bombing campaign against North Vietnamese sanctuaries in Cambodia. That sparked new protests on college campuses across the country, including Georgetown.

The officials at Saigon's Office of Overseas Study as well as our instructors from USAID had made clear to us that we were expected to steer clear of any political activity. I was in America to pursue my education, not to push a political agenda. So when campus anti-war protests broke out during my Georgetown class, I made my way upstairs to a second-floor window and watched the events play out from a safe distance.

The demonstrations immediately reminded me of 1963, when I had found myself in the middle of the protest at my high school against President Diem's treatment of the Buddhists. What surprised me this time, though, was how the police kept their distance and allowed the protest to play itself out. In Vietnam, protesters knew to carry handkerchiefs because police would almost always use tear gas to disperse them. They would also charge the protesters, beat them with clubs, and arrest them. Here, things were different. Not only did the police seldom use tear gas or clubs, but they actually kept order and cleared a path to allow the protesters to march through. I was amazed.

Before long, though, some of the student protests did turn violent. On May 4, National Guard troops opened fire on a student protest at Kent State University in Ohio, killing four students and wounding nine others. After that, the student protests escalated everywhere, including at Georgetown, where the protests seemed to double in size. Rather than quelling the protests, the Kent State killings seemed to fuel demonstrations. Still, I stayed out of the fray, watching from a safe distance or catching the evening news broadcasts on the TV at Harnett Hall.

"You're Ready for College"

I was happily settled into my routine at Georgetown and enjoying life in Washington that May when I received a message from Mr. Mahoney, the program officer at USAID who oversaw my scholarship. He was inviting me—along with the four other Vietnamese students in the Georgetown program—to a meeting. I walked to the meeting with the other Vietnamese students, including a young woman named Thuy Trinh, whom I had first met at one of the scholarship meetings in Saigon but didn't know well. As the five of us made our way from the Georgetown campus to the USAID office in a building on K Street, we wondered aloud what the meeting might be about. As soon as we arrived, Mr. Mahoney let us know.

"Congratulations to all of you," he said. "Your English is good enough and you're ready to go on to college."

With that, he shared the information we had been eagerly anticipating: where, exactly, we would be enrolling. Two of the students were bound for New Mexico, a third to Indiana. Then he turned to Thuy and me. "Both of you will be studying at Pacific University," he said, "in Forest Grove, Oregon."

Thuy and I looked at each other. In my few months in the United States, I had heard the names of many colleges. And for years I had been learning names of American universities from Mr. Hoat, my English teacher, who had explained the concept of the Ivy League and the importance of college football. But I had never heard of Pacific University—or Forest Grove. I wasn't even sure where Oregon was. We didn't speak up. The Vietnamese way was to be deferential and respectful. So we both thanked Mr. Mahoney and then walked out of the meeting, excited, eager, and a bit puzzled.

The next day I visited the Georgetown library, where I found my way to the map room. Looking around the large, impressive room, I wasn't sure where to begin, so I approached one of the librarians.

"I'm trying to find a city called Forest Grove, Oregon," I told her.

She led me to a thick, oversized atlas and flipped the pages until she found a map of the state of Oregon. She scanned a list of cities and then, using the coordinates on the map, pointed to a dot near Portland and the words "Forest Grove." "Right there," she said. I knew nothing about Oregon or Pacific University, so I felt neither disappointment nor excitement, just ready for another adventure.

Welcome to Oregon

A few days later, Thuy and I boarded a plane at Washington's National Airport and flew to Portland. We expected to have to make our own way to Forest Grove, but when we stepped off the plane, we were greeted by a representative of the university. And not just anyone—it was the dean of admissions himself, Mr. Ken Meyer.

As Mr. Meyer drove us in his station wagon, I observed immediately that Oregon was very green: evergreen trees everywhere, rivers, bridges. Not only did he give us a ride, but he hosted Thuy and me that first night in his own home, a large house in the hills of southwest Portland on a street called Skyline Boulevard. The house looked out to the west, so we watched the sun set as Mr. Meyer's very gracious wife prepared us a wonderful dinner.

That night, Thuy and I each had our own bedroom. I thought of my home in Saigon—one small room for the entire family. After nearly three months on the Georgetown campus, in one of Washington's most affluent neighborhoods, now I was in a neighborhood with large houses and two-car garages. Based on my limited experience, it seemed that everyone in America lived very comfortably.

The next morning, Mr. Meyer drove us to Forest Grove, about an hour from his house. We would be enrolling in summer school classes to prepare for our first semester in the fall. It was a small and quiet campus, and it seemed that every person I passed smiled and said hi.

Mr. Meyer took me to Clark Hall, the men's dormitory, where I would be living. There, I met my roommate, Charlie Bird. Charlie was a Pacific graduate who was studying for a master's degree in physical education. Since I was two or three years older than the other freshmen, the school had paired me with someone a bit more mature and seasoned. Charlie accompanied me as I explored the dorm and introduced myself to other students. Without exception, every person I encountered was friendly and welcoming.

"Good to have you here!" they all said. "Where are you from?"

When I told them I was from Vietnam, their eyes practically popped out of their head: "Were you in the war?"

"Pretty close," I would reply. "I could hear the bombs at night."

Everyone wanted to be my guide to the campus, so for my first campus lunch, four or five students came along. I followed them and repeated whatever they did. They tried explaining the food to me—it was typical American cafeteria fare: hamburger, hot dogs, cabbage stuffed with hamburger meat, casseroles.

"Too bad," one of the students mentioned over lunch, "you just missed Woodstock."

"What's that?" I asked.

He explained that Woodstock was a huge music festival that had taken place in New York State the previous year. Woodstock was also a means to protest the Vietnam War and to promote peace, love, and happiness. It was my first meal at my new college, and I was already seeing how the war in my country had a prominent place in the minds of American youth.

After lunch, I followed the others outside to an expansive grassy space. Some of the students who were tossing Frisbees and footballs invited me to join them. I had never thrown a football, so I asked for guidance. "How do you make the ball spin?" I inquired. One of the guys showed me very carefully how to hold the ball, with my fingers extended across it, and then throw it with a twisting motion. It took me a number of tries, but I got the hang of it. I had never seen a Frisbee before, and I was fascinated that you could make a disc fly so far with so little effort. One of the students showed me how to do that, too.

Forest Grove was a tiny town with a population of some seven thousand. I could easily walk from one end of town to the other. The railroad ran through town, and the houses were tidy and well maintained. There was a high school near the campus. It wasn't a fancy place, just an average middle-class town—a comfortable place to land in America.

The first summer school class I enrolled in was English literature, taught by a professor named George Evans. He was a wonderful, kind, mild-mannered man with shoulder-length hair. In one of our first encounters he peppered me with questions about life in Vietnam: How was I affected by the war? Were things as bad as the newspapers and television said?

As much as I liked him, his class wasn't easy for me. One of the first assignments was to read Philip Roth's novel *Goodbye, Columbus*. It was challenging. That summer, I watched the other students on campus enjoying the outdoors and blasting music from inside their dorm rooms. If they had homework, they would bring a pillow out to the quad, put on sunglasses, lie down, and read the book in a couple of hours. Not I. I spent most of the summer in the library, the only quiet place where I could study. I would bring my English-Vietnamese dictionary and slowly make my way through Philip Roth, one word at a time. My father had always taught me that when I started something, I should finish it before I started another project. That meant that if I read a book, I read it from cover to cover in one sitting. With *Goodbye, Columbus*, I had to break that rule. It took me three long days to make my way through the novel, dictionary in hand.

When I wrote a paper about the novel, my instinct was to summarize what I had read, just as I had learned to do in Vietnam, where the education system was authoritative and placed a high value on memorization and summarization. Students were supposed to be quiet, listen, and absorb what the teacher had to say. If students asked questions, they had to be careful not to challenge the traditional way of thinking. But Professor Evans explained that things were different here. I didn't need to regurgitate what I had read in the book. He was more interested in my analysis. What did I think of the characters? What surprised me? Did I agree or disagree with the decisions the characters made? I found this approach refreshing and freeing, but it also meant I had to think on my own. I was not accustomed to that style of learning.

With so much to read and think about, it didn't take long for the library to become one of my favorite places on campus, almost a second home. In addition to my coursework, I spent long hours perusing *Time* magazine, *Life*, *National Geographic*, and the local newspaper, *The Oregonian*. Just as I had found respite and stimulation at the Abraham Lincoln Library in Saigon, the Pacific University library became a place where I felt both alive and comfortable.

Professor Evans also went out of his way to help me adjust. Soon after I started in his class, he invited me and Thuy, the other student from Vietnam, to his home for dinner. His wife, Donna, was a sweet woman and a wonderful cook. Another time they had us over and Thuy cooked Vietnamese food for all of us.

In contrast to my experience in literature class, my math studies came easily and naturally. I took calculus as well as statistics and probability.

Once I learned the terminology, I didn't have to worry about translating. To do homework for other classes, I had to labor over a typewriter, pecking at one key at a time, but in math I could breeze through the homework, write my answers in pencil on paper, and turn it in.

Not all of my classes were typical academic courses. In my first semester, to fulfill a physical-education requirement, I took a semester-long swimming class. Thuy happened to enroll in the same class. The instructor, Mrs. Jean Horner, taught us various swim strokes and kicks and the rules of Olympic swim competition. I was already a competent swimmer, but it was helpful to learn these new skills.

Mrs. Horner also taught us the basics of water survival: If you find yourself in deep water, how do you save yourself from drowning? She taught us how to tread water, and to pass the class, every student had to show that we could tread water for an extended period of time. We also learned specific strategies for coping with a water emergency. One that stood out in my mind was that, while treading water, you could take off your pants, blow air into them, tie knots at the ends of the legs, and use the pants as a floatation device. She taught us how to stay afloat for a long period of time with minimal effort to avoid becoming exhausted and drowning.

I did well in the class, passing both the practical and written exams. What I couldn't have known then was that one day what I learned in Mrs. Horner's class would save my life.

Lessons from Tony and Cliff

In those early days at Pacific, I was learning just as much outside the classroom as inside. Some of my new friends invited me to watch a football game with them on the TV in Clark Hall. I couldn't make sense of what I was watching: players chasing each other across a field and piling on top of the one with the ball. My friends wanted me to understand, so they patiently explained the rules: each team had four opportunities to advance the ball ten yards down the field. They told me to watch the quarterback—Joe Namath of the New York Jets was a star quarterback at the time. Once I had watched a few games, I developed a basic understanding and started to enjoy the game.

I learned more about football from Tony Warren, one of the few black students on the Pacific campus. Tony was a star sprinter on the track team and played running back on Pacific's football team. He was friendly, cheerful, and outgoing, and he would talk to just about anyone. Everyone loved Tony, and he became a close friend of mine.

One time I dropped by his room while he had *Sanford and Son* on the TV. He told me it was a fairly accurate reflection of daily life in the black community. I couldn't help but notice that at Pacific, most of the black students kept to their own group. I wondered why so many of them would sit at the same cafeteria tables, separating themselves from the white students. I found it hard to start conversations with them. If I asked a question, many of them would answer in a few words, but they didn't seem to want to engage beyond that. I wasn't sure why.

One exception, in addition to Tony, was Cliff Wood, who was a proctor in Clark Hall. Cliff—tall, quiet, and a star of the basketball team—was a problem solver and a helper. If you got locked out of your room or if somebody was making too much racket after midnight, Cliff would step in and retrieve a key or quiet down the noisy student. He had better people skills than most other students, and I felt comfortable asking him questions. Cliff dreamed of playing pro basketball, and whenever I had a question about basketball, I would ask him, and he would patiently answer.

Cliff was also a leader among the black students, so I came to him with my questions about African American culture. I hadn't spent much time around black people, and even small things fascinated me. In the dormitory bathroom, I noticed that after they took showers, the white students used combs or brushes, but the black students had very long combs made of metal. They would use these combs to puff up their curly hair and make it look bigger. I also noticed that their accents sounded different from the Caucasian students' accents.

Another thing I noticed: the Caucasian students all called each other by their first names. I didn't understand why, but the black students always called each other "man" or "brother."

One morning in the dormitory, one of the black students I'd gotten to know offered me a friendly greeting: "Hey, man!"

When I answered by attempting to copy his accent—"Hey, man!"—he glared at me for a moment, perhaps not sure what to make of me, and then broke into a smile.

Beyond those observations, I had lots of questions about black culture. Back in Saigon, Mr. Hoat, my high school English teacher, had taught us about the discrimination blacks faced, particularly in the South, where people of color couldn't even stay in the same hotels as whites. Mr. Hoat had told us stories of South Vietnamese military officers who had trained with the US Army's 101st Airborne Division at Fort Campbell in Kentucky. They could eat in the base mess halls, but outside the base, sometimes restaurants weren't willing to serve them because they were Asian.

As a newcomer to America, I was curious to hear about this kind of discrimination, and—maybe because I was a newcomer and an outsider—Cliff wasn't hesitant to engage with me about it. He told me about the plight of blacks in the South. He told me about lynching. He told me about segregation. He told me about busing. He explained that the United States had two different school systems: the black schools were poor, lacked facilities, and had mediocre teachers; the white schools had great libraries, nice football fields, and new equipment. In the not-too-distant past, the white students had never met black students, and black students had never met white students, he said. Busing, he explained, was an attempt to correct that problem, integrating the schools by moving children from black neighborhoods to white schools, and vice versa.

"What do *you* think about busing?" I asked.

"It's a disaster," he told me. "The blacks don't want to go to white schools, and the whites don't want to go to black schools."

I had read that people referred to America as a melting pot—a place where people from diverse backgrounds mixed in a single society. "It's not a melting pot," Cliff once told me. "It's a salad bowl." People married within their ethnic group, he said, and each group retained its own distinct identity.

Once I had forged a friendship with Cliff, the other black students seemed to change their attitude toward me. They were more open and friendlier to me.

As much as I was learning about race and my classmates' wide variety of backgrounds, I also encountered students who were far less open. One, Alex, a white student who lived in a Clark Hall room near me, held a low opinion of black people. He avoided talking to Cliff and sometimes asked me why I hung around with Cliff and Tony.

"I learn a lot from them," I would tell him, "and they're nice guys."

Pacific also had a large number of Hawaiian students, and Alex didn't like them, either. He had grown up in a predominantly white area and then served in the military before college. But he did become friends with me and with a Chinese student in his program.

"You Orientals are hardworking and you know your place," he sometimes said, thinking he was offering a compliment. Alex also had a strange sense of humor. Once we were together in the cafeteria line near the milk dispenser. Seeing the chocolate milk sprout next to the regular milk, Alex shook his head. "Now they're even trying to integrate the milk machine," he said.

I didn't confront Alex. I didn't want to get in an argument with anybody about anything. I also felt that I had a lot to learn from Alex, just as I was learning from Cliff and Tony. I figured that I could learn from anybody.

Gamma Sig

Another place I made friends was in a fraternity. Pacific had two major fraternities, which shared a healthy rivalry. Alpha Zeta had a reputation as the wild house. One of the fads hitting college campuses in the early seventies was streaking, and Alpha Zeta's members did that: stripped off their clothes and sprinted across the campus. Unfortunately, the news leaked, and almost the entire student population was waiting to see them running naked. Gamma Sigma was the more academic fraternity, with less partying and scheduled quiet hours for studying. Gamma Sig's members were also known to be more close-knit and more selective in recruiting. That, I decided, was more my speed.

The Gamma Sigs may have been less wild, but that didn't mean they didn't have fun. When I went through the fraternity's rush period, the older fraternity brothers gave us various ridiculous tasks to perform before they would sign our pledge cards.

I was constantly asking the fraternity brothers to explain the meaning of words for me, and often the words I asked about were slang terms that didn't show up in my pocket dictionary. Some of the fraternity brothers looked at the English-Vietnamese part of the dictionary, but they couldn't find any of the slang terms. So one of them, Ben, photocopied the pictures of his biology textbook—the male and female bodies. On the picture, he jotted in pen the slang words for the various male and female body parts.

"I want you to learn and memorize these before I'll sign your pledge card," Ben told me. A few weeks later, he tested me. As he pointed to various anatomical parts, I called out the correct slang terms.

Another fraternity brother noticed that I spoke English in an overly formal way. He thought it was important for me to learn to speak more like my American friends. In other words, I had to increase my vocabulary of swear words. He made me a list of twenty of the most popular swear words and explained the meaning of each and the circumstances under which I might make use of it. And he told me that he would agree to sign my fraternity pledge card only if I could demonstrate how to use the words appropriately in real-life settings. The brothers decided the perfect time to test me was on a Sunday afternoon, when we were gathered around the TV to watch a football game.

"In order to pass the test," one of them explained, "you need to use at least ten swear words appropriately during the game."

We settled onto the couches in the TV lounge with beers and soft drinks and pretzels and chips to watch the game on a black-and-white TV. The fraternity brothers all wanted to have a good time, but I took the challenge seriously. Instead of paying attention to the game being broadcast on the screen, I focused on seizing opportunities to use my newly acquired swear words and pass the test.

The first wasn't difficult. Just a few minutes into the game, one of the guys stood in front of me, blocking my view of the TV.

"Goddammit!" I said. "Get your ass out of my view!"

Everyone laughed. They thought it was hilarious, particularly with my Vietnamese accent.

"That counts as *two* words," one of the guys said, marking the tally sheet.

A few minutes later, a player on the team we were cheering for fumbled the ball.

"That was a stupid f--king play!" I shouted.

The guys burst out in cheers for me. By halftime, I had already passed the test.

The final challenge of Gamma Sigma's rush proved a bit more difficult. One Sunday morning, two of the fraternity brothers took me for a drive to get lunch. About a half hour's drive from campus, we stopped at a McDonald's in an unfamiliar town—I didn't even know its name. When I reached into my pocket to pay, one of the fraternity brothers asked to see my wallet. After rifling through it, he handed me back my state identification card and my student ID, then pocketed the wallet.

"Your challenge," one of them told me, "is to get yourself back to the fraternity house. You're on your own. But if you get lost or you can't make it, use this dime to call." He handed me a single dime, and they returned to their car and drove off.

I wasn't very worried. I had always been resourceful and comfortable talking to strangers. Still, it felt strange to be left in an unfamiliar place. After the two fraternity brothers drove off, I started chatting with drivers in the McDonald's parking lot.

"Do you mind telling me where we are?" I asked someone getting out of his car.

"You're in Newberg, Oregon," he said. I had no idea where that was relative to Forest Grove, but I kept talking to people. I introduced myself to each person I approached as an exchange student from Vietnam who was studying at Pacific University in Forest Grove.

"If you're going that direction, even part of the way," I said each time, "I would appreciate a ride."

Finally, a driver told me he was headed to Tigard. That would get me partway there, so I accepted a ride from him. He dropped me in Tigard and pointed me in the direction of Forest Grove. I stood by the side of the road and extended my thumb. Finally, a driver stopped and gave me a ride to Beaverton. Another took me as far as Hillsboro, and a final driver gave me a lift for the final leg to Forest Grove. When I made my way to the fraternity and walked in, the guys burst out in cheers, slapped my back, and then cracked open a celebratory round of beer.

Some new experiences at Pacific were less momentous but still memorable. Most students returned home during Christmas break, and in my first year, Ralph Huntington, the fraternity's president, invited me and another member to spend the holidays with his family in Madras, a small town in central Oregon. As Ralph drove over the Cascade mountains that December, I gazed out and, for the first time in my life, saw real snow. Ralph pulled over to the side of the road, we all got out, and the two of them demonstrated for me something I had never learned growing up in Vietnam: how to make a snowball. Then, right there by the side of the road, the three of us spent a few minutes in a friendly snowball fight.

I was not the only one finding friends in Greek life. Thuy, my classmate from Vietnam, was enjoying the university as much as I was and had joined a sorority, Theta Nu Alpha, and a service organization called the Boxerettes. During my second year at Pacific, I began spending more time with her, inspired by a simple exchange of smiles. Thuy told me later that there was one particular moment when she saw me coming out of a class in an academic building called Marsh Hall. Coming down the steps, I spotted Thuy and we smiled at each other. There was something about that exchange that connected us. We began sitting together at meals in the dining hall. I took her to a movie, *Love Story*, and she cried during one of the final scenes, when Jennifer Cavilleri (played by Ali McGraw) was dying of cancer in the embrace of her husband Oliver Barrett (played by Ryan O'Neal).

One weekend, a friend of ours, Pam Aronson, an optometry student at Pacific, invited Thuy and me to join her and a few others for a picnic at the Washington Park Zoo in Portland. It was my first visit to such a high-quality zoo, with well-maintained landscapes and healthy-looking animals. I remembered Saigon's zoo as rundown and full of undernourished wildlife.

One of the zoo's featured exhibits was its Asian elephant collection. Watching these huge creatures, I noticed the name of one of them posted on a sign: Tuy Hoa. Immediately I remembered the newsreel I had seen as a child back in Tay Ninh about the young elephant that had been captured in Tuy Hoa province in central Vietnam. Here I was, standing in front of the very elephant I had seen on film as a child! I felt a sudden, unexpected sense of connection to Vietnam, my family, and my roots.

"You Can Say Anything Here"

Most Pacific students adopted the styles of the times: long hair, Levi's blue jeans, and tie-dyed clothing. I had always worn my hair short. In one fraternity photograph, the faculty adviser, Mr. Art Wilcox, and I stood out as the only two with neatly trimmed hair.

"How much did you pay for that haircut?" a fraternity friend once asked me just after I returned from the barber.

"Five dollars," I told him.

"Ouch, that's a lot of money! That's like two six-packs," he said. (That was how most of my friends at Pacific measured the worth of things: how many six-packs of beer you could buy with that amount of money.) Since I was subsisting on a small monthly stipend from USAID, I didn't mind finding a new way to save money. Besides, I wanted to fit in. So I started to let my hair grow long.

Around the same time, the girlfriend of one of my fraternity brothers started tie-dying clothing. She asked if I had any white T-shirts. The truth was, I had nothing *but* white T-shirts (most male students wore T-shirts all the time, except on the rare dressy occasion), so I gave her one, and she returned it to me beautifully tie-dyed in bright colors.

Another friend, who had a car, took me into Portland for a shopping excursion at Lloyd Center, a shopping center in northeast Portland, and Meier & Frank, a downtown department store. My body was particularly small by American standards, so I searched in the boys' department for clothes that would fit me. I found just the right pair of Levi's blue jeans on sale. With my jeans and tie-dyed T-shirt, I blended right in with my classmates.

Of course, the hippy lifestyle that was becoming popular at the time was about more than hair and clothing. My American classmates were friendly and lived by ideals I hadn't encountered in my upbringing: be yourself, value self-expression, take pride in being a nonconformist, don't worry what others think of you, love can change the world, be good to the earth. Nearly every student I knew also objected to America's involvement in the war in Vietnam. Their opposition came in part from their sense of defiance of any kind of authority. Once, in the dorm, a friend asked me to share my feelings about the war. I paused before answering, and he sensed my hesitation.

"Come on, Khiem," he said, "you don't have to worry. This is America. You can say anything here."

I let that sink in for a moment. "Really?" I asked.

"Sure," he said. "Watch me." With that, he pried open a window facing the street outside, cupped his hands around his mouth, and shouted at the top of his lungs, "F--k Nixon!" To make his point, he repeated himself a few times.

Of course, I had heard about freedom of speech, but in that moment, it really struck me. In Vietnam, we didn't even speak out against our parents or teachers, let alone the president of the country. I thought back to the violent protests against President Diem. The rallies I had seen at Georgetown were against policies, not individuals. But to open the window and shout the worst imaginable insult about the president of the United States? That was something.

At the time, defying authority was part of campus culture. I sometimes asked classmates whether their parents approved of their stances against the administration and against the war.

"I don't care," most of them would say. "I'm over eighteen. I can do whatever I want."

That sort of attitude certainly wasn't the norm in Saigon. But, as one of my fraternity brothers liked to remind me in practically every discussion, "it's a free country!"

Of course, one reason students were so defiant of authority was the military draft, which was very much a reality in 1970. They had all seen friends and neighbors drafted and shipped off to Vietnam. Most of my peers at Pacific were convinced that the war was wrong. "I wouldn't put on a uniform and go over there and kill women and babies," I would hear them say. I understood; they hadn't experienced the war firsthand. They were repeating and reflecting what they had heard from the news media.

A few students held different views on the war. I later learned that these students considered themselves Republicans, and many of them had family members who were serving—or had served—in the military. Sometimes in the dorm these students would get into heated arguments with other students about the war. What amazed me was that they never became violent. There were never fistfights. They didn't even call each other names. They just debated and disagreed.

And all of them wanted to know where I stood. All of them—the anti-war students as well as the pro-war students—considered me their friend. They asked me how the war had affected me, and I told them about living through the Tet Offensive, how frightened I had been, how I had witnessed the destruction of entire neighborhoods.

"That was a big victory for the Viet Cong," one of the hippies said.

"What do you mean?" my conservative classmate replied. "The Viet Cong were decimated. They were nearly destroyed!"

They were both correct, in a way. The American and South Vietnamese forces had won a military victory, but they had also suffered a major political defeat.

I never took sides in these discussions.

"Are you anti-America or anti-Communist?" one classmate asked me.

"I'm neither," I told him. "I'm pro–South Vietnam."

I always kept in mind the admonition the USAID officials had given us to avoid taking public positions on political issues. Forest Grove was such a tiny place that it didn't have its own anti-war marches, so I didn't need to worry about avoiding them. Even the rallies in Portland—mostly at Portland State University—were quite small compared to what was happening in places like California, Wisconsin, and Ohio.

The closest I got to publicly commenting on the war was when a friend who was an editor at the campus literary magazine, *Pacific Review*, asked me to write something about Vietnam. I wrote a short story titled "Then One Day, When the War Is Over…" imagining what I would have seen when I returned to my village in South Vietnam after the war's end. It appeared in the summer 1972 issue.

One thing that confused me about the hippies and their anti-war protests was the symbols they used. I noticed that a lot of my hippie friends at Pacific would greet me with a V sign, raising their index finger and middle finger. I had seen that sign only in pictures of Winston Churchill, the British prime minister, who had used it during World War II to symbolize victory.

"Why is everybody waving a victory sign at me?" I asked one of my friends.

He explained to me that those signs weren't meant to symbolize victory. They were peace signs. He drew a picture for me of a circle with one vertical line intersected by two shorter lines at angles.

"This is a peace sign," he said. "When they wave two fingers like that, it's a sign of peace, love, and happiness. They go together."

While he was at it, he told me there was another hand gesture I should know about: the middle finger. We didn't have anything like that in Vietnam, or, as far as I knew, in all of Southeast Asia. He showed me how to extend my middle finger and hold back the other fingers with my thumb.

"This is for when you want to say 'F--k you,' but silently, with the same meaning," he told me.

I spent a few minutes awkwardly trying to hold my fingers in the right position, then thanked him for his helpful tutoring. Later that afternoon I was in my dorm room with the door open, practicing flashing my middle finger. A few friends passing by on their way to dinner spotted me and came to join me, chuckling as they watched me struggle to get the gesture just right.

"You need to get some practice using that," one of them said.

The four of us stood at my third-floor window, watching a stream of students pass by below on their way to the dining hall for dinner. One of my friends called out, "Hey, guys!" and when the students down below started looking up, all four of us extended our middle fingers at them. The passersby were obviously surprised and somewhat confused, wondering what they had done to deserve this treatment. Then they stopped and responded in the only appropriate way: they raised their own middle fingers and flipped the bird at us. We all just laughed.

Later I said to my friends, "You showed me the peace sign and how to flip the bird; how about the hand signs for 'Thank you' and 'I'm sorry'?" They told me it was a good question, but they didn't really have an answer. One of them showed me the thumbs-up sign and said I could use it for "Thank you." A few others nodded in agreement.

I didn't use the middle-finger gesture much after that, but I appreciated my friends for their efforts to help me understand the finer points of American culture.

Friends and Adventures

One of my closest friends at Pacific was Jim Remensperger, a neighbor in the dorm who liked to play sports and party. He was too young to buy alcohol, and since I was over twenty-one, I became the designated beer purchaser that year. Jim was from a wealthy family in Millbrae, California, an affluent San Francisco suburb, and his father ran a business that imported scooters and parts from Italy. Soon after we met, Jim told me that he'd had an uncle—his mother's brother—who had served in the US military and died in Vietnam. Jim had been young when the uncle died, and he didn't recall many details about him. But later I would learn that we shared an unexpected connection.

In my sophomore year, Jim invited me to spend winter break with his family in Millbrae. The two of us drove in his van from Forest Grove down Interstate 5 to San Francisco, where I was thrilled to cross the Golden Gate Bridge, which I had previously seen only in photographs. I couldn't believe the size and scale of the span.

Jim's parents couldn't have been warmer or more welcoming. In their home, I noticed a framed black-and-white photograph of an American officer standing in a rice field with South Vietnamese soldiers crouching at his side. Jim's mother, Betty, told me it was a picture of her brother, Captain Kenneth Good, who had volunteered to serve as a military adviser to a South Vietnamese battalion.

Captain Good, it turned out, was the soldier who had been killed in 1963 at the Battle of Ap Bac, the very incident I had heard my father's cousin, my Uncle Bac, describe to my father years earlier. Then a second lieutenant in the Vietnamese Airborne Division, Uncle Bac had been part of a unit that parachuted into Ap Bac to relieve pressure on the South Vietnamese troops at the battle.

The coincidence gave me a sudden and deep feeling of connection to Jim's family. And they reciprocated, treating me like a part of the clan.

One special treat they gave me was the opportunity to attend my first professional football game. The Remenspergers were San Francisco 49ers season-ticket holders, and they took me to a thrilling contest in which the 49ers defeated the Detroit Lions to win the NFC division championship at Candlestick Park. Even more thrilling, Mr. Remensperger brought Jim and me as his guests to a 49ers banquet, where I had the opportunity to shake hands with John Brodie, the 49ers quarterback, and Gene Washington, a wide receiver. Each of them also gave me an autographed photo. It was my first time seeing gigantic, brawny professional football players so close up, and it was a thrill.

The Remenspergers also brought me along to celebrate Christmas with their extended family in Mission Viejo, in Southern California. There I met Jim's aunt, Captain Good's widow, Barbie, as well as their three children, Leona, Chuck, and Lori. I also met Jim's grandfather, Mr. Ken Good, who told me with pride about Captain Good and showed me the book *The Making of a Quagmire*, which David Halberstam had written about Ap Bac and which specifically mentioned Captain Good. I learned from the senior Mr. Good that Captain Good had been a graduate of the US Military Academy at West Point and that he had been nominated for the academy in 1948 by then senator Richard Nixon. He had gone on to volunteer for a tour in Vietnam, worked in the Military Assistance Advisory Group, Vietnam (known as MAAGV), as an adviser to the ARVN's Seventh Infantry Division, and was awarded the Silver Star.

Though I generally steered clear of politics, I occasionally got a taste of American democracy. One of my friends, Reed Vandehey, was a political activist with a particular interest in the Democratic Party. During a school break in our sophomore year, Reed invited me to join him canvassing for a local candidate, Les AuCoin, a Pacific graduate who was running for re-election to the Oregon House of Representatives. I went along with Reed mostly out of curiosity. I had certainly never experienced anything like door-to-door canvassing in South Vietnam, where that kind of citizen activism just didn't exist.

Reed drove me to the campaign headquarters, where he introduced me to Les, a very personable and friendly man in his thirties. One of the campaign staffers gave us a brief orientation, then dispatched the two of us to work. We spent that afternoon walking from one house to the next, asking permission to put Les' campaign signs in their yards. We encountered some strong supporters who were happy to display the yard signs. But more than a few Republicans weren't shy about expressing their disapproval, sometimes using colorful language! I'm not sure how much we helped the campaign, but the afternoon gave me an opportunity to experience democracy as I never had before. And when election night arrived, Reed and I were pleased to learn that Les had been re-elected.

In May of that same year, 1972, another friend, Joe Haber, invited me to join him for a rally in Portland for George McGovern, the US senator from South Dakota, who was then vying for the Democratic nomination for president. We drove to Memorial Coliseum in Portland, where McGovern was addressing a mock convention. He spoke against President Nixon, against the draft, against the Republicans. And he called the war in Vietnam "a moral outrage." That won huge applause from the audience. Here in Portland, halfway across the world from Saigon, the conflict in my home country remained a major issue, the one that provoked the most energy, passion, and outrage.

What struck me most was hearing a politician get up and freely denigrate the sitting president. In Vietnam, there was no such thing as a peaceful opposition rally. There, if you wanted to run against President Diem or President Thieu and you said something critical of them in public, you could get thrown in jail, if you were lucky—and killed if you weren't. The rally served as another reminder that America truly was the land of the free.

In Search of a Challenge

I had come to Pacific intending to major in chemical engineering, and the Office of Overseas Study back in Saigon had approved that choice. But toward the end of my freshman year, South Vietnam's Ministry of Education had sent a bulletin explaining that there was also a need for professionals in the banking industry. One of my relatives, the husband of my mother's cousin, ran a bank in Saigon. That option seemed appealing, so I made contact with Mr. Mahoney in the USAID office in Washington and secured his approval to change my major to business and economics.

By the middle of my sophomore year, I had settled into a comfortable routine at Pacific. I was earning good grades, I had an active social life, and I was enjoying time with my fraternity brothers and my friends in the dorm. I was in Symphonia, a music group, and wrote articles for the literary magazine, *Pacific Review*. My professors all knew me by name because I sat in the front row, I was a foreign student, and I made great efforts to do high-quality work.

One factor was missing, though: challenge. As I grew more fluent in English, language became less of an obstacle; I could get through reading material more easily than when I had first arrived. All my life, I had enjoyed working hard and taking on difficult tasks. Now that I was comfortable at Pacific, I came to realize that I needed more challenges. As happy as I was there, I knew I needed to be working harder—and I was ready to. I made an appointment with my accounting instructor, Professor Sanford Bacon.

"What's the best business school in the United States?" I asked Professor Bacon.

He told me the top three: Harvard, the Wharton School at the University of Pennsylvania, and Stanford.

"I mean undergrad programs," I said.

He didn't hesitate. "Berkeley," he said.

That was all I needed to hear. I wrote a letter to USAID and explained that I needed more of an academic challenge, and I wanted to transfer to the University of California, Berkeley. A USAID representative wrote back, telling me that if Berkeley accepted me, USAID would approve the transfer. I immediately submitted an application to Berkeley, and a couple of months later, a letter arrived from Berkeley with good news: "Congratulations! You are accepted as a transfer student to the University of California, Berkeley."

Around the same time Thuy, too, started considering transferring to another school. Her interest was in finance, but she wasn't confident Berkeley would accept her. Instead, she applied to the University of Oregon in Eugene, which had a highly ranked business finance program. By then we had grown very close. When she gained admission, we had a serious talk about our future. I saw it as a test for our relationship. I wanted to see if we were truly in love, and I figured we would know based on how much we missed each other when we were far apart. In fact, it was difficult from the beginning. My saddest moment was saying goodbye to her when a Pacific admissions officer gave her a ride to Eugene to start her studies there.

"You're the New Math Teacher"

Before I left Forest Grove, I had a couple of important experiences. One was working as a math grader. I had excelled in my math classes, and at one point I noticed that my calculus instructor, Professor Mike Clock, was handling a large volume of students' homework.

"Do you have an assistant who helps you with grading the homework?" I asked him one day. He told me that he'd had a student assistant doing so in the past, but now he handled grading homework on his own. I offered to help, and he let me try. He gave me a stack of homework. I carried it back to my dorm room and shut the door. I corrected each paper using a pen with red ink. I could see some of the mistakes the students were making, so instead of just marking problems correct or incorrect, I jotted down tips to help them learn from their mistakes. Not long after that, Professor Clock stopped me to tell me how much the students appreciated the helpful tips. "You don't need to add the comments," he said. But I didn't mind if it helped them. Then he hired me as a regular grader; I started putting in two or three hours a week, earning extra money in the process.

Near the end of my sophomore year, as I was preparing to move to Berkeley, I spotted a notice on a campus bulletin board: wanted: math tutor. I inquired and learned that the job was for Upward Bound, a summer enrichment program for underprivileged high school students that Pacific hosted each summer. I applied and had a meeting with the program's director, Paul Hebb.

Paul was in his midthirties, slim, with long brown hair. I liked him immediately. He was laid-back and easy to talk to. He explained that the program was funded through the federal government's Office of Equal Opportunity. The students, who were in their last three years of high school, generally came from low-income minority families and were mostly from Portland; they lived for the summer in the dorms and ate in the dining halls. Upward Bound was trying to supplement their studies with tutoring and extra help to prepare them for college. I had found that many Americans had a fear of math, but numbers came naturally to me, so I was excited for the opportunity to help younger kids with their math studies.

Paul called Professor Clock, my math professor, as a reference. Professor Clock must have said nice things about my work because soon after that, Paul offered me the job as tutor. I was to start just after we completed final exams that spring.

My first day with the program didn't go as planned. Paul had hired me as a tutor. But when the math teacher didn't show up for work, Paul didn't miss a beat. "Khiem," he said, "you're going to be the new math teacher."

I didn't hesitate. I had been prepared to tutor, and I figured that teaching just meant I would get more time with the students. I stepped into the classroom and looked at the small group—mostly black students, along with a few Native Americans and Caucasians. They must have been wondering, *Who is this short guy with the foreign accent?* But I tried to put them at ease. I introduced myself and then told them about the class.

"I want to tell you three things," I said. "Number one, we're going to have fun."

"Math? Fun?" one of the students yelled from the back.

"I guarantee it," I said. The kids all looked skeptical. "Second, we're going to make you better at math when you return to your school at the end of the summer. And third, I'm available. If you don't understand anything in class, just say so." And then, I borrowed a line from my fraternity brother: "It's a free country!" They laughed, and that broke the ice.

To start the first lesson, I gave them an intriguing introduction: "Instead of teaching you math, I want to quiz you about how much you know football."

Their eyes lit up. They were expecting dull numbers and equations, and I was talking about sports. I told them to take notes and raise their hand when they had the answer—it would be worth bonus points.

"Okay, on the first down, your football team gains five yards, but on the second down they lose three yards, so what's the result?"

They all raised their hands and gave me the right answer: the team had gained two yards.

"Good!" I said. "Then in the next play, your team fumbles the ball!" I heard some moaning but continued. "Then the opposing team gains five yards and loses fifteen yards. What happened to them?"

"They lost ten yards!" a student shouted.

I explained that when you gain yards, it's a plus sign; when you lose yards, it's a minus sign. I wrote the calculations on the blackboard. After a few minutes, I told the students, "This is what math is all about!"

"I didn't know math was so easy," a kid in the back called out.

"That's because it was taught to you the old-fashioned way," I told him. "I teach math the real-life way."

One kid smiled. "Khiem," he said, "you're good at this!"

That's how I won them over. By relating the concepts to the world they already knew, I gained their trust and their love.

In the process, I also made a number of close friends. One was Paul Hebb, who'd hired me and who became a kind of mentor. After I started earning money, I wanted to buy a car. Paul was a jack-of-all-trades who knew a lot about cars and auto repairs. I found the car I wanted in a classified ad: a white 1967 Volkswagen Beetle decorated with blue flower decals—a hippie car! I offered $375, contingent upon having Paul check it out and give his approval. Paul went with me to see the car, and I watched him check it over from headlights to rear fender.

"It looks okay," he finally said. "Just needs a new muffler." Paul helped me find the right muffler and then he installed it for me.

He was more than a boss—he became a friend. Paul asked me to come back to Forest Grove to teach for Upward Bound for the next two summers. In later years, whenever he inquired about how the Volkswagen was running, I always offered the same reply: "Good muffler, good car!" And we broke out laughing.

Another friend I made that summer was the Upward Bound program administrator, Bobbi Nickels. Paul provided the leadership and Bobbi was the detail person. She had a remarkable memory, kept meticulous records, worked long hours, and made sure everything ran perfectly. I also liked that Bobbi laughed at my jokes, even the corny ones. When Bobbi's parents visited her in Forest Grove, she made a point of introducing me to them.

That summer I also got to know Dennis Real, a friendly teacher with a great sense of humor who became my first American friend of Latin American origin. (The preferred term at the time was "Chicano.") As we worked side by side and Dennis routinely peppered me with questions about my country and the war, we quickly grew close.

That August, after I finished my summer teaching for Upward Bound, I packed all of my possessions—clothing, books, a few keepsakes—into the front trunk and on the back seat of the VW Bug, said goodbye to my friends and Forest Grove, and headed for Berkeley.

Berkeley Life

Arriving in Berkeley, I knew immediately that I wasn't in Forest Grove anymore because it was so difficult to find a parking spot. Berkeley was a busy place, buzzing with life, and the university was at the center of it all.

I made arrangements to stay at the International House, which hosted students from all over the world, offering a room and three daily meals. While the vast majority of Berkeley students were Caucasians, unlike at Pacific, it also attracted a wide range of international students: there were people from Europe, China, India, Africa, and Latin America. Walking into the breakfast room felt like entering the United Nations General Assembly, and everyone I met was very smart.

That included two brilliant Vietnamese students. One was Pham Xuan Quang, a high school teacher from Saigon who was there on scholarship, studying toward a doctorate in mathematics. He was a contemporary of my English teacher, Mr. Hoat, and had taught at Chu Van An as well as at our rival school, Petrus Truong Vinh Ky. I called him Teacher Quang.

The other was Tran Tat Lanh, another PhD student, an absolute genius who was easygoing and even self-deprecating. He later wrote a doctoral thesis in mathematics that was only nine pages long, a proof of a complicated theorem.

These people were serious academics. Nobody at Berkeley was sitting around watching football on TV or catching the latest episode of *Sanford and Son*. They went to class and studied. When fall quarter started, I moved into one of the high-rise dormitories. Everyone worked much harder than Pacific students. The professors were quite demanding, and many classes were large—some so big that on certain days students watched teaching assistants on video monitors. One of my classmates quipped about one professor who graded papers on a curve: "It's a wonder he doesn't cause any traffic accidents."

I had to adjust my social life to this new level of academic challenge. At Pacific, there had been a party almost every evening, and I'd rarely studied on weekends. At Berkeley, there was no time for that. Besides sleeping, eating, and walking back and forth between my dormitory and classes, I spent my days and nights in Moffitt Library, the undergraduate library, reading, writing, and carefully checking my papers for grammar, syntax, and spelling.

I was majoring in business administration with a focus on accounting and finance. Berkeley had other academic requirements, so I also took writing classes and Introduction to Sociology, as well as a memorable course called Government and Politics of Southeast Asia, taught by Professor Karl Jackson. In that class, I met Tom Chirug, a brilliant student who had been a Rhodes scholar and then returned to Berkeley to work toward doctorates in political science and economics. He had a particular interest in Vietnam, so we became friends, and he taught me a great deal about politics. He gave me his address—his parents' home—and I wrote it in my address book so that I wouldn't lose contact with Tom once I left the US.

Another friend I made in Professor Jackson's class was Jim McWalters. When he heard that I was from Vietnam, his eyes lit up. "My wife is from Vietnam!" he told me. Jim had served as a marine in Da Nang, met Hong when she was working at the PX on his base, and married her in Vietnam before returning to the United States. It was the first time I met an American married to a Vietnamese person in the United States. Before long, Jim invited me over for dinner. Hong prepared a delicious Vietnamese dinner for herself and me, and grilled a steak for Jim, who wasn't fond of Vietnamese food. They had a toddler son, Michael, so when I needed a break from the dorm and my studies, I would stop by Hong's place to play with Michael and enjoy home-cooked Vietnamese food.

While I got to know some students in my classes, I found it harder to get to know students outside the classroom than at Pacific, where I would typically run into the same people four or five times a day. Berkeley was a huge university with a very large campus, and people were busy. Everyone was on a mission to get a degree of one kind or another. Nobody was sitting back, drinking a beer, and shooting the breeze.

In particular, I was struck that so many of the foreign students at Berkeley stuck together and didn't take advantage of the opportunities to get exposure to American students and American culture. On a campus of some thirty thousand students, they tended to socialize with one another, live with one another, eat their own ethnic foods, and converse in their native languages. They were getting an excellent education, but seeing how much they were missing made me feel grateful to Pacific University and my Gamma Sigma fraternity brothers for giving me the opportunity to assimilate and learn about American society and culture.

That's not to say that I wasn't working hard, too. Berkeley was extremely challenging academically, but I did well, even earning a place in the university's Scholastic Honor Society and the notation "honor student" on my transcript. I was also exploring some of my intellectual interests independently—in particular, I began to read books about history, particularly the American Civil War.

Since I was spending so much of my time in the library, after a while, I felt that I didn't have any social reasons to stay in the dorm, so I moved out and found a room in a boardinghouse not far from Jim and Hong's place.

Despite the university's size, I did manage to connect with some of my instructors. One of my favorites was Professor George Strauss, who taught organizational behavior. He was the director of Berkeley's Institute of Industrial Relations. One of his predecessors in that position, Clark Kerr, had gone on to become chancellor of Berkeley and then president of the entire University of California system, so I assumed that Professor Strauss probably had a promising future. He was a tough professor but also went out of his way to make sure that his students learned the material. He was the author of the textbook that we used in the class, and he could be quite intimidating.

I worked very hard in his class, but in spite of my efforts he gave me a grade of B minus. I had never received a college grade below a B. I checked my total points earned against the course syllabus and thought I deserved a B, so I paid him a visit during office hours and asked him to review my grade. Professor Strauss opened a desk drawer and pulled out a ledger. He looked through it and then added up some numbers as I nervously watched. Finally, he looked up at me. "You're right!" he said. "I'll change it to a B." It felt like a small victory.

As hard as I was working, I did try to have fun once in a while. In the fall of my senior year, some friends invited me to join them at a concert by the rock band The Who. We all chipped in for gas and tolls and drove across the Bay Bridge to the Cow Palace, an arena just south of San Francisco in Daly City. It was my first rock concert, and I immediately noticed two things: lots of police officers, and lots of marijuana smoke. It seemed that every second person was smoking dope, some holding joints with small metal clips, some using pipes. I couldn't believe how thick the air was with marijuana smoke. But what surprised me even more was that the police officers didn't seem to care—or at least, they didn't intervene.

I also noticed the music volume. There were dozens of huge speakers blasting the music at us. My friends were all excited about seeing the drummer, Keith Moon, who was known as the best rock 'n' roll drummer and left the audience mesmerized.

When I got back to my room, my clothes and even my hair reeked of marijuana smoke. The smell was so strong that my friends and neighbors asked if I had been smoking dope. (I hadn't, but I couldn't help but inhale the secondhand smoke.) Once I took a shower and changed clothes, I got rid of the aroma, but it was a couple of days before the ringing in my ears went away.

The music I actually preferred was classical, so I got a season ticket (with my student discount) to see the San Francisco Symphony, which played at Zellerbach Hall on the Berkeley campus. (Coincidentally, the mother of my Pacific friend Joe Haber—who had taken me to the McGovern rally in Portland—was part of the Zellerbach family, for whom the concert hall was named. I was impressed by the idea of having a big building on the Berkeley campus named after you.) I had enjoyed classical music since childhood, when one of my wealthy classmates in Saigon had played it on a record player. The same friend's father had disapproved of his listening to the Beatles and advised him to listen to Frank Sinatra instead. "You can understand the lyrics," he explained, "because Sinatra enunciates every word clearly."

Two kinds of people showed up for the classical concerts: affluent East Bay residents in suits and dresses, and people who looked like me: students who might have been wearing a nice button-down shirt instead of a T-shirt and shorts. I would sit with a few friends from my dorm in the cheap seats on the upper level, enjoying the music and the brief respite from my homework and busy schedule.

I also made it to an occasional Cal football game, but the real thrill was in January of my junior year when I saw Berkeley's basketball team play UCLA at Harmon Gymnasium. UCLA had such a strong team that they blew out Berkeley by nineteen points. It was UCLA's fifty-seventh win in what turned out to be an eighty-eight-game streak. It was a thrill watching their center, Bill Walton, the best college basketball player anyone could remember.

Montana

While I adapted to life in Berkeley, I also kept in touch with Thuy, calling from a pay phone to the boardinghouse where she was living in Eugene. I had to drop one coin at a time to avoid being disconnected.

In case she and I had any doubts that we were meant to be together, they were dispelled by the way fate kept throwing us together. We had both been selected to be among the thirty USAID scholarship recipients from all of South Vietnam. Then we had both been in the group of five chosen to go to Georgetown. From that group, we were the only two sent to Pacific University.

And in the winter of 1973, we had yet another fateful encounter. Every Christmas break, USAID would send its scholarship students to one of a number of seminars held in various locations around the country. In December 1972, I was sent to a seminar in Bozeman, Montana, that focused on the natural wonders of America's national parks. It turned out, through no work of our own, that USAID sent Thuy to the same seminar. Together with USAID students from places like Nepal, India, Iran, and Pakistan, we stayed in dormitories at Montana State University.

As part of the trip, USAID arranged for us to travel by a large snowcat to Yellowstone National Park, where we got to see Old Faithful and some of the park's other natural wonders. I had never seen anything like the geysers, canyons, and hot springs we encountered that day, and I was overwhelmed by their beauty and the power of nature they revealed.

The organizers also arranged for us to stay over the Christmas holiday with local families. It was a way of learning more about America and giving us a homey place to spend the holiday. As fate had it, out of all the students, they sent Thuy and me to the same house! We stayed with a lovely couple, Jack and Gladys Rosenthal. Jack was a real estate developer, and the couple lived in a large and beautiful home. (The Rosenthals assured us they hadn't intentionally arranged to have the two of us—they'd just picked a male and a female student randomly from the list.) Jack also took us for a flight in his small single-propeller airplane. I felt lucky to be there, and sharing the experiences with Thuy made them even more memorable.

Far from Home

I also did my best to maintain contact with my family back in Vietnam, mostly via mail—though it could take a month for a letter to get from one country to the other. When I wrote home, I avoided discussing politics or the military situation, fearing censors might not let the letters through. My parents and siblings exercised the same precaution in their letters. In one, my father shared the news of a promotion at work. When I had left Saigon, he was working as a typist for the appellate court system and moonlighting ferrying PX goods for my mother. Now he had passed an exam and earned a new position with the Ministry of Foreign Affairs. In the new job, he would likely be posted abroad for two years or more at a time. For now, he was working in the ministry's Saigon office, no longer as a typist but as an administrative assistant.

Not long after that, he wrote to tell me that he had been posted in South Vietnam's embassy in Vientiane, Laos. At the time, Laos had relations with both North and South Vietnam, and both countries had embassies in the capital. I detected a bit of the political tension he was coping with in his letter: he instructed me that when I wrote back, I shouldn't discuss politics, just report on my health, my studies, and whatever I was doing.

As for my mother, her letters didn't dwell on difficulties, so I assumed that she and my siblings were doing well. She reported that my uncle Bac had been promoted to the rank of major in the South Vietnamese Airborne Division.

Of course, Vietnam was never far from anyone's mind at Berkeley, where demonstrators seemed to gather daily in Sproul Plaza, the campus's open central area. Every day as I crossed the plaza, I saw ten or fifteen different groups, each with its own speaker, each with its own banner blasting President Nixon or the war itself. One group had a mock iron cage meant to represent a South Vietnamese prison and portray South Vietnam as confining prisoners of war and depriving them of human rights. Just to get to class I often had to cross a gauntlet of anti-war protesters or watch women's liberation protesters burning bras.

I was too busy studying to participate in politics, and, in any case, I didn't want to risk attracting the disapproval of the South Vietnamese government and losing my scholarship. When classmates asked for my opinion on the war, I would say that it wasn't truly a Vietnamese conflict. I had learned the word *proxy*, and I would explain that this was a proxy war, with the United States and the free world on one side and the Soviet Union and Communist China on the other. Vietnam just happened to be the chosen location. Most of my American friends would agree, but the handful of Republicans I knew would tell me I was wrong, and then, as I sat and watched, the vocal pro-war and antiwar students would go at each other.

Meanwhile, my Berkeley classmates constantly talked about the military draft lottery. A classmate explained to me that the Selective Service System held a lottery to randomly assign every male a draft number according to his date of birth. If you had number 1, you would be called first to join to the army, unless you had a deferment. If your number was 365, you could feel more confident that you might avoid being drafted—at least for now.

A table in the dining hall fit eight students. I was often the only man at the table who wasn't worried about being drafted. One night at dinner in the dining hall, one of the guys at my table couldn't stop smiling. His number was in the high two hundreds. Another student at the table had a number in the twenties. The first told me that now he could drop out of school without worrying about the consequences.

"If I get drafted," said the second guy, "I'll go to Canada."

Berkeley students were almost unanimously anti-war, anti-establishment, and anti-military. My friends knew I was from Vietnam, and they had watched the news broadcasts showing American GIs using Zippo lighters to burn down huts and decimate villages. When we discussed the war, they would use black humor: "Khiem, I'm going to go over there and kill women and children." They simply hated the war and had little respect for their fellow Americans fighting in Vietnam.

I listened without judgment and didn't debate the merits of the war with them. They were my friends, and each of them faced a difficult choice—the kind of choice I would soon face myself.

Besides the draft and the war, another huge political story was attracting everyone's attention that year: Watergate. President Nixon had won the fall election over George McGovern by a landslide, but now his campaign officials faced charges of acting illegally to win the election, and the president himself was accused of acting to cover up those crimes. It seemed that every day some new piece of news emerged about Watergate. And the news kept getting worse and worse.

In the spring of 1973, I noticed a group of activists near Sather Gate holding a banner that read impeach Nixon. I wasn't familiar with that word, *impeach*, so I asked some friends, who kindly took the time to explain to me that the House of Representatives could bring charges against the president and the Senate could essentially try him and vote to remove him from office. Another friend suggested that I read Irving Wallace's novel *The Man*, which included a description and explanation of the impeachment process. I checked it out from the library but had to wait until final exams were over before I had the time to read it. Then I spent a week making my way through Wallace's informative and compelling novel. I felt lucky to have such a good friend pointing me the right way.

That May, the Senate began many weeks of hearings on Watergate that dragged into the summer. Paul Hebb had invited me to return to Pacific to teach at Upward Bound, and I was happy to accept. I drove north in the Volkswagen, happy to be reunited with Paul and Bobbi Nickels, the program administrator. We spent much of our free time that summer watching the televised Watergate hearings, and I got to know the personalities: Sam Earvin, a senator from North Carolina, and Howard Baker, from Tennessee, and others. In Vietnam, I had watched coup after coup after coup, and the most important political activity took place behind closed doors. But here in America, there was respect for the law, and the entire country could watch this process play out on television. The experience increased my admiration for American democracy.

Besides teaching, I spent time that summer with Paul, Bobbi, and my friend Dennis Real. I also made another close friend in the program: Marcus Glen, a teacher and counselor who was friendly and outgoing and a gifted pianist.

Being in Oregon also gave me the chance to drive the two hours to Eugene and spend time with Thuy. Sometimes she took a Greyhound bus to visit me. Though we only saw each other a few times a year, we wrote letters often and thought of ourselves as a couple.

Two of my students at Upward Bound stood out that summer. One was Donald, a very serious student. After he solved a difficult algebra problem in class, I told him I was giving him a nickname. "Donald," I said, "you did such a good job that from now on I'm going to call you 'VIP.'" He flashed a big smile. "You know what VIP means?" I asked.

"Very important person," one of the kids said.

"No," I replied. "Donald's a nice guy, but he's not a very important person, not yet."

Nobody could guess. So I finally told them. "Very intelligent playboy," I said, adding, "Write that down."

Everyone smiled and chuckled, and Donald blushed a bit. But the name stuck, at least in our class. Toward the end of the summer, he sought me out to thank me and tell me how much he enjoyed the class. "Khiem," he told me, "I learned more in your math class than in an entire year in school."

Another student who made an impression was Johnny, one of the few Native Americans in the program. I found that even the other minority students underestimated Johnny and the other Native American students. They had somehow come to believe that Native Americans had less potential. As a newcomer and outsider, I carried no such preconceptions. I assumed that all students were capable of achieving nearly anything if we taught them well enough.

Johnny was quiet and didn't mix much with the other students. One afternoon, he stayed after class to tell me how much he admired me because I was in college and that he wanted to become a math teacher.

"What can I do to get better at math?" he asked.

I told him what had helped me, how my father had given me extra homework, way beyond what my classmates were doing. I suggested that when he went back to school in the fall, he should really focus in his math class. When the teacher assigned homework, I said, you should do extra problems—not just the ones the teacher assigns. Don't wait to get an assignment, I said; do the problems on your own, and if you're stumped, go talk to the teacher. Teachers love this type of student, I said, and they are more than willing to help them.

"If you do that," I said, "I have great faith that you can succeed in math and become a teacher."

What Next?

As I neared the end of my college years, I faced the most difficult decision of my life. All around me, my classmates were filled with excitement for what lay ahead after graduation. Some of my wealthier friends were expecting cars as graduation presents from their parents. Others would be taking off for a summer traveling through Europe. And many of them had earned admission to prestigious graduate programs: medical school at the University of California, San Francisco, Columbia Law School, and the graduate business schools at Harvard and Stanford.

Amid all of their excitement, I lay in bed every night, wondering what my next move should be. I had three options: return to South Vietnam, where I faced the possibility of being drafted into the military; stay in the United States illegally; or flee to Canada.

When I accepted the scholarship from USAID, I had promised that when I completed my studies, I would return to my home country. I wanted to honor my word. I also felt an obligation to help rebuild my country. I hadn't come to America only for myself. I had always dreamed of using my education to become a leader in South Vietnam.

When I asked friends in Berkeley for advice, nearly every one of them was adamant that I should stay in the US or go to Canada. Many even offered to let me live secretly in their homes or their parents' homes. (The exceptions were the very few friends who were in Berkeley's Young Republicans group; they all encouraged me to return to Saigon.) But, I wondered, if I stayed in Berkeley, what would my future be? I wouldn't be able to obtain a green card. If I applied, the Immigration and Naturalization Service would certainly discover that I had overstayed my visa and had promised USAID that I would return to South Vietnam.

If I decided to stay, I wouldn't be able to get a job—at least a meaningful one. Maybe a restaurant would hire me to wash dishes. But then what? I had worked hard for four years and had earned A's and B's at one of the best universities in the country. I didn't want to live as an illegal alien.

Should I flee to Canada? The Canadian government might have accepted me, as they accepted many Americans who opposed the war, but I didn't want to be labeled a draft dodger. Besides, I didn't have any friends in Canada, so it didn't seem like a bright future.

And if I returned to Saigon? Sure, I might face danger, but at least I would probably find a good job and decent pay. After all, I would return with a business degree from Berkeley. I would be in a very small pool of top job applicants. And I would be with my family and my old friends.

Sitting up late at night, alone in my boardinghouse room, I kept juggling my options. And the more I debated with myself, the more I felt that the only honorable option was to return to Vietnam, though I was unsure what the future would hold.

While I struggled with my difficult decision, Thuy, still my girlfriend, faced no such dilemma. As a woman, she didn't face the peril of being drafted by the military, so the prospect of returning to South Vietnam didn't bother her much.

I had seen our separation as a test of our relationship, a chance to see whether we were truly meant to be together. It turned out that we missed each other a great deal and wanted to spend our lives together. Facing the end of her studies in Oregon, Thuy was ready to go home and see her family in Saigon, where she had no doubt a good job would be waiting for her. So she returned to Vietnam in June 1974. Her move was yet another factor pushing me toward returning: I was confident I wanted to marry her. I made returning to Saigon my plan A.

In the spring of 1974, I began my search for a job in South Vietnam, starting by sending my résumé to a number of American companies with operations there. Among them: Coca-Cola, Pepsi, IBM, and several oil companies—Shell, Esso, and another called Cal Tex. The responses, in the form of one-page typewritten letters, were consistent: *Thank you for contacting us. Congratulations on your fine academic record. Our operation in Saigon makes its own recruitment and hiring decisions, but we will be happy to forward your application to that office.*

One exception was the letter from Pectel, a company Shell had created to do petroleum exploration on the continental shelf off Vietnam. It turned out that the head of the company's Vietnam operation would be traveling from Houston to Saigon and had a stopover in San Francisco. He invited me to meet him at the San Francisco International Airport to discuss opportunities with the company. I drove from Berkeley to SFO and met him in an airport restaurant. He explained that hiring was a slow process because of the South Vietnamese government's red tape, but he gave me his business card and told me to be in touch when I arrived.

Eventually I gave up on the idea of landing a job before I got to Saigon, but with my credentials and timing, I wasn't worried about my prospects once I arrived there.

I hadn't abandoned plan B: grad school in the United States or Canada. During my last quarter at Berkeley, I took the graduate business school exams and applied to the MBA programs at Berkeley, the University of Oregon, and the University of British Columbia. I did well enough that all three schools offered me admission. But the reality was that those programs were never a serious possibility for me. For one thing, I couldn't afford the tuition. Without the kind of financial support I had enjoyed for four years from USAID, I was on my own. And besides, soon after I finished my undergraduate degree at Berkeley, my visa would expire.

What ranked highest in my mind were two things: the contract I had signed when I accepted the USAID scholarship, in which I committed to return to Vietnam at the end of my studies; and my desire to use the education I had received to play a role back home. The South Vietnamese and American governments had fulfilled their parts of the contract by giving me the education and financial support. Now it was my turn.

I also had confidence that things would remain stable in Vietnam. The Paris Peace Accords of 1973 had led to a cessation of hostilities and an international agreement that North and South Vietnam would exist as separate countries. I had high hopes for peace and prosperity.

As I approached graduation, I made arrangements to spend one final summer in Forest Grove teaching for Upward Bound. Before I left, though, I took the last final exam of my college education, for an advanced accounting class. My friend Jim, the one who had been a marine and married Hong, was in the same class and took the same exam. Afterward, he invited me to his house to celebrate this milestone. Hong cooked a wonderful Vietnamese dinner for herself and me and a fancy steak for Jim. And he and I toasted our accomplishments with a beer, or two, or three. In fact, we had so many beers that I barely made it back to my boarding house, just a few blocks away.

Near the end of the year, I paid a visit to Professor Strauss in his office. I told him that I would be returning to South Vietnam and wanted to thank him for everything he had taught me. I had brought a copy of the textbook he had written and asked him to sign it for me. With a serious expression on his face, Professor Strauss signed the book with a personal message: "Mr. Tran, it was my pleasure to have you as my student. Stay safe and good luck!" With that, we bid each other farewell. That book became one my most treasured possessions.

I decided not to stay for graduation since I didn't have family around to celebrate with me. Ready to move on, I packed up the Volkswagen and drove north again, to Forest Grove.

One Last Oregon Summer

My colleagues and friends at Pacific University were unanimous in their opinion that I should not return to Vietnam. Paul Hebb, the director of the Upward Bound program; Dennis Real, my fellow teacher there; Bobbi Nickels, the program administrator—they all implored me not to go. George Evans, who had been my first English professor at Pacific back when I read *Goodbye, Columbus* in my freshman year, begged me to stay in the United States.

"I'll hide you in my basement," he said. "We just don't want to lose you."

Paul Hebb, a lifelong liberal Democrat, offered to drive me to British Columbia.

"Whatever you need," Paul said. "Just say the word."

Dennis pleaded with me. "The Viet Cong may get you, and you'll end up fighting on the other side, against me," he said.

I answered Dennis with a smile. "Don't worry about that," I said. "If I see you across the field with a gun pointing at me, I'll just say, 'Hey, Dennis! Remember the summer of seventy-two?'" (It was a play on the title of the blockbuster 1971 movie *Summer of '42.*) We all laughed.

The truth was that I had reached my decision. As I made up my mind, I constantly thought of my father's wise counsel: "You must keep your word. You must not dishonor your family. You must serve your country after all it has given you."

One morning after a meeting, I broke the news to my Upward Bound friends. "I know you're all trying to help me, and you all want what's best for me," I said. "But I have already made my decision. I'm returning to Vietnam."

I wasn't sure that any of them could understand my decision, but they had to respect it.

Knowing that I would soon leave the United States, I took the opportunity to attend to some details. For one thing, I wanted to get the best pair of eyeglasses I could before I left the country. Pacific University had its own College of Optometry, so I made an appointment there and selected a gold-framed pair of glasses. They weren't cheap, but I knew they would have been far costlier and harder to get in Vietnam.

I also knew that it would be important to have strong references for my job hunt, so I asked Charles Trombley, Pacific's dean of students, and Paul Hebb, my boss at Upward Bound, to write letters of recommendation. They both agreed, and both wrote glowing testimonials for me. I was grateful and felt sure the letters would be helpful.

While I struggled with my personal upheaval, the world outside was facing a crisis of national proportions. I spent much of the summer watching the developments in Watergate on a small black-and-white television Paul Hebb kept at the Upward Bound office. Toward the end of that summer, on August 9, President Nixon resigned and Vice President Gerald Ford was sworn in as the new president. With Paul, Bobbi, and the others, I watched as President Nixon bid farewell and flew off in a helicopter.

"It's amazing there are no tanks in the streets," I said to Paul.

"What do you mean?" he asked.

I explained that in third-world countries, there was no such thing as a peaceful transfer of power from one president to another. "Usually, if there's a military coup," I said, "you have tanks and soldiers in the street. You have brutal police crackdowns, curfews, bans on public gatherings." In the US, former presidents, like Truman, Eisenhower, and Johnson, just went into peaceful retirement, but in Vietnam and most other third-world countries, when a leader lost an election, usually his only choice was to flee the country for his safety and spend the ill-gotten money in his foreign bank accounts.

What I didn't share with my friends was that President Nixon's departure was actually causing me great concern. Nixon had promised to punish North Vietnam if it violated the Paris Peace Accords of 1973, but Ford had made no such promise. And the anti-war movement on America's campuses was being felt strongly on Capitol Hill. Politicians of both parties were speaking out against the war and for slashing military aid to South Vietnam. The previous June, Congress had passed a law, the Case-Church Amendment, that prohibited US military activity in Vietnam, Laos, or Cambodia without congressional approval.

Although the signing of the Paris Peace Accords had signaled the end of the war, in reality, South Vietnamese forces had to face more than 130,000 North Vietnamese troops who had been allowed to remain in the South while the US withdrew all of its forces and greatly reduced military aid to its former ally. I worried that things were looking bleak for my home country, but I mostly kept that to myself.

I worried about my family, but there was little I could do. As a Vietnamese expression put it, "We are pushed and pulled, grabbed, and crushed by the jaws of history." As citizens of a small, weak, and poor country, there was nothing we could do. We could try our best, but whatever came our way, ultimately, we had no choice but to accept our fate.

At the end of the Upward Bound session, I sold the Volkswagen and packed my suitcases. Paul Hebb drove me to the Portland airport. As we made our way to the airport, a radio news bulletin reported that Gerald Ford, the new president, had chosen Nelson Rockefeller, the New York governor, as his vice president. At the airport, Paul walked me to the gate. We shook hands and said goodbye.

Last Stop, DC

Before returning to Vietnam, I flew first to Washington, DC, for a three-day session run by USAID. Just as it had organized an orientation program, USAID ran exit sessions for graduated students, mostly from third-world countries, who were now all obligated to return to their countries.

About thirty of us sat around a big conference table. We began introducing ourselves: name, country, degree, major, number of years of US study. Looking around the room, I tried to imagine what the future held for these accomplished peers of mine. A student from Nepal had earned a master's degree in library science; I thought of him as the future director of the Nepalese library system. The Indonesian student sitting next to him, who was a medical doctor and had earned a master's in public health, was probably going to be the minister of health. A young lady from India told the group that she had just finished her master's degree in banking; she would become the president of the Reserve Bank of India, I thought.

There were no limits. These bright young students would make excellent ambassadors to the United States, representatives to the United Nations, and foreign ministers, and fill many more important posts.

As for me? I hoped for the best. Perhaps I would work my way up in the Ministry of Economy, or Ministry of Finance, or the National Bank of Vietnam. Or someday I would return to the United States as an ambassador or representative to the United Nations. Or maybe I would be drafted into the South Vietnamese army as a grunt. With the prospect of war still hanging over my country, my fate was anyone's guess.

As it happened, one of my Pacific fraternity brothers, Roger, was attending law school at Catholic University in Washington, so he and his wife Dee hosted me for the last two nights of the exit session. We enjoyed catching up, though I could sense their concern about my returning to war-torn Vietnam. We didn't discuss the issue, and I tried to enjoy my last few days in the US with friends I loved.

When the program was over, a USAID official handed me my return airline ticket. I flew from Washington to San Francisco, where my Berkeley classmate Jim and his wife Hong came to be with me during the four-hour layover. At the Pan Am counter, before I boarded the flight to Saigon, the agent weighed my suitcases, then shook her head and told me that my luggage exceeded the airline's weight limit.

I tried to save myself with some quick math. "I weigh one hundred pounds," I said, and then I pointed to Jim. "He weighs two hundred fifty pounds, so combined, my weight and luggage are less than his weight combined with under-the-limit luggage." She laughed but was unconvinced. That's when Jim stepped in. He told her—honestly—that he had once been a Pan Am manager in Saigon. That was enough to convince the agent to waive the weight restriction. I said goodbye to Jim and Hong, with whom I had shared so many happy times in Berkeley, and I headed for my gate and my homeland.

We flew to Honolulu before going on to Tokyo. Stepping into Narita International Airport, it hit me that I was returning to Vietnam. I wandered around the airport, struck by all of the Asian-looking people around me. I flew on to Hong Kong, and from there, finally, to Saigon.

As the airliner touched down at Tan Son Nhat Airport, a wave of emotion came over me. I didn't feel sad, exactly, but I was deeply unsettled. I was excited to see my family and Thuy. I was looking forward to reuniting with the high school friends I hadn't seen in four years. At the same time, I had become accustomed to a certain standard of living, and I knew life in Vietnam could not match that. As my mother put it, I was "jumping from a vast ocean to a tiny pond." I wondered what the future would hold.

Eight Months in Saigon

The Shock of Re-entry

The culture shock began as soon as I stepped off the plane. The late-summer air had a thick and humid feel that I hadn't experienced in years. And the military presence was immediately palpable. All around me, I saw hundreds of sandbags, barbed wire, and soldiers armed with M-16 rifles. The airport was clearly in the grip of security forces. I had grown accustomed to American airports, where I'd rarely seen a police officer, let alone soldiers with guns. Within seconds of arriving, I knew I had gone from the Land of the Free to the Land under Military Control. It had been just over four years since I'd left, but the security presence in the airport was many times what it had been in 1970.

The next shock came when I handed my passport to the uniformed clerk at the passport authority desk. The man stamped it, and I waited for him to hand it back to me.

"Can I get that back?" I asked.

"No," the man said. "It will be sent to the Ministry of Interior for safe-keeping." The Ministry of Interior, unlike the similarly named department in the United States, was an überpowerful government agency, like the FBI, CIA, and National Guard all rolled into one. Its power was second only to the military's. I had unwittingly surrendered my passport. Taken aback, I wondered how I could ever go abroad again. Seizing passports was part of the government's effort to control the population: anyone who wanted to go abroad had to undergo an investigation before being authorized.

Speeding through the streets in a taxi, I thought of all the ways in which I would have to adjust back to the Vietnamese way of life. Americans were open and spoke freely. Here, I would need to relearn to be more careful and less explicit in my expression—to be indirect rather than direct. In America, I had learned to stand erect and offer a firm handshake to anyone. Here, I would have to remember to bow in deference to my elders and authority figures. In America, people handed over business cards casually, with one hand. Here, I would have to remember to present mine more formally, grasping it with both hands as I politely offered it.

Finally, I would have to be more circumspect. It was well known in Saigon that the secret police were always listening. It was common for people to be arrested for saying the wrong thing and to be sent to jail without ever facing a trial. One could never know who might be an undercover government agent. As the Vietnamese expression went, "A protruding nail gets hammered." If you stood out and called attention to yourself, you could become a victim. I had grown accustomed to putting these things out of my mind for four years, but I would have to readjust.

My father was still abroad in Laos, near the end of a four-year posting for the Ministry of Foreign Affairs. But all five of my siblings were still living at home with my mother: my sisters Binh, who was then nineteen, and Thao, seventeen; brothers Khoi, sixteen, and Khoa, fifteen; and my youngest sister, Mai, thirteen. (It wasn't unusual in Vietnam to have two or even three generations living in a single house, and none of them had married yet.) All of my siblings were excelling academically, just as I had. My mother proudly told me that among the five of them, they had earned six awards for being among the top students in the class.

As for my mother, she was still reselling PX goods—canned fruit, chewing gum, Coca-Cola, beer, cigarettes, and more—with some assistance from my siblings. (Though American troops had left Vietnam, the Defense Attaché Office, which supported the US military aid program, was operating out of Tan San Nhut airbase, where the PX still functioned.)

I also had a happy reunion with Thuy, who had accepted a job at the Saigon office of USAID, the same organization that had provided our scholarships. I paid her a visit at her home in a working-class neighborhood called Phu Lam, about four miles from my family's home. After knowing Thuy for four years, I finally got the opportunity to meet her mother, whose name was Vu Thi Thong. Thuy's father had died in a military vehicle accident when she was only nine, and Thuy's mother had raised Thuy and her seven siblings on the salary she earned as a typist. Thuy had told them all about me, and they welcomed me warmly.

I didn't take their kind reception for granted. For generations, the custom in Vietnam had been for parents to arrange their children's marriages. But that was changing with the times, and besides, Thuy and I had both spent four years in the United States, where arranged marriages were practically unheard-of.

My mother and siblings were just as welcoming to Thuy. They had heard from me how much I liked her, and they accepted her almost immediately as part of our family.

I took a few days to visit neighbors, friends, and relatives, filling them in on my experiences in America and hearing about what they had been up to for the previous four years. I had brought the same gift for almost everyone. That summer, before leaving the United States, I had purchased about fifty silk neckties for a few dollars each at a small department store in Forest Grove. South Vietnam's high tariffs made silk ties prohibitively expensive, so every recipient seemed delighted to receive the gift. Most Vietnamese men wore ties about twice a year—on the Tet holiday and at the occasional wedding or funeral—but that made it a step above an ordinary gift.

Not all of the visits were happy, though. I stopped by the home of an elementary school classmate, Chien, hoping to spend time with him, but his brother informed me that Chien had joined the South Vietnamese Airborne Division and had gone missing during the 1971 incursion into Laos. The family had held on to the hope that he was missing in action and North Vietnamese forces had captured him. After the 1973 Paris Peace Accords had called for a release of all POWs, they had hoped Chien would be released. Now it was 1974, and the family had come to the tragic conclusion that Chien must have been killed, his body never recovered.

I also learned of another tragic loss. Another Chu Van An classmate, Tung, had been killed in action during 1972's Red Fiery Summer, an operation the Americans referred to as the Easter Offensive. Tung, I remembered, had flunked the second part of the baccalaureate exam and had been promptly drafted into the army. He had been killed when the North Vietnamese army overran Quang Tri City, South Vietnam's northernmost city. Now his mother told me that Tung was buried at the South Vietnamese military cemetery at Bien Hoa, about thirty-five kilometers northeast of Saigon. I made a mental note to visit and burn incense at his grave.

Hearing the news of my two classmates brought home the reality of the war with painful immediacy. I could only console my friends' families with the well-accepted Vietnamese philosophy that each of us has a predestined fate that we should accept.

But I recalled a statement I had read in college by William Jennings Bryan, the American politician of the early twentieth century: "Destiny is not a matter of chance; it is a matter of choice. It is not a thing to be waited for; it is a thing to be achieved." Of course, to my two friends' families, their children's deaths were matters of neither fate nor choice. They were simply realities they had to accept. After living for decades with armed conflict and daily death tolls, I realized, people had to rely on something, however superstitious, to cope with the horrors of war.

A Big If

One of the first people I visited was Uncle Bac, my father's cousin. When I had left Saigon, he had been a captain in the South Vietnamese Airborne Division, an elite fighting unit headquartered next to Tan Son Nhut Air Base. Now he was a lieutenant colonel and commanded a battalion. When I asked about the battles he had fought since I had left in 1970, he smiled wryly and said he had gone abroad, too.

"Really?" I asked, surprised that someone of his rank traveled internationally.

He nodded, still grinning. "Sure. I was in Cambodia for the invasion in 1970, and then I went to Laos for the 1971 incursion." Uncle Bac went on to tell me about his role in the 1972 Easter Offensive, among the bloodiest battles he had fought.

I told him of the awful pictures and accounts of the war I had seen in American newspapers and magazines, and then I asked him to give me his assessment of where South Vietnam stood at the moment.

"We have our full military strength," he said, "and we still have military aid from the United States. The only thing we don't have is US troops." As a condition of 1973's Paris Peace Accords, US troops had withdrawn from Vietnam. Then Uncle Bac gave me his prognosis: "We don't need the American soldiers to fight here. If America continues sending military aid, we should be able to hold out against the Communists."

To me, that sounded like a big if. I supposed that as a midranking officer of an elite fighting unit, Uncle Bac didn't want to sound pessimistic. As his nephew, I wanted to show respect and not openly challenge him. So I kept my thoughts to myself.

Uncle Bac also asked me about Americans' attitudes toward the war. I explained that an overwhelming majority of young people in the US were opposed to the war. "They don't want to get drafted," I told him. "They don't want to be accused of killing women or babies."

"What about the older generations?" he asked.

I told him they were the heroes of World War II and the Korean conflict;

those older people were committed to stopping Communism. The question, now that Gerald Ford was president, was whether he would stand up to a Communist attack and support South Vietnam. Nobody knew the answer.

When I asked some friends who were serving in the South Vietnamese military, they expressed more skepticism about South Vietnam's prospects. Our military no longer had the help of America's B-52 bombers and the firepower of the Seventh Fleet's warships—factors that had provided a major tactical advantage. The army's artillery power was much more limited than before and now lacked the American medevac helicopters that had so effectively whisked the wounded to military hospitals. One friend gave an assessment that stuck in my mind: "The Americans trained us to fight as a rich army," he said. "Now they're gone, and we've got to adjust to fighting as a poor one."

As I contemplated the realities of the war, I thought of my classmate Tung and decided to visit his grave. One Sunday, I rode to the Bien Hoa Military Cemetery on a motorcycle I had purchased, a 49cc Honda. (In Vietnam, anything 50cc or higher required a license, so many Japanese-made motorcycles sold there were rated 49cc.) Being at the cemetery brought back memories of my visit in 1970 to Arlington National Cemetery, outside Washington, DC. Approaching from a distance, I saw a massive statue called *Thuong Tiec* (Sorrow Remembrance), which depicted a sad and weary Army of the Republic of Vietnam soldier seated and staring into the distance, with his rifle in his lap.

I parked my motorcycle and followed a road leading to a hilltop pagoda. After ascending a flight of steps, I took in the view. Under the soft morning sun, the cemetery looked peaceful and tranquil. I looked out at the curved rows of graves, laid out in concentric circles around a circular monument and obelisk. It wasn't nearly as overwhelming as Arlington, I thought, but observing the serene landscape reassured me that my country was properly honoring these soldiers who had sacrificed their lives.

Wanting to find where Tung was buried, I made my way to the information booth, only to learn that it was closed on Sundays. Disappointed, I took a final look, quietly said a prayer for Tung, got on my bike, and headed back toward Saigon.

Teaching Again

The officials at USAID in Washington had recommended that I drop by the USAID office in Saigon when I returned to Vietnam. So I paid it a visit. The people there welcomed me warmly and gave me a beautiful certificate—a large document that looked like a diploma with printed text, "This is to certify that Khiem Manh Tran has completed a four-year course of study in the United States under the sponsorship of the United States Agency for International Development." In the background was the US-AID logo: two hands interlocked in a handshake.

When I started interviewing for jobs, I often noticed a framed version of that same certificate hanging in the air-conditioned offices of the top personnel at South Vietnamese government agencies. I didn't have an office yet, so I stored mine at home with my important papers.

The people in the USAID office told me that they would keep me on their guest list and that I should expect invitations for special events—their Fourth of July celebration, for example, and other various gatherings. They also encouraged me to get in touch with the VAA, the Vietnam American Association, which was known to have Saigon's best English-language classes. Perhaps I could do some work teaching English in the evenings.

I did land an interview with the VAA, but the official I spoke to explained that the current need wasn't for English teachers but rather for someone to teach accounting to USAID's Vietnamese employees—people with a working knowledge of English who needed to do accounting using American systems and terminology. I got an interview with the manager of USAID's training department, Mr. Peterson; we got along well, and he hired me.

I had learned accounting in English, so I made contact with Mr. Hoat, my high school English teacher, who was now a top administrator at Van Hanh University, a Buddhist institution in Saigon. He was pleased to see me and expressed interest in hiring me. I politely told him that I had a lot of interviews scheduled already and asked if perhaps he could help me find a Vietnamese accounting textbook. He did, and over a few days, I mastered all of the Vietnamese terms I needed to know, and I began teaching accounting three nights each week. Just as I had enjoyed teaching at Upward Bound, I found the job fulfilling, and Mr. Peterson was helpful and supportive, lunching with me occasionally to discuss my students' progress.

Landing a Dream Job

While I taught accounting at night, during the day I looked for a full-time job. I started my job quest with Shell because the Pectel executive I had met at the San Francisco airport had suggested I get in touch with the Saigon office. Shell was the largest company in South Vietnam, and I knew landing a job there would guarantee me a promising future. I sought out Mr. Tri, the executive recruitment officer and labor relations manager for Shell Vietnam. When we finally made contact, he told me that he had already received my résumé, and he scheduled a time to interview me.

In my excitement for the interview, I made one mistake: I neglected to account for "rubber time," Vietnamese people's lax approach to punctuality, and scheduled another interview, at the National Bank (South Vietnam's equivalent of the US Federal Reserve), for three hours before my Shell interview. On the day of my interview, the personnel manager at the bank was running so late that I knew I would be late for my appointment at Shell, so, panicking, I phoned Mr. Tri from the bank. I explained the delay and asked if I could reschedule.

"If you had said your motorbike broke down—the usual excuse—I wouldn't have given you a second chance," he said. "But it sounds like you're telling the truth." He agreed to reschedule the interview, and I breathed a sigh of relief.

When we did finally have the interview, it went well, and Mr. Tri arranged for me to meet with Shell's chief human resources officer, an aristocratic Vietnamese gentleman named Mr. Giu. The interview was at Shell's impressive headquarters, a neoclassical French-built edifice on Thong Nhut Boulevard, just a block from the prime minister's office, two blocks from the US embassy, and five blocks from the presidential palace. The offices were luxurious, particularly by Vietnamese standards. Mr. Giu had an oak-paneled corner office, with a secretary and an administrative assistant sitting just outside his door. Mr. Giu was impressed enough with me that he sent me on to interview with Shell's financial manager, Mr. H. Haerry.

Mr. Haerry was a Swiss national who signed his letters simply "H." Nobody called him by his first name. It was always "Mr. Haerry" or "Dr. Haerry." (Later I learned that he traveled in a white Peugeot with a Swiss flag decal—for protection—driven for him by a Vietnamese driver.) We had a good conversation, and then he sent me back to talk once more with Mr. Tri, the recruitment officer. "Congratulations," Mr. Tri told me. "Mr. Haerry has approved your hiring." I thanked him—particularly for agreeing to re-scheduling the appointment when I was running late. He waved off the gesture, but I made a mental note that I owed this gentleman a great debt of gratitude. Someday I would find a way to repay him.

I was thrilled to have the offer, but before I accepted, I had a few more interviews at other organizations, including South Vietnam's Agency for Development and Investment and the Vietnam Credit and Commerce Bank, the country's largest private bank, which also offered me a position. IBM, the American technology company, also made me a generous offer.

Still, I was leaning toward Shell, which I felt offered the best opportunity. Shell paid better than any other company in the country. It was also known to have the best employees—most of Shell's executives had studied abroad, as I had.

Before I accepted the offer, though, I checked with Mr. Tri to be sure I would be granted a military deferment through Shell. Since Shell's business was so critical to the nation's economy and the war effort, working there should certainly merit a deferment "When we have asked for deferments in the past," he told me, "we have never been refused."

I accepted the job and started at Shell on October 15, 1974, as an auditor working for the finance department.

Shell's operation in South Vietnam had about one thousand employees spread through multiple locations: Saigon and the largest installation/depot in Nha Be, Hue and Da Nang in the north, Nha Trang and Qui Nhon in the central region, Can Tho and Vinh Long in the Mekong Delta, and elsewhere. My position called for a lot of travel, often for a week at a time. I would travel to an installation or depot to check on an operation. When an oil tanker bound from Singapore stopped in the port of Saigon and then Da Nang, for example, I was assigned to observe the procedures, all of them spelled out in a well-organized English-language manual issued by Shell's London operation. I learned a great deal and took no shortcuts.

Sometimes I rented cars to travel—often with my boss, Minh, the head of the finance department's internal auditing section—and other times I would fly via Air Vietnam, the national airline. When flying, I would sometimes look out the airplane's window and see the craters that bombs had left across the landscape; in the rainy season, they became ponds filled with rainwater, and looking down, I could see the reflection of the sky in the thousands of ponds dotting the countryside. I remembered flying over the American Midwest and gazing out plane windows at healthy, green crops. In my mind, I compared America's verdant farmland with my country's landscape, so scarred by war.

On one of my inspection trips to Da Nang, my uncle Bac happened to be in the city with his battalion. I invited him to dinner, and we shared a delicious meal and a good visit at one of the best restaurants on the beach. When the check came, I insisted on paying. Uncle Bac had been so generous to me in the past. This was my first opportunity to return the favor. From the look on his face, I could tell that my uncle was proud of me.

My supervisors, too, were pleased with my work. Mr. Haerry confided after I had been at Shell for nearly six months that he planned to have me succeed the head of the internal audit department before long. Somehow, he sensed that there might be a need for a succession in the not-so-distant future, and he wanted me to be prepared. I thanked him and kept this promising bit of news to myself.

As jobs go, it was heaven. I was earning 135,000 piasters a month, four times my father's salary. Still living with my extended family, I paid my part of the household expenses, sharing the burden with my parents. When Shell's internal monthly publication ran an item announcing my hiring—with my photo and the caption "American University Graduate"—I suddenly became famous within the company. A senior executive dubbed me "Shell's most eligible bachelor."

The hours were very reasonable. I would work from 7:30 a.m. until about 11:30 a.m., then break for lunch, joining the executives in the top-floor dining room, which had the atmosphere and menu of a four-star restaurant. The kitchen served a variety of cuisines—British, Vietnamese, French, Chinese. Every dish was excellent, and the company subsidized our meals.

I usually dined with a few young colleagues, including Thang, who

had been a few years ahead of me at Chu Van An High School. He had
also spent a high school year in the United States on an exchange student
program, American Field Service. (His younger brother, Vui, a high school
classmate of mine who had also spent a year in the US, had gone on to join
the South Vietnamese navy.) Another lunchtime companion was Minh, my
immediate supervisor and the head of internal auditing.

Shell's leadership was loosely divided between the young executive
group, casually referred to as the "young warriors," and the "old-timers,"
executives over fifty who had been educated under the old French system.
These older men were fluent in French but less comfortable with Shell's
new official language, English. We "young warriors" were mostly educated
in English-speaking countries, were savvier about new technology and
management issues, and were generally more aggressive, innovative, and
assertive. The two groups operated in relatively separate social realms.
When one of the prominent younger executives invited me to a house
party, he explained to me that in the next five years, about half of the old-
timers would soon reach Shell's mandatory retirement age of sixty, creating
new opportunities. "Khiem," he said, "prepare yourself!"

On rare occasions, I lunched with Mr. Tri, the executive recruiting
manager. Another time, Mr. Giu, the aristocratic chief human resources officer, waved me over to his table to ask me how things were going for me
at Shell.

At Shell, we worked six days a week, Monday through Saturday, and had
Sundays off. After a half-hour lunch, we would return to work until four,
when we finished the workday in time to beat traffic, which, in Saigon, could
be awful. The company gave every executive Wednesday and Saturday after-
noons off to give us a chance to take care of personal business. I often used
my Wednesdays to visit the Abraham Lincoln Library, still one of my favorite
places in Saigon. I had spent so many years reading *Time* magazine at Pacific
University and Berkeley that I yearned for my weekly dose of American news
and culture. I read *Time* cover to cover each week—not in translation anymore, but the way any American would—and I also read the *Washington Post*,
a newspaper that had gained a stellar reputation thanks to Bob Woodard and
Carl Bernstein's reporting on the Watergate scandal. By the time the periodicals made their way to Saigon, the news was weeks old, but that didn't bother
me; most of it was still new to me.

Finally, I was in a dream job I had been preparing for all of my life—through my early years of studying math, my diligent high school studies at Chu Van An, my two years at Pacific, and, in particular, my two years studying accounting and business at Berkeley.

Thuy, too, was enjoying her new career. After about three months working for USAID, she had landed a position as a financial analyst at Esso, Standard Oil's operation in Vietnam. Thanks to her American education, the management treated her with respect and paid her a much higher salary than she had been earning at USAID. She also had great potential for advancement.

What neither of us realized yet was that her decision to leave the USAID job would turn out to be a fateful choice, cutting off what might have been a life-changing opportunity for the two of us.

A Poor Man's War

As Thuy and I both happily launched our careers, it was impossible to ignore the ominous march of events happening outside the office where I was spending much of my time.

The Paris Peace Accords had allowed North Vietnam to keep some 130,000 troops in South Vietnam, over President Nguyen Van Thieu's strenuous objections. To induce Thieu to sign the peace agreement, President Nixon had promised Thieu that America would come to South Vietnam's aid if the North violated the agreement. Now that US troops had withdrawn, the North began shrewdly testing to see if President Ford would indeed step up. In December 1974, the North Vietnamese attacked the province of Phuoc Long, north of Saigon, along the Cambodian border. After they captured Phuoc Binh, the provincial capital, on January 6, 1975, the US military opted not to honor Nixon's promise to intervene.

That emboldened the North Vietnamese to press on. In March 1975, they seized Ban Me Thuot, a major city in the central highlands. Again the US did nothing. Not only had American troops withdrawn from South Vietnam, but the US had drastically cut its military aid to Saigon. As my uncle Bac explained it to me, we were going to have to fight a poor man's war—to fight the Vietnamese way rather than the American way. The American way was to use overwhelming firepower—artillery, air support, everything. Now, without American support, our military was forced to conserve bullets and bombs. That would make it far more difficult to fight the North. Watching one defeat after another, President Thieu was ordering South Vietnamese troops to withdraw to more defensible positions.

The heavily censored South Vietnamese press wasn't reporting on all of the losses. I got more accurate accounts by listening to the BBC broadcasting from London, or sometimes Voice of America, which broadcast in both Vietnamese and English. And every time I visited the Abraham Lincoln Library, the pictures in *Time* magazine looked bleaker and bleaker.

By late January 1975, a general sense of panic had taken hold of Saigon, and it became clear to me that the best option for Thuy and me was to find a way to get out of South Vietnam before things got worse. I understood that if I couldn't escape now, my decision to return to South Vietnam—made the previous summer from the safety of Forest Grove—would turn out to have been a huge mistake.

On the other hand, if I managed to get out, I could consider that decision to have been a good one. After all, I had honored my commitment to return to South Vietnam after graduation, I had reunited with my family, and I had joined Thuy and met her family. I had landed the job with Shell, made some money, and gained valuable work experience. And if we got out, Thuy and I would have the chance to rebuild our lives in America.

In my family, we were at once trying not to panic and doing our best to prepare for whatever might come. My mother had endured her share of political turmoil and had also lived under Communism. She took practical steps, such as stocking up on rice and other dry goods that could provide sustenance during a prolonged war. My father, who had recently returned from his four-year posting in Laos, was actively trying to work his connections at the ministry of foreign affairs to find a way out for us. But he was having little success. I, too, got to work trying to secure an exit plan—for Thuy and me, our parents, and any of our siblings who wished to join us.

As the threat from the North became clearer, the American embassy in Saigon and its affiliated organizations began to evacuate any Americans not considered "essential personnel." Without announcement, USAID, the Defense Attaché Office, the US Information Service (which operated the Abraham Lincoln Library), and other American organizations soon followed suit.

With American agencies and organizations limiting evacuations, I decided to inquire whether Shell, my new employer, could help us to escape the country. I asked my old friend Thang, who informed me that the British embassy had already evacuated Shell's top five Vietnamese executives, but the rest of us would have to wait.

Finding little hope with Shell, my next stop was the USAID office. They knew me as an alumnus of their scholarship program, and Thuy and I had friends from our cohort who were still working there. But the moment I entered the office, I could see that the same panic that was engulfing the rest of Saigon had seized USAID, too. The office had always been a tidy, organized place lined with four-drawer filing cabinets and desks with typewriters neatly arranged on top. As I walked in now, though, everything looked different. I spotted employees dumping out files and shredding the contents. Hundreds of files and typewritten pages were strewn across the floor. I saw handwritten notes indicating how various stacks of paper were to be destroyed, depending on the sensitivity of the information: burn, shred, trash.

Two peers from our USAID cohort who had become USAID employees were assembling lists of their family members for evacuation. Their lists included fiancées and spouses of employees, brothers-in-law and sisters-in-law—anyone they wanted. And no supervisor was checking the lists.

In the midst of this bedlam, I found Dung, the woman who administered the USAID program.

"Will Thuy and I be able to get on the list?" I pleaded.

"Not now," she said. "There will be an opportunity in the future, but for now, the list is limited to current USAID employees."

Of course, neither Thuy nor I could have predicted it at the time, but her decision just months earlier to leave her USAID job for a position with Esso now had dire consequences. If Thuy had still been working at USAID, she would almost certainly have been on the list, and she could have put me on it, too. In fact, she might have been able to use her connections to enable both of our extended families to evacuate. I had never doubted that her decision to join Esso was the right one, but now, with twenty-twenty hindsight, I wished things were different.

I did have another connection with USAID. I had been teaching accounting for the VAA, which operated under the purview of USAID. I tried to telephone Mr. Peterson, my boss there, who had become a friend and mentor. We had even dined out together. I practiced reciting my appeal to him: "Mr. Peterson, I'm working for you. The VAA is a USAID organization. In a way, I'm a USAID employee—I would like to be put on the list for evacuation."

I dialed his number and waited. Someone picked up, but I didn't recognize the voice.

"Mr. Peterson, please?" I said.

"Mr. Peterson left the country two weeks ago," the voice replied.

I was shocked that he had left without saying goodbye. The person who answered the phone told me that Mr. Peterson had left in a hurry;

he just didn't have time. It turned out that USAID had chosen to evacuate their expatriates first, then other employees, and later people who had connections to USAID employees.

Devastated, I kept trying to find connection and options for escape. I went to the home of Vui, my friend who was a navy officer. But he wasn't there—his superiors had ordered him to stay at the naval headquarters.

The entire city was in a state of panic. And to make matters worse, thousands of people who had fled cities like Hue and Da Nang when North Vietnamese forces took over were now streaming into Saigon, which had grown in population by hundreds of thousands. Some of them took refuge with relatives or friends, but others had no option but to camp out on the streets, which were now overflowing with hordes of people, all desperate to flee the country.

On the way to work every day, I passed the French embassy, which had previously been surrounded by a six-foot-tall wall. Now that wall had been built up twice as tall, and a crowd milled about outside it, trying to press in to find a way out of the country. But it wasn't an option for us. The French were mostly offering help to people with French citizenship or ties.

The American embassy wasn't an option either. The crowds surrounding it grew by the day, and they were simply too large and dense to penetrate. But the Canadian embassy had a relatively small throng around it. One day, I brought the letter I had received offering me admission to the University of British Columbia's MBA program. I managed to get in and show it to one of the Canadian personnel.

"Do you have your passport and visa?" he asked me.

I explained that I had surrendered my passport at the airport and hadn't applied for a visa. "Can you help me anyway?" I asked.

He shook his head. "If you don't have a passport and Canadian visa," he said, "then I cannot help you."

Every day, I rode my motorcycle to work. On the way, I passed the US embassy, where, outside the walls topped by barbed wire, a throng of thousands seemed to grow by the day. Marine guards struggled to maintain control, and now and then someone from the crowd would attempt to scale the fence, desperate to get inside. Within the walls of the embassy, the scene likely resembled what I had witnessed at the USAID office, with employees working around the clock to destroy documents, desperate to prevent intelligence information or the identities of CIA agents or others from falling into the hands of the Communists.

I did my best to try to find a way to communicate with one of the marines posted at the embassy's perimeter. Maybe, I figured, if I could make an appeal in fluent English, someone might feel moved to listen to me and let me inside to make my case. But there was no way. I couldn't even get close.

Once I arrived at the Shell office each day, there was no work to be done. The main purpose of showing up was to see if any new prospects had emerged for fleeing Vietnam. Would Shell be arranging for a boat to evacuate the executives? Was my name on the list? Some days I would show up to discover that another senior executive was gone, having arranged an exit by plane. Even people with whom I had close working relationships didn't give any warning; they simply disappeared without saying goodbye. For all I knew, perhaps some of them had secretly been working as CIA agents and that connection gave them priority.

I tried every possible option. I dropped in at IBM, where I had been offered a job before I'd accepted the Shell position. There, I met with the executive who had interviewed me, and we exchanged forlorn expressions. I looked at him; he looked at me. I didn't need to explain why I was there. We both wanted to get out. I asked if IBM had evacuation plans. He had nothing to report.

The one place that offered a glimmer of hope was the Vietnam Commerce and Credit Bank, another company that had made me a job offer before I'd landed at Shell. After hearing a rumor that the bank had arranged for a ship to evacuate its employees, I made an appointment with the man in the personnel office who had first interviewed me.

"We don't know yet if there's a plan," he told me. "Only the top people are privy to what's going on."

I tried to go upstairs to appeal to the executive who had offered me the position, but a security guard wouldn't let me go up the elevator, so I returned to the same personnel officer. I gave him my business card. "I hope everything works out for you," I told him. "If you could call and let me know where I can get on the boat, I would appreciate it." I thanked him again and added, "I will remember you for the rest of my life."

We had good reason to be so desperate to get out of South Vietnam. By mid-April, rumors were circulating about the horrific events unfolding in neighboring Cambodia. On April 17, 1975, the Communist Khmer Rouge, under the brutal leadership of Pol Pot, had occupied Phnom Penh, the capital, overthrowing Prime Minister Lon Nol. According to the rumors—which turned out to be true—the Khmer Rouge were killing government officials and Cambodian soldiers, then marching city dwellers to the countryside, where they forced them into agricultural work and murdered hundreds of thousands. They murdered anyone wearing eyeglasses, which they considered a sign of being an intellectual. We heard reports of the violence on the BBC and Voice of America, and some survivors made their way to Saigon with reports of the ongoing tragedy.

Most well-informed Vietnamese were also well acquainted with the Cultural Revolution in China, when Mao's regime had stripped millions of intellectuals of their homes and livelihoods and sent them to the countryside to work as farmers and laborers.

Finally, watching so many American organizations and government agencies evacuate their employees to safety raised widespread suspicions that the United States foresaw a bloodbath in South Vietnam.

For me personally, the stakes were even higher. In the Communists' eyes, the worst thing was to be American or associated with America. Everyone who worked with me or lived in my neighborhood knew that I had gone to college in America. That marked me as a prime person to be interrogated and tortured. Everything I had worked so hard for all my life would make me a target. In addition, I had worn glasses since I was in seventh grade. If the North Vietnamese Communists cleared out the cities and singled out intellectuals, I would not survive. They probably wouldn't even waste a bullet to kill me. One of the Khmer Rouge's preferred methods was a lethal blow to the head.

In the midst of the nationwide panic, I tried my best to attend to my family. My mother continued to be a calming presence as she saw the unfolding events as yet another cycle of history. She did not express a particular desire to flee the country. "I have lived a long life," she would tell us. She had witnessed a dozen or so regime changes, from the last emperor of Vietnam to the Communists to the nationalists to the military and beyond. As long as at least some of her children remained in the country, she preferred to stay put.

My father, on the other hand, worried about his own fate, since he had spent his career serving the South Vietnamese government; that made it likely the Communists would deal harshly with him.

In early April 1975, with our future looking increasingly uncertain, I gave each member of my family the name and address of Paul Hebb, my friend who had run the Upward Bound program at Pacific University.

"If we're separated and you get out alive, and you make it to America," I told them, "write to Paul. He will help you, and he will help us find each other." I told them how to address mail to him: "Paul Hebb, Pacific University, Forest Grove, Oregon."

I gave Thuy the same instructions. She and I intended to stay together, but we knew it was possible that traveling solo might offer us each better prospects for survival. Things were getting so desperate that we had an agreement that if one of us was presented with an opportunity to get out of Vietnam without the other, that person should seize it. It wasn't ideal—of course we preferred to travel as a unit—but we knew that opportunities were getting scarce, and if one of us got out, we could always try to get the other out. In case we found ourselves separated, we each agreed to seek out Paul.

Paul seemed an obvious choice. He had been a protective mentor who'd tried to talk me out of coming back to Vietnam in the first place. He had been my last contact in Oregon, driving me to the airport and wishing me well as we shook hands that morning at the Portland airport. That had been only half a year earlier, but it seemed like something from another life, another planet.

Besides, Paul's name was easy to say, spell, and remember. Jim Remensperger was a close friend and his family was remarkably generous. But I feared that my relatives, none of whom were very fluent in English, might have trouble remembering his polysyllabic name and his Bay Area street address.

Around the same time, I wrote letters to both Paul Hebb and Robert Remensperger, my friend Jim's father, asking for help. I asked them to contact the Immigration and Naturalization Service as well as the US embassy in Saigon to try to arrange visas for Thuy and me. I closed the letters with fateful words. "*I hope for the best,*" I wrote, "*but if the worst ever comes, I would like to say goodbye to all of you.*"

With anxiety rising all around me, I tried to follow my mother's lead and project calm assurance. But it was difficult to avoid the reality that our options were quickly disappearing.

Then, on April 25, when things looked bleakest, an unexpected lifeline appeared. I returned from work to discover that an envelope had arrived at our home: a telegram from the United States. I opened it to find a typed message from Mr. Remensperger. The message was brief but incredible: "*Your papers are at the US Embassy. See you in San Francisco.*"

I felt overwhelmed with gratitude at this sliver of possibility. My letter had somehow gotten through. My friends in the United States, watching events in Vietnam unfold from across the world, were thinking about me and my family and trying to help. But even if there really were papers waiting for me at the embassy, how would I get to them? I had passed the embassy repeatedly in recent days, and there was always a mob trying to get in, with armed US marines struggling to control the crowds and keep the compound secure.

When a person is about to drown, though, he'll grasp at anything that floats. Holding that piece of paper from friends who seemed a lifetime away, I felt a small glimmer of hope.

The next day, I rode to the embassy with the telegram in my pocket. But the mobs had grown even larger and unrulier. I parked my motorcycle two blocks away and tried to wend my way through the crowd, but reaching the embassy fence was simply impossible.

Sure, there might have been papers waiting for me in the embassy. What Mr. Remensperger could not have known, though, was that there was no way for me to get them, and even if I could get them, I would have been one of hundreds of thousands trying to escape Saigon.

Three days after Mr. Remensperger's message arrived, I received a second telegram. This one was from Jack Rosenthal, who, along with his wife Gladys, had hosted Thuy and me when we'd attended the USAID seminar during Christmas in Bozeman, Montana. *"We are working very hard to get you out,"* it said.

Again I felt grateful for the expression of concern and altruism, but I sensed that however hard our American friends were working, it wouldn't be enough.

The Last Chance

April 29, 1975, was a day that would forever change Vietnam, my family, and my life. That morning, I told my two brothers, Khoi and Khoa, that we ought to make one last attempt to find some way out. Around 5 a.m., the three of us left our house together and walked toward the center of Saigon, where I was determined to make it into the US embassy. My hope was that we could board a helicopter at the US embassy to be evacuated as quickly as possible. I had the telegram from Mr. Remensperger folded in my pocket as proof that my papers were waiting for me.

As we neared the US embassy, though, I saw that the crowd on the surrounding streets was larger than it had ever been. It was difficult to imagine any way to get in.

Then, just a few blocks from the embassy, we came across an unexpected sight: a US Army bus with an American driver in civilian clothes at the wheel. It was packed with passengers but wasn't yet moving.

"Is it all right for us to board?" I asked in English.

The driver nodded, and the three of us stepped in. Seeing no seats available, we stood near the driver. I gathered that the bus had been designated for Vietnamese employees of various US agencies and their families. Since the teeming crowds made it impossible to board vehicles on the embassy grounds, buses like this one had spread out to locations where they would be more accessible.

"Where are you headed?" I asked the driver, again in English.

"The airport." he said.

This is it, I told myself. *This bus is going to be the escape I have been looking for.* If we could get to the airport, we could board a flight. If we could board a flight, we could escape Saigon and whatever fate awaited us when the Communists seized control. *If this bus can get me to the airport,* I thought, *I can have a chance to rebuild my life.*

The driver spoke to someone on his radio and reported that the bus was filled to capacity.

I heard a voice crackle on the other end: "Proceed."

Saigon's streets were more congested than I had ever seen them. The bus moved at a crawl.

My heart pounded as the bus—and time—seemed to stand still. Helpless, I tried to channel my energy to mentally push the bus through the traffic, but there was nothing I could do. I stood there, willing myself to the airport, imagining my brothers and myself on the flight to freedom, heading to America.

And then, almost as quickly as this opportunity had appeared, my hope was shattered.

We were halfway to the airport when the driver received a message, seemingly in code.

"What's going on?" I asked.

"The airport's come under rocket attack," he said, shaking his head. "We need to turn around."

My heart sank. Suddenly the driver made a U-turn and drove back toward the city center. There, he stopped, parked the bus, and opened the passenger door. One by one, we filed off the bus and onto the chaotic streets of Saigon.

Nearby, at the American embassy, the throngs had become a mob. To control the crowd, the marines were tossing tear gas grenades, attempting to protect the embassy and disperse the crowd. On the roof, helicopters came and went, whisking away whoever made it inside and up the steps, presumably to an airplane or a ship that would take them away from South Vietnam. When the last helicopter took off late that night, there were still thousands of people surrounding the embassy, all desperate to leave.

As my brothers and I slowly walked toward our home, I had a hopeless, sinking feeling like none I had experienced before. Along the way, we saw people looting abandoned businesses and homes. Some were carrying typewriters and other heavy equipment. We saw a man pushing a three-wheeled pedal cart loaded with a refrigerator. Others were hauling chairs, tables, and mattresses. The city was descending into chaos.

When we finally arrived at home, the rest of the family was listening to the radio. Duong Van Minh, a general who had been installed as president just days earlier, taking over a collapsing regime, had announced South Vietnam's unconditional surrender.

The war was over.

There was no way out. The Communists had taken control of Saigon.

Living Under Communism

Part Four

Destroying the Evidence

I had always been told that if you had a good education, nobody could ever take it away from you. But my education could no longer serve or protect me. Under Communism, I knew, the American education I had worked so hard for was no longer an asset but a liability. I needed to do whatever I could to hide or destroy any evidence of my years in America.

I started to do that the night Saigon fell, while the rest of my family was huddled around the radio, listening to Radio Saigon, which was now controlled by the Communists and was broadcasting victory celebrations and speeches. I quietly gathered whatever papers I could find from my years at Pacific University and Berkeley, every souvenir and memento from my four years in America. Hiding them or even burying them wasn't an option—so many friends and neighbors knew I had spent time in America that I needed to destroy every piece of evidence.

I carried the stack of documents outside to the kerosene stove in the back of the house, which my mother used for cooking. Standing alone in the darkness, I set my papers on fire, one at a time.

I burned my transcripts from Pacific and Berkeley with the names of every course, every instructor, and the A's and B's I had earned by working late into the night in my dorm rooms and in libraries.

I burned the address book with the names, addresses, and telephone numbers of dozens of American friends I had made in Washington, DC, and in Oregon and California—my only source of contact information for Tom Chirug, my Rhodes Scholar friend from Berkeley; Paul Hebb; Bobbi Nickels; Denis, my fellow teacher from Upward Bound; Jack and Gladys Rosenthal, who had hosted Thuy and me in Montana; and the Remenspergers.

I burned a small American flag made of red, white, and blue fabric with gold trim—a gift from a Berkeley friend, one of the Young Republicans who had been among the few people in my life in America who had supported my decision to return to Vietnam. "I don't know when I'm going to see you again," he had said when he'd given me the flag, just before I had left Berkeley eleven months earlier. "I hope this reminds you of your good memories of America."

I burned letters. I burned the recommendation Charles Trombley, Pacific's dean of students, had written for me. I burned the offers of admission from the MBA programs at Berkeley, the University of Oregon, and the University of British Columbia. I burned the certificate Georgetown University had given me for completing the course I'd taken in preparation for my college years. I burned the larger certificate USAID had given me when I had returned to Saigon—identical to those I'd later spotted on the walls of many Vietnamese executives' offices. I burned the contract I had signed with USAID a few months earlier to teach accounting to its employees. Finally, I threw two last souvenirs into the fire: my autographed photos of John Brodie and Gene Washington of the San Francisco 49ers.

Standing alone and watching the flames, I felt heartbroken. The bright future I had seen for myself had turned quite dark. Feeling very much alone, I contemplated what the future might hold.

Communists in Our Midst

I woke up the next day in a new world. People in Saigon reacted to the regime change in different ways: some were apprehensive; some greeted the news with calm. Most people felt relieved that the war was over, but no one knew for certain what the future would hold—for the country or for any of us individually.

Many of us had personal reasons to worry. I was concerned because of my US education. My father worried because he had worked for the South Vietnamese government. Our neighbor three doors down, the widow of the police officer who had run South Vietnam's forensic science unit, was concerned about her fate because of her late husband's ties to the South Vietnamese police. Anyone considered an intellectual worried about a cultural revolution. More and more, we were hearing rumors and seeing the evidence of the violence in Cambodia, and we couldn't help but fear that we might suffer a similar fate at the hands of the Communists.

While most of the people around me were worried and uncertain, others were celebrating. On April 30, we noticed a large number of North Vietnamese soldiers carrying AK-47 rifles congregating at the house five doors down. All day, men in uniform came and went. My family knew the family in that house well—or we thought we did. The man who lived there, slightly younger than my own father, was like an uncle to me. I called him Mr. Nam—Vietnamese for " Mr. Fifth." As far as I knew, he was in the business of transporting and selling flowers from Dalat, a city in Vietnam's central highlands. I knew his children, who were the same age as some of my younger siblings, and when I had returned from the US, I had made a point of giving him one of the silk neckties I had brought back as gifts. I had also shared with Mr. Nam the good news when I'd landed my job at Shell Oil.

What I hadn't realized all that time was that Mr. Nam was a member of a Communist sleeper cell. I was incredulous. So were the rest of our neighbors. Unbeknownst to us, for years we had all been sleeping a few doors away from a secret Viet Cong cell. Even the high-ranking police officer, now deceased, hadn't been aware of it, as far as I knew. It turned out that what we were experiencing wasn't uncommon. Back in 1954, when the Geneva Accords had divided Vietnam and led to the north-south migration that had brought my family south, thousands of Communist sympathizers had stayed put in South Vietnam, slowly infiltrating South Vietnamese society and ultimately laying the groundwork for the North's victory.

The New Normal

Adjusting to the new reality involved taking an inventory of the family. In the weeks leading up to the Communists' conquest of Saigon, nearly everyone in my orbit had been scrambling to flee the country. As far as I knew, one of my siblings had made it out—though we had no idea where, or if, she had landed.

In the panic of the twenty-ninth of April, the same day I had been with my two brothers on the bus heading to the airport, my father had made a last-minute attempt to get our family onto a boat docked at the port of Saigon. Riding his motorcycle, he could shuttle only one passenger at a time, so he had started with Thao, who was eighteen and the second-oldest of my five siblings.

"Wait here," my father told her, then sped back toward our home to retrieve my mother and the rest of us. By the time he returned with another family member, the boat had left with Thao on board, heading toward the South China Sea. We had no idea what had become of her after that.

Thuy also had a sibling who had apparently been able to evacuate. The second-oldest of her brothers, Thu, who had been a captain in South Vietnam's military intelligence, had managed to gain passage on another boat. Her oldest brother, Thi, a captain working for the South Vietnamese Joint General Staff, had not been able to escape and now faced a difficult fate because of his involvement in the military on such a high level.

As we all struggled to accustom ourselves to our new reality, people put all kinds of plans on hold. Travel was postponed. Social events were canceled. When Thuy and I had returned to Saigon the previous year, we had planned on getting married soon. But the panic of the previous few months had upended those plans. Still, despite the turmoil around us, we were in love, and we wanted to formalize our relationship. With so many unknowns, so much uncertainty, we both felt a strong desire to settle at least this one significant piece of our lives.

There were also practical reasons for us to marry soon. I lived in constant fear that my American connections and my jobs with Shell and the VAA (part of USAID) might attract the attention of Communist authorities and get me arrested and thrown in jail. That would have left Thuy alone. If we were married and the authorities arrested me, at least we would be recognized as husband and wife. We had each other.

Still, it wasn't the time for a big celebration. The victorious Communists were busily setting up their local government, and South Vietnamese citizens were wary about displaying wealth or throwing lavish parties. Instead, our two families had a low-key, simple gathering in my family's home—no guests, no bridesmaids or groomsmen, no uncles, aunts, or cousins; just the immediate family members. My parents were there, along with two of my three sisters and my two brothers. Thuy's mother, one of her brothers, and one of her sisters were present. Instead of wearing the colorful and elaborate traditional Vietnamese wedding dress, Thuy just wore her everyday clothing. So did I. We had no formal ceremony, just an acknowledgment by all present that our lives were joined. My parents accepted Thuy as their daughter-in-law, and her mother accepted me as her son-in-law. The simple event was followed by an above-average meal: rice and vegetables with a bit of chicken or maybe pork. And we were husband and wife.

While we felt that the wedding formalized our union, it didn't change our legal status. The Communist regime was so new that it hadn't yet established the basic workings of government—things like issuing marriage licenses. The government, such as it was, was too busy figuring out what to do with more than a million men who had served in the South Vietnamese military. They were focused on rooting out suspected CIA agents. The people working in the new government might have been quite proficient at shooting AK-47 rifles and fighting wars, but they were less capable in government administration.

Thuy and I did settle into a new home. Not long before the fall of Saigon, my father had bought the family a new home, and he hadn't yet sold the old one. Before the wedding, the rest of the family relocated to the new home, and for the time being, Thuy and I settled into the old Tran family home as newlyweds.

Although we had a home, our financial picture was bleak. When they had taken over Saigon, the Communist government had frozen all commercial bank accounts, and later they'd announced that there was no reserve for withdrawal. Overnight, any money we had in the bank had disappeared. Gone. The Communists declared that any treasury notes issued by the South Vietnamese government were null and void. A few months later, the government issued new currency and required all citizens to exchange their South Vietnamese piasters for the new currency, the *dong*. If an individual's cash holdings exceeded a limit set by the government, the excess was declared invalid and confiscated. Anticipating these measures, many people had sought out black market deals on US dollars or gold, currencies that were likely to hold their value no matter what the political situation brought.

Adjusting to Life under Communism

With no good alternative, I continued to show up each day for work. Immediately following the Communist takeover, the government had nationalized Shell and renamed it the Petroleum Company of Southern Vietnam. In those first weeks, I simply sat at my desk with nothing to do, except on rare occasions when someone asked me to perform some menial task.

Those of us who were holdovers from Shell were filled with apprehension and fear: apprehension because nobody knew what would happen next, fear because troops with weapons were occupying what had previously been a typical corporate office.

Immediately, the company slashed my pay. I had been earning 135,000 piasters per month in the old Republic of Vietnam currency. With the change in currency, five hundred of the old piasters were worth a single dong. The company cut my salary by 83 percent—from 270 dong a month to just 45 dong. And the high rate of inflation made things even worse.

My father kept showing up for his job as an administrative assistant for the former South Vietnam's Ministry of Foreign Affairs. But before long, the Communists summarily fired him and his fellow holdovers and told all of them to relocate to what they labeled the New Economic Zone to practice farming. Some of my father's older colleagues had worked as civil servants for upward of thirty years and had been nearing retirement. Now they were stuck with no income, no pension, and no prospect of retirement.

Thuy, who was still working at Esso—now redubbed the Machinery, Parts, and Supply Company of Southern Vietnam—suffered a similar pay cut, so we suddenly found ourselves living in poverty, though we had a bit of savings.

We found creative ways to supplement our salaries. I still had my Honda motorcycle, but the Communist government had declared gasoline a strategic commodity, so it was difficult to obtain unless you were an employee of the government or a government-owned enterprise, and even then each employee was limited to two liters per month. For extra money, I would buy gas and then resell it around the corner for three times the pump price. Instead of riding my motorcycle, I rode a bicycle the ten miles each way to and from work. That arrangement gave me a steady source of extra income.

The government also distributed food ration cards to employees. They could be used to buy staples such as rice, flour, and orange juice (donated by Algeria). Another option: fish heads and lobster heads. (The Soviet Union had made loans to North Vietnam during the war. To repay some of the debt, Vietnamese would catch fish and lobster and send the choice fish filets and lobster tails and claws to the Soviets, leaving only the heads for the Vietnamese market.) The Vietnamese joke went, "*Ban gi cung mua, mua gi cung ban*," which meant, "Buy anything the government sells, and sell everything you just bought on the black market." We did just that, and it helped us pay the bills.

The Petroleum Company of Southern Vietnam

Before the fall of Saigon, the British had evacuated Shell's top Vietnamese executives, and every expatriate (non-Vietnamese) employee had also fled. About twenty Vietnamese executives had managed to leave the country on their own. After the many departures, some thirty executives remained from the old operation.

It wasn't long before the new management sent all of us holdovers to a "re-education" program where they tried to indoctrinate us politically. They divided us into two groups—one for executives, one for the rest of the workers. I was grouped with the executives. The Communist leaders delivered memorized lectures, long diatribes about the history of the Communist Party and its successful struggles against the Japanese, the French, and the Americans. They ranted against the United States and American "imperialists," seemingly unaware that Shell was a British company, not an American one.

When it came time for questions and answers, one colleague in our group raised his hand. He mentioned the cultural revolution happening in the People's Republic of China and how the government had sent intellectuals from the city to do hard labor in the countryside and learn the value of hard work. "Is our government going to follow China and send us to the countryside?" he asked.

The speaker hesitated, then replied. "We don't follow China. We don't follow the Soviets," he said. "We have our own policy: showing generosity toward the reformed and dealing harshly with the reactionaries."

All of us silently exchanged glances, wondering what his answer had meant. In any case, I admired my colleague for speaking up.

In the same building where I had grown accustomed to the elegant dining room and well-educated, worldly colleagues, now I was figuring out how to work with three different kinds of colleagues: older Communists originally from North Vietnam, South Vietnamese Communists, and younger Communists who had received their training in Russia and Eastern Bloc countries.

The older Communists from North Vietnam were sterner and more regimented than the others. They were indoctrinated to hate capitalism and America. They also held the top positions and wielded the most power.

The Communists who were born and raised in the South were less bitter and less vindictive toward the southerners.

The most open and tolerant people among the new arrivals were the younger Communists with training from the Eastern Bloc. They had been educated in places like the Soviet Union, Bulgaria, Yugoslavia, and East Germany, where they had studied everything from chemical engineering to economics and management. Later, I would compare notes with one of them—Chong, who had studied in East Germany—about our similar university experiences abroad: in the countries where we had gone to college, most people had automobiles and lived in houses, everyone had enough to eat, and parties featuring alcohol were commonplace.

The Communists' top concern was security. The new regime had to account for a million former ARVN soldiers and millions of M-16 rifles, as well as countless explosive devices and other weapons. There were also former civil servants in every city and hamlet. Less than a week after their victory, the new government ordered former military personnel, police, administrative officers, and others to register at various locations around the country. Later, the government ordered former ARVN military officers to report for what they thought would be a week or a month of "re-education." Instead, they spent years in the jungle or in prison in North Vietnam. (This treatment was in marked contrast to what I remembered learning about the aftermath of America's Civil War: the Union army gave Confederate soldiers rations, issued them printed parole papers, and allowed them to go home and take their horses with them.)

As the government nationalized businesses like Shell, it required every worker to submit to the government a detailed personal profile known as a *ly lich*. It was a kind of personal background sheet that listed names of relatives, financial details, religious preference, and political affiliation. The government required that the *ly lich* include any ties to the United States. Omitting such pertinent information was considered intentionally lying to authorities and could land a person in jail.

The government controlled everything—jobs, the food supply, access to education, housing—and used information on the *ly lich* to determine who was entitled to what. It was the controlling document that governed our lives, and everyone had to fill one out: high school students, executives, workers of all kinds. I learned that the biographies that the South Vietnamese holdovers produced were likely to attract particular attention because the Communist authorities considered petroleum and its related products to be strategic commodities linked to national security, which was their most prominent concern.

The security department at Shell—now the Petroleum Company of Southern Vietnam—instructed me to fill out my *ly lich*. Since almost everyone at Shell (and my Communist neighbor, Mr. Nam) knew that I had graduated from an American university, I knew I needed to be transparent about my American connections. After I submitted my *ly lich*, I was summoned to the security office, where a security officer peppered me with questions in order to reveal more details of my biography. Once the file was complete, management shared the information with the local police precinct.

"Do You Work for the CIA?"

Some of the older Communists from the North had spent years on the Ho Chi Minh Trail in Laos and Cambodia overseeing the fuel supply for North Vietnam's tanks and trucks. That was the entirety of their experience working with petroleum, and most of them lacked education beyond the fifth grade. They had been indoctrinated in Communism, they had fought for years against the US military, and they viewed people like me—who had been educated abroad and spoke English—as enemies and possible CIA agents.

One incident made me realize the frightening—and ridiculous—nature of their suspicions. In my office, I had a bookcase that was filled mostly with Shell's detailed and thorough technical manuals, all bearing the company's scallop logo. On another shelf, I kept a collection of professional magazines and journals. One I perused regularly was published by America's Institute of Internal Auditors. In my first months with Shell, I had asked management to pay for a subscription to the publication in order to help me keep up with developments in my field. Mr. Haerry, the finance manager and my supervisor's boss, had approved it, so one shelf of my bookcase held a few back issues of the magazine.

The older Communists made it their business to keep an alert eye on my colleagues and me. One day, one of them showed up in my office and approached the bookshelf, closely perusing the titles. I was certain that he had little, if any, grasp of English, but that didn't stop him. He pulled out a magazine for certified public accountants, flipped through it, then casually returned it to the shelf. Then he pulled out an issue of the corporate auditor's magazine and scanned the pages. Suddenly he held it close to his face, furrowing his brow as he examined a page closely. He looked at me, then back at the page. Clearly something had caught his attention, but he didn't bother to tell me what it was. He simply slipped the magazine back into its place and made his way out the door.

Half an hour later, two agents from the Office of Organization showed up at my door. One of them told me to follow him to the security office.

There, he sat me down and began interrogating me.

"How long did you live in the United States?" he asked.

I told him I had studied there from 1970 to 1974.

"What did you study?"

"I studied accounting and finance."

"What did you do besides study?" he asked.

I told him that I did what college students do: I went to sporting events, movies, and parties.

Then the questions got more pointed: "Do you know of any CIA agents hiding in our company?"

What was this about? "No," I said strongly.

"Are you a CIA agent or have you ever worked for the CIA?"

"No," I said. Then I turned the questions around. "Why are you asking me this?" I asked.

"We have proof that you are connected to the CIA."

How can that be? I wondered. "What proof?" I asked.

With that, the security agent who had visited my officer earlier walked in from an adjacent room, carrying something in his hands: my stack of *Internal Auditor* magazines. He opened an issue and turned to a page at the front. Holding the page so I could see, he pointed at a list of the magazine's contributors.

"CIA," he said, looking up at me. "Do you work for the CIA?"

If his question hadn't been so preposterous, I would have broken out in laughter. I shook my head. "It stands for 'certified internal auditor,'" I told him. Each of those contributors had passed a test to be certified with that designation, one of the most sought-after certifications in the accounting industry. I hadn't passed the test yet myself, so I didn't have the designation.

I tried to explain. "I worked in the auditing section of Shell," I said. "This is a professional magazine I read to do my job."

The agents looked skeptical, and I felt concerned. I was familiar with how Communist security people thought: *If he's not a CIA agent now, he could become one at any time.* "If you don't believe me, ask someone else who speaks English," I said. "Ask Mr. Chong." Chong was a young Communist who had attended college in East Germany and had a decent grasp of English. In fact, he sometimes had me come into his office, closed the door, and practiced his English with me, out of the hearing range of our Communist colleagues.

The agent who had been questioning me paused for a long time. Then he spoke. "We will investigate," he said. "In the meantime, write down your full explanation, date it, and sign your name. You must be truthful, or you will be punished."

I spent the next hour writing down everything I had told him. I signed the page and handed it to the agent. He admonished me not to talk to anybody about what had happened. I returned to my office, relieved but also newly reminded of the bleak reality in which I was living. I was past feeling demoralized.

At home that evening, I decided not to tell Thuy what had happened, not wanting to add to her worries. Knowing that I was under surveillance, I also opted not to go out to visit relatives or friends. If I had, the security authorities would have probably called in the people I visited for interrogation. Furthermore, it would have confirmed the Communists' suspicions that I had something to hide. I told Thuy that I didn't feel well. We had a quick dinner, and I went to bed early.

The next day at the office, nobody mentioned the magazine incident. A week passed, then a month. I never heard about it again.

Go to the New Economic Zone!

About a year after the government nationalized Shell, the company began firing people. I had been lucky to be number one on many lists in my life, but this time being first meant something else. The Petroleum Company of Southern Vietnam put me at the top of its layoff list. By this time, I had given up my old office to a Communist official and been assigned a desk in a large, open work area. One day, a security staffer came to my desk and asked me to follow him to the security office in the basement.

"Your services are no longer needed," the security officer told me.

"Why, may I ask?" I asked politely.

He handed me a typewritten page with the reason: "Improving internal security." The paper also instructed me to register with the local police for "local supervision."

That was it. My time there was finished. No severance package. No goodbye party. What had started out before the fall of Saigon as an exciting and promising position had developed into a meaningless job for a state-controlled enterprise. I assumed that the internal security people suspected that either I was a CIA agent or I would become one. In the eyes of the Communists, I had no business working for an organization that handled what they labeled "strategic commodities with national security implications."

The security official did offer me some advice. He told me that my background (by which he meant my US connections and Western education) would make it very difficult for me to find employment in the new Vietnam, which had almost no private enterprise. "The best option for you," he told me, "is to leave the city, go to the New Economic Zone, and work in an agricultural cooperative, growing rice."

The Communist government had created the New Economic Zones program after the fall of Saigon to remove southerners from their homes and relocate them to uninhabited, mountainous forested areas. It had collectivized the farms, and now that farmers had no incentive to work hard, rice production had dropped to historically low levels. Vietnam was quickly on its way to becoming one of the planet's poorest countries.

I was determined to avoid being sent to work the land. I was small, not particularly strong, and had gotten far using my brain, not my muscles. I knew that if I were to be forced to relocate to the New Economic Zone, my fate would be bleak.

"I'm not very strong," I told him. "I don't think farming is for me."

He explained that plenty of Chinese intellectuals had learned valuable lessons from their work on collective farms.

I said I would give it some thought. Then a security officer escorted me back to my desk to gather my personal items. When I entered the open work area, it suddenly became quiet. I suspected that my old Shell coworkers were already aware of my firing. Everyone looked down at their work. No one made eye contact. Nobody approached to shake my hand and say goodbye. My colleagues were afraid that the security officer might suspect that they somehow had a connection with me. Looking straight ahead, without ceremony, I left the room and headed for the building front door, where I paused to look around. Some eighteen months earlier, I had felt such promise here. I turned back to the exit and saw a familiar face just ahead of me. Mr. Tri, the recruitment manager who had kindly let me reschedule my initial Shell interview, was walking out of the building. He had been fired that day too.

Feeling the same hopeless, sinking sensation I had experienced when I got off the American bus that I had hoped would take me to the airport on April 29, 1975, I stepped outside and headed home.

"When Do You Want Me to Start?"

Despite what I had told the security official, I didn't really give any serious thought to joining a collective farm in the New Economic Zone. I knew myself. I wasn't a strong person or a big one. I had never been particularly muscular. For my entire life, I had used my brain, not my muscle, to survive and thrive. Rather than heading to the countryside, I accepted my unemployment. With nowhere to report to each morning, I stayed home and slept late. Each morning Thuy would quietly slip out and head to work, leaving me to rest.

After only a couple of days of this, I was awakened by a knock at the door. When I opened it, I saw a familiar face: Mr. Doi, an independent contractor I knew from my time at Shell. Mr. Doi's company manufactured underground storage tanks for gas stations. Somehow he had heard that I had lost my job, so he invited me to come to work for him at his company, which was called Storage Tank Co.

One door closes and another opens.

"When do you want me to start?" I asked.

"You can start tomorrow," he said.

"You've got a deal."

I worked as an accountant in an office that was a sharp contrast to the plush suites where I had spent the previous year and a half. The production facility was in an open yard, about twenty feet from my desk, and all day I put up with the loud sounds of crews cutting and pounding steel sheets and then using blowtorches to weld them together, usually in sticky ninety-degree heat. When I wanted to consult with a colleague, I had to shout. It wasn't exactly what I had envisioned when I was studying accounting at Berkeley. But it was a job.

Less than a year after I started the job, my former employer, the Petroleum Company of Southern Vietnam, was threatening to take over and nationalize the storage tank company. Knowing that would not bode well for me, I quit, and soon I found yet another opportunity. Another former colleague connected me with his brother, who was working as a govern-

ment contractor for an irrigation project in the city of Can Tho, in the
Mekong Delta, aimed at diverting water from a river to irrigate rice fields.
Workers with shovels and buckets were dredging a small tributary. My
friend's brother, whose name was Nhiep, needed someone to handle the finances—dealing with the bank, managing payroll, and other such matters.

Can Tho was four hours by intercity bus from Saigon. (Though the
Communists had renamed it Ho Chi Minh City, most people continued to
call it Saigon.) But getting to Can Tho wasn't as simple as merely buying a
bus ticket. The Communist government had cracked down on travel, and I
needed to secure a permit to make the trip. Nhiep, my boss on the project,
handwrote a letter on my behalf—countersigned by the Communist head
of the project—to request a travel permit for me. I took it to my local police headquarters and asked for a permit.

"How long will you need it?" the officer asked.

Not sure, I said a year. The officer approved the permit, and each week,
I traveled to Can Tho, where I slept on the floor of a house five nights a
week, returning to Saigon for the weekend. It was a job. I worked in a tiny
thatched-roof hut, without air-conditioning or even an electric fan, near
the dredging operation. Each week (and eventually every day) I visited the
local bank and withdrew cash to pay the workers' wages.

It was only five months before the dredging project was complete.
Seeking employment again, I paid a visit to the printing house that had
printed pay statements and time cards for the dredging project. (I had inquired with the same business years earlier about a small printing project
for Shell.) The owner, a man named Hoang, knew that I had attended university in the United States and worked at Shell. His business was growing
quickly, and he desperately needed someone with my experience to keep
the books straight. He offered me a higher salary than I'd earned at either
of the previous two jobs, and I eagerly accepted.

"You can start today," he said.

Mr. Hoang was well connected in Communist circles. His wife had
fought on the Communist side in the war against the French and had remained in Saigon after the country's 1954 partition. Her comrades from
the war days, now mid- and high-ranking Communist officials, constantly
dropped by the print shop to visit and reminisce. They also gave Mr. Hoang
and his wife lucrative government contracts. One was with Vietnam Air-

lines, the new state-owned carrier. Since I was proficient in English, they assigned me to proofread the English-language section of the international tickets and luggage tags for that contract.

I quickly learned how important payoffs and kickbacks were in the commerce of a Communist country. Mr. Hoang, a kind and soft-spoken gentleman, would pay government officials 10 or 15 percent of each contract in cash. He had a driver who would take him around Saigon to visit high-ranking officials and pass out envelopes, each containing thousands of dong. The lucrative contracts made him a very wealthy man.

Part of my job was visiting banks to withdraw cash for these payments. The Communist government kept a tight rein on cash withdrawals by businesses and individuals. It quickly approved check payments from one enterprise to another, but withdrawing cash was another matter, subject to extensive inquiries: What would the cash be used for? Why cash instead of checks? Who would be keeping the cash? Typically, businesses explained that they required cash to pay wages and to buy supplies on the black market. (Government-run stores had serious supply shortages.)

Once, when I was visiting a bank, the branch manager, a northern Communist woman in her forties, complained to me that she was exhausted from her daily bicycle commute. That afternoon, I recounted the conversation to Mr. Hoang. "We're going to need a lot of cash from this branch," I said, "and as branch manager, she has the authority to approve it." I suggested we surprise her by buying her a used motorcycle to make her life a bit easier. Mr. Hoang loved that idea, so I went to the used-motorbike dealer where I had bought my Honda. I told the salesman to give me the most reliable bike he had. I paid him in cash and then rode the motorcycle to the branch manager's house, near Tan Son Nhat Airport.

"You're going to have to learn how to use this," I told her, "because it's yours."

She was overwhelmed and grateful. And after that, we never had trouble getting our cash withdrawals quickly and without questions.

Thao's Fate

As we adjusted to our new lives following the Communist victory, I was continually preoccupied with one mystery: What had become of my sister Thao, whom my father had taken to a departing boat just before Saigon fell? With no word from her, none of us knew her fate. Had the ship made it out to sea? Had Thao survived the journey? And if so, where had she landed? I knew that the language she knew best, besides Vietnamese, was English, though she was far from fluent, so I hoped that she had somehow found her way to the United States. My family had no way to reach out to her, but Thao was never far from our thoughts.

Then, out of the blue, we got a piece of an answer in the form of a cryptic telegram. It arrived in December 1975, about eight months after my father had left her at the port of Saigon. And it consisted of just a few words: "Thao attends old university."

We all puzzled over that. Of course, everyone was elated to have some word from her. She was alive! But whoever wrote the telegram had been careful to compose a message that would survive the scrutiny of Communist censors. Also, telegrams were expensive, so the writer was being economical with language. But what could it possibly mean? Which university? Georgetown? I didn't think she would go there. Berkeley? It would have been too difficult for her to get in.

My assumption—and my hope—was that the mysterious message meant that Thao had somehow made it from Saigon to Oregon and was at Pacific University. Perhaps she had followed my advice to make contact with Paul Hebb and Paul had connected her with my many friends there. Reading the words of the telegram over and over in our Saigon home, it warmed my heart and gave me some hope to think of Thao in Forest Grove, on the campus where I had read Philip Roth in the library and watched football with my fraternity brothers and taught Upward Bound students. But I had no idea whether my supposition was right.

A few months later, we heard from Thao again. This time she sent an aerogram, on which her handwritten message took up only about a quarter of the page. Thao confirmed that she was indeed at Pacific University and that she had met Paul Hebb! There was more: Thao wrote that she was living in Forest Grove with Bobbi Nickels—my friend Bobbi, the remarkably capable and organized administrator of the Upward Bound program. I paused to imagine that—my old friend generously taking in my sister, who had somehow, miraculously, found her way from the port of Saigon to Oregon. I felt grateful that my sister had survived and that my friends had extended such kindness.

Thao also wrote that she was preparing to take the TOEFL, the Test of English as a Foreign Language, in hopes of gaining acceptance to Pacific University, where she wanted to study mathematics. I had no doubt she would get in. Thao was bright, hardworking, and motivated, and I had many friends and supporters there who would certainly help my sister along the way.

Of course, I was relieved and happy to know that my sister was alive and safe, and might well have the privilege of experiencing the kind of education I was lucky enough to enjoy in America, and I was optimistic for her future. I also had some secondary reasons to celebrate the news of her situation. Under Communism, any Vietnamese family felt lucky if they had a relative abroad, particularly in America or Western countries. We were living with such limited means and prospects that someone like Thao could well become a source of financial assistance to us in the future. If Thao were to gain admission to Pacific, excel there, graduate, and find gainful employment, our entire family could well benefit. And if Vietnam were to renew diplomatic relations with the US in the future, perhaps Thao could sponsor the rest of us in emigrating to America.

Never mind that at that moment Communist Vietnam considered the United States its enemy and the US had instituted an economic embargo on Vietnam. Thao's news offered a ray of hope in the midst of a dark night.

After that, Thao periodically sent us letters and packages. Sometimes they contained American dollars, which we could exchange for Vietnamese currency, sometimes over-the-counter medicines, which we could sell on the black market. (Medicine was often difficult to find in Communist Vietnam, and it could be difficult to know whether it was counterfeit.)

The best surprise was when a package arrived from Thao with a pair of Levi's blue jeans for me—exactly my size, and just the style of Levi's that were popular then on campus. I put them on, and they fit perfectly. I knew Levi's were high-quality jeans that would last me a long time. And when I wore them, I thought of my sister walking, learning, and shopping on the streets of Forest Grove. The image brought a smile to my face.

Seeing Mr. Tri

While working for Mr. Hoang at the printer, I was presented with another unexpected opportunity to do something kind for another person. At lunchtime one day, I was at a sidewalk food stand ordering *banh mi thit*—a Vietnamese baguette sandwich with cold meat—when I spotted a familiar figure walking toward me: Mr. Tri, the former Shell recruitment manager. I greeted him enthusiastically and invited him to join me for lunch—my treat. Ever the proud gentleman, Mr. Tri thanked me but politely tried to decline my offer.

"Mr. Tri, you may have forgotten that I owe you a great debt of gratitude," I said. When he looked puzzled, I reminded him of the time I had phoned to explain that I would be late for my interview with him and he had kindly offered me a second chance. "I'll never forget that," I said. "Please accept this sandwich as a token of my appreciation."

With misty eyes, Mr. Tri thanked me. "Double the meat!" I said to the sandwich maker. My father had always taught me to be grateful, to reciprocate favors, and to repay my debts, so it felt good to repay Mr. Tri's kindness. As it turned out, it was the last time I ever saw him.

If the Lampposts Could Walk

Mr. Hoang prospered and kept me busy handling cash and balancing the books. For a job in Communist Vietnam, it paid a decent wage and gave me opportunities to utilize at least some of my skills. But that never lessened my desire to get out of the country as soon as humanly possible.

Of course, I was hardly alone. Everyone in Saigon—especially anyone considered an intellectual—was desperate to get out. That desire was so strong and so universal that the Communists worried about "losing gray matter"—in other words, suffering a mass exodus of engineers, physicians, pharmacists, educators, and other educated professionals.

But the government made no effort to make it attractive to stay. Every intellectual lived in constant fear of being arrested and thrown in jail at any time. The Communists treated any former official of South Vietnam with suspicion and assumed anyone with US ties was a CIA spy. To make matters worse, the economy was in shambles.

A South Vietnamese comedian at the time put it best: if the lampposts could walk, they would have left Vietnam. The question wasn't whether to leave; it was how.

There were three options for anyone trying to flee the country: the official way, the semi-official way, and the illegal way. The small percentage of people who were able to escape the country in a legally sanctioned way were mostly French citizens and Vietnamese who were married to French citizens. They could secure papers from the French consulate and arrange to travel by air from Saigon's airport. Most of these people were very wealthy, but what they couldn't do was sell their homes. If a homeowner left the country, the Communist government would take possession of the "abandoned" house—in many cases, mansions in Saigon's most affluent areas—without offering any compensation to the owners, who were grateful for the chance to leave.

The semi-official way out of South Vietnam was to pose as a person who had permission to leave. The ethnic Chinese, for example, would pay Communist officials in gold to be allowed to board ships. Many ethnic Chinese living in Vietnam were wealthy, and the Communists were eager to let them go so that the Communists could collect their gold and property.

The third escape option—the illegal way—was to build a boat in secret or find someone who had built a boat. Many people did this under the guise of being fishermen. They would pay off the local police, who would allow them to build boats as long as they did their best to hide the construction from higher authorities.

Since such a large number of people were frantically trying to leave the country, all kinds of scam artists emerged, trying to take advantage of unsuspecting people in their most desperate moments. Being under so much stress and having such limited options made one's judgment cloudy, rendering many people vulnerable to seeing potential even in the most unlikely schemes.

It wasn't uncommon at the time for people to turn over large sums of money or gold to strangers who promised to provide passage from Vietnam in a boat, only to have the swindler make off with the loot and disappear. And since this was all transpiring in secret, victims had little or no recourse. A person couldn't complain to the Communist police that he had tried to pay a scam artist to take him out of the country. The police would have arrested the victim for trying to flee the country.

With that in mind, I started my efforts to find a way out by pursuing what seemed like the most legitimate options. One person I made contact with was an associate from my years at Shell, an ethnic Chinese man who owned a number of gas stations in Can Tho, the city in the Mekong Delta where the dredging operation had been. He was very wealthy, and when I had visited in my Shell days to inspect his stations, he had always offered superb hospitality. After the Communists took over, I paid him a visit and asked him about his plans. He had decided to take advantage of the opportunities for ethnic Chinese citizens and pay about ten *taels* of gold for each of twelve people in his family to get places on a boat. (A *tael* is a Vietnamese measurement equal to about 37.5 grams.)

"Is there any way I can go with you?" I asked.

He told me to wait. "The first wave will be the Chinese," he said, "but there will be a second wave and a third wave."

I knew others who got out easily—people married to French nationals, for instance, who managed to get their names on flight lists and soon disappeared, heading off to Paris. One colleague at the Petroleum Company of Southern Vietnam didn't show up to work one day. A year later, one of my other colleagues received a letter from the man's son with news that his father would be visiting him in Paris—coded language meaning that the colleague would be resettling in France.

Another time, three colleagues failed to show up at work, and we all understood that they had left Vietnam. I didn't think any of them had connections to France, nor were they Chinese, so I was uncertain how they had managed to escape the country. Six months later, one of them paid a visit to the office. It turned out he hadn't actually left the country. He had tried to escape on a boat, but in the process, he had been arrested and thrown in jail for nearly six months.

In many cases, it was impossible to know whether someone had made it to freedom, died at sea, or perhaps wound up in prison.

Some friends who made it out would send enigmatic messages, wary of government censors. "Visiting friends in Australia," for instance, meant "I survived the journey and have emigrated to Australia."

One of my high school friends told me that two of his younger brothers had managed to secure spaces for themselves on an illegal boat and wrote to him four or five months later from Indonesia. "My gosh, it's so easy," I said to him. "Why can't we do it?"

The Pilot's Plot

In 1976, I finally came upon a promising opportunity to escape Vietnam. I was visiting San, a colleague from my days in the Shell accounting department, when he introduced me to one of his neighbors, Hanh, a wealthy woman who was looking for a particular kind of help. Her husband, who had been a lieutenant colonel in the South Vietnamese army, had been sent to a re-education camp in the North and seemed unlikely to return anytime soon. Now Hanh was eager to find a way out of the country, and on my friend's recommendation, she wanted to hire me to investigate what seemed like a promising exit opportunity. She had made contact with a pilot named Manh who had flown commercial jets for Air Vietnam, the airline of the old regime. Manh had lost his job when the airline was nationalized. Now Manh was plotting an escape, with plans to build a boat in secret.

The pilot had asked Hanh to provide half the cost of the boat, a total of twenty taels of gold. Hanh had heard from my friend San that I had attended university overseas and worked as a Shell executive. Before she invested her fortune in the project, she wanted to hire me to investigate Manh, the pilot—to verify his identity and background and confirm that he was indeed building a boat. The reward for my efforts would be significant: if the project proved viable, she would pay my way on the boat.

I didn't hesitate to take on the project. It would certainly be worth the investment of time and effort if the reward was a chance at getting out of Communist Vietnam.

Hanh introduced me to the pilot, and I went to work checking his credentials. I started with an acquaintance who worked at Tan Son Nhat Airport for Air Vietnam, who confirmed that Manh had, in fact, flown for Air Vietnam. I visited Manh at his home near the airport, where he showed me a photo album with pictures of him at various airports the airline serviced. Over seven or eight meetings, I got to know him and peppered him with questions about the boat he said he was building. When he learned that I might be one of the passengers, he asked if I might be able to help him obtain some important items for the journey.

The first thing Manh requested was a map. His plan was to build the boat in Rach Gia, a city on the Gulf of Thailand where there was a great deal of boatbuilding activity. His escape plan was to embark from Rach Gia, cross the Gulf of Thailand, and land in Malaysia or Indonesia. He wanted to determine the shortest route from Rach Gia to Malaysia. The second objective was to steer clear of the coast of Thailand, since many Thai fishermen had turned to piracy, attacking desperate Vietnamese refugees packed into boats to escape Communism. They could fish all week for rewards that were minuscule compared to what they could get from looting a single refugee boat for gold, diamonds, cash, watches, and other valuables.

"We need a map of Southeast Asia," Manh told me, explaining that having one would enable him to plot the voyage more accurately. The problem was that under Communist rule, it wasn't easy to secure such a map; the government had nationalized Saigon's two largest bookstores, and if a customer attempted to purchase a map of Southeast Asia, the clerk—probably an undercover police officer—would likely ask why the person needed it.

I had no good ideas about how to acquire a map, but I kept my eyes and ears open. Then, late one Friday afternoon in the spring of 1976, I met a friend at a sidewalk café in the affluent Le Quy Don neighborhood, just around the corner from the Abraham Lincoln Library, where I had spent so many hours perusing *Time* and *Life* magazines. We were conversing over cups of coffee about the awful reality of living in Communist Vietnam and trading insights about escape options when I spotted a familiar face: a woman about my age whom I recognized as an employee at the Abraham Lincoln Library. I remembered that she worked in the periodical section and had often helped me track down magazine issues when I couldn't find them on the shelves.

Seeing her gave me an idea, so I caught her eye, greeted her, and invited her to join me for a cup of tea. She agreed, and I waved my friend away so I could speak to the library worker privately.

"Are you still working at the library?" I asked.

She told me she was. The library had closed to the public, its American staffers long gone. And the US embargo made it impossible to obtain current American publications. But the Communist government was using the library as a resource for government research, and it still maintained the li-

brary's old collection of magazines and newspapers. That was all I needed
to know.

"Does the library still have back issues of *National Geographic*?" I asked.
She nodded. "Yes, it does."

I had spent long hours reading *National Geographic* at the Abraham Lincoln Library and at the campus libraries at Pacific and Berkeley. I remembered once reading a *National Geographic* cover story about the cultures of
Southeast Asia. It had included a pull-out map of the region.

"I have a favor to ask," I told her. I asked her to search through the
back issues of *National Geographic* and see if she could locate the one with
a detachable map of Southeast Asia, one that included the Gulf of Thailand. In exchange, I said, I would pay her fifty dong, probably more than a
month's salary for her.

"I'll try to find it," she said.

"I have coffee here every Friday at this time," I said. "I'll look for you."

I returned the following Friday and the one after that, sitting at a table
and scanning the passing faces for hers. No sign of her. Then, on the third
Friday, I spotted her walking toward me with a big smile on her face.
Okay, I thought. *Success*. I handed her the newspaper I had been reading.
She walked inside the café, stepped into the bathroom briefly, and then
emerged, returned to my table, and handed the newspaper back to me. Discreetly, I peered inside the paper and saw that she had indeed delivered
the goods: the *National Geographic* map of Southeast Asia. Exactly what I
wanted. Trying to be inconspicuous, I handed her the fifty dong, and she
slipped the money into her bag.

I couldn't help but wonder how she had managed to sneak the map past
her Communist bosses, so I asked: "How did you get it out?"

She smiled shyly. "I hid it in my underwear," she said. I smiled,
thanked her, paid for my coffee, and headed for home.

Map in hand, I paid a visit to Manh, who beckoned me inside his house.
He shut the door and closed the blinds, and the two of us sat at a table where
he opened the map and pointed to Vietnam and Malaysia. Using a compass,
he charted the shortest route between Rach Gia and the Malaysian coast.
It was clear to me that he knew what he was doing, and watching him renewed my confidence that Manh and his project were legitimate.

"There's one more thing I need you to get," he told me. I paused, waiting for my next assignment. "We're going to need a rescue reflector signal mirror."

"What the hell is that?" I asked.

He explained what he was looking for: a small, rectangular mirror with a hole in the middle that was used at sea to signal to other boats. Again, his knowledge reassured me that he knew what he was doing.

"Where can I find one?" I asked.

"Do you have any friends who were in the South Vietnamese navy?" he asked. Every ship had a signal mirror, he told me, and any ex-naval officer would probably have one.

As it happened, I did have a close high school friend, Thanh, who had served as a junior commissioned officer in the navy. I had visited him shortly after my return from the United States but hadn't seen him since the Communist takeover. Thinking Thanh might be able to help me find the mirror we needed, I paid a visit to his house, where his wife, Hue, answered the door. Visibly pregnant, Hue told me that several months earlier Thanh had been ordered to a re-education camp with the understanding that he would return after ten days. She hadn't seen him since and was growing increasingly concerned.

Of course, I expressed sympathy and said I hoped that he would be okay. "By the way," I said gently, "did Thanh happen to leave any navy equipment at home?"

"He did," Hue said, and she explained that he had stored it all in a duffel bag under their bed.

"May I take a look?" I asked.

Hue knew that my friendship with her husband went back many years, so she didn't hesitate. She pulled out the drab green duffel. "Go ahead," Hue said.

I opened the duffel. It was stuffed full of documents, including practically new, detailed, American-made charts of various areas of Vietnam's coastal and port areas. I dug a bit further inside and almost immediately found exactly what I was searching for: a rescue reflector signal mirror in its original package. The box was dark blue, the navy's color.

"This is exactly what I'm looking for," I told her.

"You can have it," Hue said. "I don't even know what it is, and I don't need it."

I wouldn't take it for free. I insisted on paying her two hundred dong; she was my friend's wife, and I wanted to help.

Mirror in hand, I returned to Manh's house. "This is wonderful!" he said. I asked if he'd had mirrors like that in the planes he flew. He had, he said, but only in case of an emergency water landing—to signal a rescue boat. Sitting in the room and using the light from a lamp, he demonstrated how to use the mirror as a signal. I left the mirror with him.

Soon after, I told Manh that I needed him to let me see the boat that he claimed he was having built. Hanh, who had hired me to check out his escape plan, was getting anxious, and she needed some proof that the boat was actually under construction before she would turn over the twenty taels of gold Manh had requested.

"Are you crazy?" he asked. "I can't let anyone know that I have anything to do with building a boat." It was true that it was illegal to build a boat without a legitimate reason, and he could end up in jail if the police learned about his project.

"Who's building it?" I asked. The pilot explained that the builder was a fisherman in Rach Gia who had obtained a boatbuilding permit by claiming that his own boat had been stolen. (More likely, a relative or friend of his had used it to flee the country.)

"I still need to see it," I insisted, "or Ms. Hanh will not put up any money."

Manh explained that the only way for me to see the boat would be for me to accompany him on a visit to Rach Gia, where he would show me the vessel. But the Communist regime kept such a tight grip on travel that we would need to obtain travel permits in order to make the trip. "I can let you see the boat," he said, "but I can't allow you to question anyone there about it, because that puts us in danger of exposing the plan."

Seeing a boat but not being able to talk to the boat builder didn't sound like proof. I asked Manh if he could share photos, but he reminded me that the Communists maintained tight control on cameras, so photography, too, might raise suspicions.

We were at an impasse, and it lasted a few months, until Manh insisted that the time had come. He needed Hanh to hand over the twenty taels of gold if she wanted in. It was time to pay up or forfeit her spot on the boat, and mine.

"What choice do we have?" Hanh asked me. I told her I would investigate. I asked Manh to take me to Rach Gia to see the boat. To secure the travel permits, he came up with a convincing cover story for the government officials: he told them that the two of us were researching opportunities for turning pineapples—a local crop in Rach Gia—into an export product.

After securing the permits, we traveled by bus to Rach Gia, where Manh hired a boatman to take us on a slow journey up the river. At one point, Manh discreetly whispered to me to look to my right. "See that boat right there?" he said. "That's our boat." I looked up and saw a medium-size vessel under construction on a dry dock. The hired boatman didn't slow down, just continued along up the river until Manh instructed us him to take us back.

I wasn't sure what to make of what I had seen. Yes, he had shown me a boat that was under construction. But I had no way of knowing whose boat it was. The trip had done little to dispel my doubts. Manh and I found our way back to the interprovincial bus and sat next to each other, but we didn't communicate, acting like we were strangers so as not to attract any attention.

Back at Manh's house in Saigon, I confronted him. "Listen, there's no proof," I said. "Yes, you showed me a boat, but it could belong to anybody. There's no proof that you have anything to do with it."

He simply shrugged. "If you don't want to join us, that's fine," he said. "I have plenty of other people who are interested." He said it would be only about sixty days before he secured the two engines and the boat would ready to depart. I didn't know what to think anymore. I told him that I needed some time and would get back to him.

I reported to Hanh what I had seen. "I cannot say for sure that Manh is financing that boat," I admitted. "I just don't know." Soon, Manh himself paid her a visit and pressured her to make up her mind. Hanh asked me to go to Rach Gia on my own, without Manh, but I explained that, as a stranger to that province, if I tried visiting alone I would be risking arrest. I wasn't sure what to tell her, and I also had my own confusing motivations. I desperately wanted this scheme to be legitimate, because if it was, it would be my own ticket out of Vietnam. Perhaps my own desires and desperation were clouding my judgment. "This decision," I finally told her, "comes down to a matter of trust."

A few weeks later, Hanh made her decision. She would take the risk, and she turned the twenty taels of gold over to Manh. Delighted, he instructed us both to start preparing for the journey and gave us a departure date about three months away. The boatbuilding permit was for a fishing boat, he explained, and if he gave the impression of being in a rush, government agents might catch on to his real intentions.

I waited, anxious about the plan and eager to get on with my life. With no good options to escape Vietnam together, Thuy and I had agreed that if only one of us successfully made it out of Vietnam, that person would make every effort to help the other escape. But my secret hope was to appeal to Manh at the last minute to give Thuy a place along with me on the boat.

Three months passed with no word from Manh. When I paid him a visit to inquire, he had no good news for me. He explained that the local authorities in Rach Gia were demanding even more money in bribes.

"I'm going to need five more taels of gold," he said.

"Five taels *more*?" I asked. "I don't know if Hanh will go for that."

I went to her to ask, and she refused.

"Five more taels might speed things up," I said.

She shook her head: "A deal is a deal."

Another month passed. Then two more. Hanh and I together dropped in on Manh. Clearly, he was living well, but he had no news for us about a departure. In fact, he demanded even more gold. He wanted an additional ten taels.

We left, frustrated and angry. After all these months and meetings, after I had tracked down the map and the signal mirror, after all the meetings with him and the strange trip to Rach Gia, it all became clear in my mind: we had been duped. Yes, Manh was a former airline pilot. That much was true. But he wasn't building a boat. He was running a scam.

I reviewed every exchange in my mind. The pilot had had all the answers. His story had sounded credible. He had covered every detail. I apologized to Hanh. I had done everything I could, but the truth was that my own judgment was clouded because I wanted so badly for his story to be valid. I wanted to believe we would be escaping soon.

A few weeks later, Hanh and I made one last attempt to meet with Manh. This time, his son came to the door. "He's not home," he told us, his manner somewhat hostile.

"Do you know when he'll be back?" I asked. He didn't. Two weeks later, we returned. Again, the son said he was away.

Hanh said to me with finality: "We've been scammed!"

We had no good options. We weren't in a position to report Manh to the police. That would mean revealing that we were trying to leave the country ourselves. It was time to accept our losses and move on. Hanh had lost twenty taels of gold. I had lost the fifty dong I had paid for the map and the two hundred dong I had paid my friend Thanh's wife for the mirror. In all, it was roughly the equivalent of a tael of gold.

I had also lost something else: some of my faith in people. Manh had once been an airline pilot, a responsible person with a career and family and a good salary. But when economic conditions deteriorate, people can lose touch with the morals that guide them. I didn't know his motivation: Had he been intentionally defrauding people like us from the beginning? Or had he been operating a legitimate scheme that somehow failed, forcing him to flee with our money? I realized that I might never have answers, but I knew one thing: I needed to put this bad experience behind me and find a more promising way out of Vietnam.

In fact, I spent nearly every waking moment thinking about how to get out. Nearly every conversation turned to questions about fleeing: *Have you heard anything? Do you know anything? Do you know anyone who has connections?* At night, my dreams were about seeing my friends from Berkeley—or re-uniting with Paul Hebb and Bobbi Nickels from Upward Bound. One night, I dreamed that I had a job working in San Francisco for Bank of America. Whenever I woke up in the middle of the night, I would lie in bed, worrying and planning and thinking about how I could possibly get out.

Plan B

About six months after I gave up on the pilot, another escape option came my way. I first heard about it through Thuy's brother Nam, who was five years younger than she was. Nam, who was about twenty-one, was an honest, upstanding guy who was devoted to his sister. One of his best friends was named Phat. I had seen the two together often, at Thuy's house and elsewhere. Their friendship went back so far that Thuy's mother and siblings treated Phat like a relative.

One day, Phat told me that he had an uncle who was planning to get out of Vietnam and had already managed to line up the boat that would take him. He took me to meet his uncle, whose name was Dat, at the uncle's house on Tran Quoc Toan Street. The uncle explained that his family owned a fishing boat in Vung Tau, a coastal area about ninety-five kilometers southeast of Saigon. He was in the process of accumulating enough fuel to travel from Vung Tau to the Philippines or Indonesia.

"How are you collecting the fuel?" I asked.

Phat's uncle Dat explained the scheme: The Communist-run cooperative placed quotas on how much fuel fishermen were allowed to purchase. His family would purchase the maximum allowed each day and then take the boat out to sea, turn off the engine, and buy fish from other boats. In a few weeks, they could accumulate enough fuel to make it to the Philippines or Indonesia. Did I want in?

I explained that I didn't have the money to pay now, but that Thuy and I had graduated from American colleges and would likely earn good salaries in America. Could we pay him once we were established there?

He thought about it for a moment. "Since Phat and Nam are friends, I can do that," Dat finally said. "But I'll need some gold for the immediate expenses. What can you give me now?"

I told him that all we had was one tael of gold. He agreed. "I trust you," he said. "We can make it a handshake deal."

Later, I asked Phat if he trusted his uncle. Of course, he did. I asked Nam what he thought. "I trust Phat," he said. "He's my best friend." I used some of my dollars to buy a tael of gold on the black market to give to Phat's uncle Dat.

A week later, I met Phat, Nam, and Dat at Soai King Lam, a well-known upscale Chinese restaurant in Cho Lon, a suburb of Saigon. I sat next to Dat. As we enjoyed a meal together, I discreetly handed him the tael of gold under the table. We had a deal. Now the wait began.

Three months later, Phat gave me word that it was time to go. I hadn't uttered a word about the deal to Thuy, fearing that if I did, she might inadvertently let it slip out. But when Phat told me it was time, I shared the news with her that we finally had an escape plan. She knew that the connection was Phat, her brother's close friend, so she was hopeful. Phat's uncle Dat told us to meet him at noon on a particular day at a restaurant on Phan Thanh Gian Street, a main artery running directly to the Bien Hoa highway, which went to Vung Tau. The restaurant's location made it a popular meeting spot for travelers heading from Saigon to the Southeast. Dat promised to pick us up there in a car and take us to the boat.

We left home that morning, not telling anyone of our plan for fear that the secret would get out. My heart was pounding as we arrived at the restaurant around 11 a.m. Thuy and I each carried a small travel bag, enough for a trip of a day or two. We were trying to blend in with the other travelers.

We waited at a table, eagerly looking for Dat. Noon came. No sign of Dat.

One o'clock. No Dat.

One thirty. Still nothing.

At two o'clock, Dat still hadn't shown up. We didn't have a telephone number to call or an address to visit. Our only plan was to meet at this restaurant, and he wasn't there. I got a sinking feeling, the same feeling I'd had when Manh, the pilot, disappeared.

I looked at Thuy and shook my head, discouraged. "We got cheated," I said.

Disappointed, frustrated, and angry, we boarded another bus for the ride back home. When we arrived, I immediately tracked down Nam, Thuy's brother, who had vouched for Phat.

"Where's Phat?" I demanded.

Nam didn't know. "I usually see him every week," he said, "but I haven't seen him in at least two weeks."

I didn't know what to think. Nam assured me that what happened wasn't Phat's fault, but my own feeling was that Phat was in the scheme. Phat knew I had worked for Shell and that I had money to spend—the USAID money I had saved for years by living frugally during college and money from my Upward Bound work. Having resources made me a prime target. In this case, I had been successfully targeted by my brother-in-law's best friend.

I had always been a trusting person, but these experiences were making me question my capacity to judge character and eroding my trust in people. And the more time that passed, the more I feared getting arrested. When the Communists had first taken power, I might have estimated that my odds of being arrested were five out of ten. When I was fired at the Petroleum Company of Southern Vietnam and the authorities could no longer assume the company's security force was watching me, my chance of being arrested had jumped to seven in ten. I worried about how long my luck would hold out. One thing I knew for sure: the Communist authorities dealt harshly with dissidents who openly opposed their one-party rule and demanded free elections and democracy. My intention was to avoid anything that might call attention to myself.

As the political and economic condition worsened, the Communists moved from arresting ex–government officials and military officers to apprehending (without filing charges) civilians: writers, novelists, journalists, and others. They also targeted ethnic Chinese, including some of the gas station and fuel truck owners I had met through my work at Shell.

Then came my contemporaries who had gone abroad for education. Some of them had taken midlevel government jobs, and now they were under arrest. Or they had reported for re-education training and had not returned.

One of my USAID accounting students told me the Communists had taken away Mr. Hoat, my favorite high school teacher, who had taught me about the United States and arranged our Sunday encounters with English speakers.

I tried to visit an ethnic Chinese merchant I knew from my Shell days, assuming he would be plotting an escape. But he wasn't there. His daughter told me that the police who had arrested him had also made off with the family's cash, gold, and diamonds.

These were the hazards of living in a police state: at any moment, you could be taken away from your family—for no reason, with no formal charges, and for an indeterminate period.

The arrests would happen in the middle of the night. Before curfew, a local police officer would drop in on the house and chat with the home-owner to make sure the person would be home later. Then, after midnight, the police would return and make the arrest. The people in the neighbor-hood would hear the desperate screams of a woman protesting as authorities dragged her husband away.

Hearing about one arrest after another, one shattered family after another, one missing father and husband after another, I began to wonder: Was I next? The more time passed, the more desperate I was to get out.

The Philippine Connection

Early in 1979, another escape opportunity emerged. At that moment, Communist Vietnam was increasingly isolated. The United States had imposed a trade embargo on the country. Vietnam was at war with Cambodia, and its relationship with China had gone from bad to worse. As a result, the Vietnamese government was targeting its own ethnic Chinese citizens, confiscating their property and seizing their bank accounts.

Rumors were circulating that the Chinese government would be sending a ship to the port of Saigon to evacuate ethnic Chinese citizens. Eager to prevent the spectacle of a Chinese ship pulling into central Saigon to rescue Chinese people (an occurrence that might have sparked a riot), the Vietnamese government offered an alternative location: Phu My port, about 129 kilometers from central Saigon. China refused this offer, and the conflict escalated. Eventually, in March 1979, a shooting war broke out on Vietnam's northern border with China.

Around that same time, one of my high school friends, Kha, shared another rumor: the Philippines was planning to send its own ship to Saigon to evacuate some of the thousands of Filipino nationals who hadn't been able to get out before the Communist takeover in 1975. Kha knew a Vietnamese woman who was married to a Filipino man, and he thought they might be able to help us pass as Filipinos.

Together, Kha and I paid a visit to the couple, who lived in a modest house about twenty minutes from my home. I spoke to the Filipino in English while Kha talked to his wife in Vietnamese. I asked the husband how he might be able to help us. He confirmed what we had heard: that at some point in the near future, the Communist government would allow a ship from the Philippines to dock at the port of Saigon, and people who were certified as Filipino citizens could board and return to the Philippines.

"How can we pass as Filipino?" I asked. He explained that we would need Filipino passports, but we could also claim to have lost our passports and instead present papers certifying our Filipino citizenship. I asked what such papers would look like.

The Filipino man pulled out a letter-size sheet of paper with Embassy of the Republic of the Philippines as the letterhead, with a Saigon street address, and a passport-size photograph of his wife. I read the letter, which consisted of a couple of paragraphs—in both Vietnamese and English—attesting to the bearer's Filipino citizenship.

I read the Vietnamese version carefully. It looked genuine: no grammatical errors or typos. I read the English version. Again, no red flags, no spelling errors. The document bore an official seal and had a stamped impression over the photograph and the signature of the chief of consular affairs at the Philippine embassy in Saigon. To an untrained eye, the certificate looked utterly authentic.

"How can we get certificates like this?" I asked.

The man told me that Kha and I would need to have passport photos taken, and he offered a tip to help us pass as Filipino men: "Let your hair grow a little bit longer, then comb it back with gel." That was the style popular with Filipino men. "I wish your skin were a little darker," he said, "but you'll be fine."

"How much will this cost us?" I asked.

"One hundred US dollars each," he said. "Cash."

It was a lot of money, but I was feeling increasingly anxious, and this scheme seemed to be my best option at the moment to escape Vietnam. After leaving, Kha and I compared notes: what the man had told me in English matched exactly what the Vietnamese woman told him in Vietnamese.

Kha and I skipped haircuts for a few weeks, then visited a shop that took passport photographs. Following the man's instructions, we slicked back our hair with gel before posing for the pictures. Then, as instructed, we brought four copies to the couple, along with one hundred dollars for each of us.

"Come back in a week and I'll have your certificates," the Filipino man said.

A week later we returned to the apartment and he presented us with the certificates. They both looked flawless, just as authentic-looking as the example the man had originally shown us, complete with the seal, the impression, and the signature. We were in business.

"When do you expect the ship to arrive?" I asked the man.

"That, we don't know yet," he replied. "It all depends on the negotiations between the two governments."

We waited for word. After a week, none came. I asked around to see if anyone had heard about when the Philippine ship might come. I heard nothing. We went back to visit the couple at the apartment. They reported that the governments were still in talks.

That was when I began to worry. Two hundred dollars was a lot of money. We paid another visit to the couple, but they had no news for us. They couldn't control the governments, the man said, and they had delivered what they'd promised: the certificates.

Almost every night, I listened to the BBC's Vietnamese-language broadcast, hoping to hear about the Vietnamese-Filipino government negotiations or, better yet, the Filipino evacuation ship. But no such news came. After a couple of months of this, it struck me that once again, I had placed my trust in strangers who had taken advantage of my vulnerability. I had known Kha for many years, and he had vouched for the Vietnamese woman. But we had based the entire plan on a rumor that turned out to be a fabrication. There was no ship from the Philippines. There was no plan to rescue Filipinos. I had paid one hundred of my precious dollars for what I had hoped would be an escape from the increasingly bleak reality of Vietnam. What I got instead was a piece of paper with my name typed on it next to a photograph of me with slicked-back hair, trying to pass for a person I wasn't.

Tragedy on the River

My fourth attempt to escape began with the highest of hopes.

It started with a friend, a woman named Huong, who had been a colleague at Shell, where she had been a well-paid clerical worker. We had grown close in the months just after the Communists took over the company. I once visited Huong at her house, about fifteen minutes from mine, to discuss in secret opportunities to flee Vietnam. It turned out that I had been at Huong's house many years before: her youngest brother, now studying in Japan, had been a friend of mine back at Chu Van An High School. Having that extra connection helped to deepen our friendship. I trusted her as a well-regarded colleague, and knowing that I had once been a friend of her brother's made Huong trust me even more.

Eager to find any way to escape the country, I tried to keep in touch with a wide variety of friends and acquaintances, hoping that one connection or another would lead me to an exit route. With that in mind, I dropped in on Huong once a week or so to see if she might have come across any options. On one of these visits, she introduced me to a friend of hers, Toan. Like me, Toan was desperate to escape Vietnam, and he told me he had a lead. He knew a boat owner who was looking to sell spaces on a boat that was nearly ready to depart. Toan didn't have enough gold himself, but I expressed interest, and he said he would arrange for an intermediary to contact me.

I trusted Huong, she trusted her friend Toan, and Toan apparently trusted this intermediary, so I agreed to talk to him. Was it a reliable connection? Again, I was like a drowning person. Every piece of information about escape was like a piece of wood floating in the water. They don't come by often, but when one does, you grab onto it, hoping it will save your life.

Soon I met the intermediary, a tough-looking man in his twenties named Nguyen Quang Song, who visited me at home to explain his proposal. He said that he represented the boat owner. If I wanted in, he required a down payment of two taels of gold per person. I told him I had only five—not enough for the three people I wanted to transport: Thuy, my father, and myself. Song said he wasn't certain that would work, but he would take my offer to the owner he represented.

A week later, Song returned. He told me the owner had agreed to take five taels of gold for the three of us. I accepted those terms, but I was not comfortable parting with that much gold in advance. I suggested that I turn over the gold to my friend Huong for safekeeping. Once we were safely on the escape boat, Song would be able to retrieve the gold from Huong. We had a deal.

I delivered five taels of gold to Huong, then shared details of the plan with Thuy and my father and told them to be ready.

Song gave me instructions: the three of us should meet the boat in Nha Be, an out-of-the-way area across the Saigon River from where we lived. The organizer had planned the escape for a moonless night, when the sky would be darkest, making it easier to escape without attracting notice.

The designated time came in November 1977. The three of us—my father, Thuy, and I—rode our bicycles through the dark streets for the five kilometers to the Saigon port, took the ferry across the Saigon River, and then rode another three kilometers to the spot on the river in Nha Be where we had been told to report. There, in the shadows of the riverbank, we found a small motorboat manned by Song and two other men in their twenties. Song instructed us to get in and explained that they would take us to the boat, which would be leaving sometime later.

It all made sense at the time: the moonless night, the remote location, the middle-of-the-night departure. Clearly, Song and his crew people were doing everything possible to avoid attracting attention and raising the suspicions of the Communist authorities, which could lead to arrest and severe jail time.

Soon the small craft left the shore and motored toward the middle of the wide river. It was so dark and the location so isolated that I had no idea where we were. After half an hour, they docked the motorboat near what I thought was an islet in the river.

"We're close now," Song told us. "The big ship is just around the bend, on the other side of this island." He said it was time for him and his partners to escort us to the ship, one person at a time.

Vietnamese tradition is to honor older people, to demonstrate respect for one's elders, so without hesitation or discussion, I said, "Dad, you go first." Silently my father stepped out of the boat. Song and one of the other men went with him. I watched the three of them walk away, one just ahead of my father, one behind him, as they strode through the tall grass of the island and into the darkness. The third man stayed in the boat with Thuy and me. The minutes passed. The time seemed to crawl as Thuy and I waited anxiously, eager to leave the motorboat and join my father on the larger vessel that was to carry the three of us away from Vietnam and to our new lives.

Another ten minutes. Still no sign. Finally, half an hour after they had disappeared into the darkness, the second man appeared, followed by Song. At first I felt relief, but then, just before Song stepped back aboard the boat, I noticed something chilling: he was clutching a knife and had blood on his hands. I watched him lean down to rinse his hands in the river. As he and the other man clambered back into the boat, I was overcome by a feeling of dread.

"We've got to move to another place," Song told us. "It looks like the police are watching us here." He ordered Thuy and me to move to the bow. We did, and as we sat there, I was seized with fear and confusion, but there was little I could do. They were three men, all bigger than me. Song steered the boat back out toward the deep water in the middle of the river. I tried to figure out what to do next as a whirlwind of thoughts spun in my head.

Suddenly, Song changed his tone. "You're under arrest," he said to Thuy and me. "We're *Cong An*," he said, using the term for the security police. Bewildered and panicked, I looked over at Thuy, struggling with how to react. Then Song said to his partners, "Hey, I forgot to bring the handcuffs."

It suddenly became clear: These men weren't police. And they weren't taking us to a boat. They were criminals. And they hadn't escorted my father to a boat. As I could tell from the knife and his bloody hands, they had murdered him.

Song approached Thuy and me and used rope to tie our hands behind our backs.

"Where's my father?" I demanded.

"He's on the big boat," Song insisted.

"Then why are you doing this to us?" I asked. He didn't answer. "You and I had a deal. You take the three of us to the boat, we board, then you will go to Huong and she'll give you my five taels of gold."

The other two men shot Song looks of puzzlement. Clearly, he hadn't let them in on this part of the plan. "What are we going to do now?" one of them asked.

"Let them drift," Song replied.

Song approached me and roughly ordered me to stand up. As I rose, he suddenly struck my chest with both of his hands, knocking me off the boat and into the water. As I struggled to climb back in, he pushed Thuy over, too, and she hit the water with a splash. With the two of us floating side by side, Song spun the boat around to get close to me, trying to use the engine's propeller as a weapon to slice into my body. It would likely have killed me if the rotor had struck my body, but somehow I avoided contact. Obviously frustrated, Song gunned the engine and sped away, leaving Thuy and me to float in the dark, desperately treading water in the middle of the deep, dark river.

The water was cool, but not dangerously so. Somehow the rope tying my hands had loosened, and I was able to pry my hands free. Struggling to stay afloat in the darkness, I recalled the swimming class Thuy and I had taken for PE in our freshman year at Pacific. I flashed back to the day Mrs. Horner had taught us how to survive in the water, and I did exactly what she had shown us: I squirmed out of my pants. I knotted the bottom of each leg. I blew air into the pants and waved them overhead to fill them with air, trying to capture as much air as possible. Nearby, in the blackness of the water, Thuy, who had managed to free her hands, too, was doing the same thing.

There, in the middle of the night, with practically no light, I floated beside my wife, trying to reassure her. "Hang on, Thuy!" I called to her. "Stay with me! Don't leave me, Thuy. If we can float until morning, we can find our way to safety." Together, we floated. And floated. I wondered how this could possibly end. I thought of my father and wondered where he was. Had they really killed him? I thought of the big ship that was to take us out of Vietnam, a ship that apparently didn't exist. I couldn't believe that I had fallen victim to yet another scam. I wondered whether I would see the morning, whether we would ever escape Vietnam.

Struggling to keep my head above water, I could not make out the riverbank. I had crossed that river in barges enough times to know that it was very wide, far too vast for me to swim across. Trying to stay afloat, on the precipice between life and death, I had no sense of how much time passed—a minute or an hour. After a time, something unexpected happened: I spotted Song's boat again, heading toward us. I wondered what their plan was now. Would they attack me again? Did they want to make sure we were dead, too? But something had changed. The men had come back not to harm us but to save us. Song was in the stern, handling the engine. One of the others gestured with his arms for us to swim toward them. "Come on," he said. "Let's get you back on the boat."

One of them reached out and helped Thuy onto the boat. The other pulled me up.

I didn't understand what had made them return to retrieve us. The same men who had apparently murdered my father and threw us in the river to drown had come back and saved our lives. Why had they changed their minds? Maybe the three of them had quarreled. Perhaps the other two men had been in on Song's plot to rob us of our money, but they weren't aware of the five taels of gold Song was to collect from Huong later. Most importantly, maybe they hadn't expected Song to kill my father and leave both of us to drown. Now they had one murder on their hands. Maybe they thought Buddha would never forgive them if they were responsible for two more deaths. Robbery was one thing; murder was quite another.

I looked at the men and quietly thanked them. Thuy and I sat on the deck of the boat, not knowing what to expect next. Silently, Song steered the boat toward the riverbank, to the place where we had first boarded it. There, Thuy and I got out of the boat, and the three men quickly disappeared into the darkness. We found our bicycles, just where we had left them a few hours earlier, when we'd thought we were leaving Vietnam forever to seek out a new life.

As we rode toward home, I was consumed by a heavy burden of guilt. I had been the one who pursued this plan through my friend Huong from Shell. I had presented it to my father. I had been so blinded by desperation to get out of the country that I had failed to consider that this might be a scam—and a deadly one. I couldn't get the image of Song's bloody hands out of my mind.

I felt a combination of anger, sadness, disappointment, and betrayal. In my twenty-seven years, I had never felt worse. My father was gone, and I couldn't help but think that the fault lay with me. To make matters worse, my hope of ever escaping Communist Vietnam had vanished.

We arrived at our house at dawn. Leaving Thuy there, I bicycled to Huong's house. I wanted her to know immediately the tragic result of our escape attempt—and I wanted to retrieve my five taels of gold before Song got to her.

When I arrived at Huong's house, she was already awake. She was also startled to see me, having assumed that I was safely on a boat leaving the country. Seeing how upset I was, she invited me inside. We sat down and I quickly blurted out my report: "Song killed my father! He threw Thuy and me into the river to try to drown us. Somehow they changed their mind and pulled us back out of the water."

Shocked and horrified, Huong asked for details: How many men had there been? Where had they taken us? What had transpired? As I recounted the events of the previous evening, she listened quietly, occasionally murmuring, "Oh my God!"

I asked for the five taels of gold, and Huong retrieved it from her bedroom and handed it to me. Then the doorbell rang and her friend Toan showed up, surprised to see me. "You're still here?" Toan asked.

Huong interrupted: "The people you connected him with are *murderers!*"

Toan seemed stunned. "Murderers? Why?" Huong recounted my horrific story to Toan, who shook his head. "I didn't know Song personally," he said. "I only knew his cousin."

Shattered, I bid goodbye to the two of them and headed home. Later that morning, Thuy and I went to my parents' home and I broke the shattering news to my mother. I told her how I had heard about the boat through a friend, how we had all been excited and confident that this was our opportunity. Then I recounted what had happened—how my father had gotten off the boat with two men and one had returned with bloody hands and a knife.

My mother was in shock, but she was also a worldly woman who had heard of many people who had lost their fortunes or their lives in their attempts to flee Vietnam. Even at this moment of pain and tragedy, she remained remarkably calm and level-headed.

The worst part for all of us was that we had no idea where my father's body was. Because it had been so dark and because I hadn't been the one steering the boat, I had no idea where the island was where we had last seen him. I couldn't begin to look for my father's body, and there was no one to ask. It would remain a mystery.

I was also concerned about the criminals who had killed my father and defrauded the three of us. With them still at large, I feared for our safety.

Two days after my father's murder, I answered a knock at the door and opened it to see Song himself.

"I didn't kill you or your wife; I pulled the two of you out of the water and saved your lives," he said. "I've come to collect the five taels of gold you had left with Huong."

I told him that I would give him two taels of the gold if he would help me recover my father's body so we could give him a proper burial.

Again, he claimed that my father had boarded the big ship and was on his way abroad. If so, I asked again, why had he tried to kill Thuy and me? We could have boarded the big boat, too, and he could have collected the five taels of gold. Reminding Song that in our culture, a proper burial was of utmost importance, I implored him to help. We needed to recover the body as soon as possible to avoid decomposition, I told him.

Again Song demanded the gold. "If you don't give it to me," he said, "I'll write an anonymous letter to the police to report your attempt to escape." Then, he warned, I would be arrested, lose the gold and my house, and probably spend years in jail. I knew he was threatening me, but I also feared that he might be right. Song knew that he had me in a jam. Reporting him to the police would mean revealing that I had been trying to flee Vietnam—an admission that might subject me to arrest. The government was known to send many of those who attempted escape to long terms in Communist detention.

Then a strange thing happened: I looked at his hands and noticed that he was missing one of his thumbs. I remembered the novel *Dieu ru nuoc mat* (The song of tears) by the well-known Vietnamese author Duyen Anh. It described a murderous gang that punished offending members by cutting off one of their thumbs.

It hadn't occurred to me before that Song always had that hand in his pocket. Now I knew why. It was the red flag. I wished I had discovered this fact before we had gotten on the boat with him. Song seemed not to notice that I had caught sight of the thumb. He repeated his threat to alert the police unless I gave him the gold. Then he walked out.

★ ★ ★ ★ ★

By that time, I had lived long enough under Communism to recognize that Communists placed value on owning up to one's mistakes before the authorities discovered them. So as soon as Song left, I went to the district police office. I realized that revealing that I had attempted to escape meant risking punishment—even jail. But this man had murdered my father and then had been brazen enough to come back and try to extort money from me. He might well try to do the same thing to others, and I couldn't live with myself if I didn't try to stop him. I also feared that if Song remained at large, he might try to kill Thuy and me.

"You're not going to like what I have to tell you, and I may face punishment," I told the officer on duty, "but I need to tell you this."

A police officer escorted me to a small room with a desk and two chairs. Another officer joined him and started asking questions. I recounted the awful night: the scheme, the boat, the murder, the near drowning. They listened. One officer took a lot of notes. The interview dragged on for three hours.

"Do you think that Song will return to your house?" one of them finally asked me.

"Yes."

"Why?" he asked.

"He still wants the gold," I said.

"Do you think he would help to recover your father's body in exchange for the gold?"

"I doubt it," I said. "It would be evidence of murdering my father."

"Then why he would he return to your house?"

"To rob me of the gold and kill me!" I said. "I hope you can prevent that."

The police officer thought for a few moments, then told me that they would assign a public security agent to watch our house. If Song showed up, they would arrest him. He thanked me and sent me home.

The next morning, a man I recognized arrived at our home: a local security agent named An, who was around twenty and lived in our neighborhood. He typically dressed in street clothes, not a police uniform. As a local security agent (*Cong An Khu Vuc*), An was responsible for watching over our neighborhood. I had met him before. He was a friendly southerner who knew everyone in the neighborhood. I had noticed that he paid special attention to former South Vietnamese army officers who should have been in the re-education camps, former South Vietnamese political party members, and anyone engaged in anti-government and anti-Communist activities.

I invited An inside and put on some tea, and we chatted. He asked me to describe Song, and I gave him a description of what I remembered, including the missing thumb.

"He probably belonged to one of the notorious, murderous gangs under the old regime," An said. "He's armed and dangerous. You'd better be careful!"

At that moment, I heard a noise outside. Peering out into the front yard, I spotted none other than Song standing at my front gate. "He's here!" I whispered to An.

"Don't worry," An replied. "I'll be hiding in the back room and listening. Talk normally. Leave everything to me."

I let Song inside. He immediately demanded the gold. I reminded him that I would give him two taels of the gold if he would help bring my father's body to a funeral home. Again I told him that time was of the essence. I had been the one to involve my father in the escape plan, I explained, so I felt great responsibility for his death. As the oldest son, it was my responsibility to give my father a proper burial. "That's my wish," I told Song, "and my final offer to you."

Song seemed aggravated and angry, but if he felt the instinct to kill me, he was more interested in collecting my gold. As he stormed out of the house, another plainclothes officer appeared and grabbed him from behind. (Apparently, two of An's colleagues had been hiding in a nearby house.) The officer put Song in an arm lock, then arrested him, locked him in handcuffs, and marched him off for questioning.

Later, at the police station, an investigator told me that Song had denied killing my father. He had insisted that my father had made it to the big boat.

"He got on the boat?" I said, incredulous. "If my father got on the boat, then why did they throw us in the water and try to drown us?"

The investigator shrugged. "Without a body," he said, "we can't do anything."

I asked if I could speak directly to Song, and the investigator agreed to allow me. He brought me inside to a holding cell where Song was sitting. Song gave me a cold stare.

"My father is dead. We can't change that," I told him. "But would you at least tell me where his body is?" I reminded him that in Vietnamese tradition, it is considered utterly shameful for a son to deny his father a proper burial.

He shook his head. "Your father got on that boat," he said. "He's out in the open ocean."

"If that's true," I asked, "then why didn't you take my wife and me to the boat as well?"

He had no answer. In a last-ditch effort, I tried bribing him for the information, offering Song half the gold if he would lead me to my father's body.

"I don't want your gold," Song said curtly.

Our conversation ended there. Without a body, the police couldn't—wouldn't—charge Song with a crime. The Communist police, busy with more pressing state security issues, weren't inclined to offer any more help.

And without a body, we couldn't bury my father, so I kept looking on my own. A couple of days later, I rode to the area where Thuy and I had boarded the motorboat that night. There, I tried to gather clues from the locals and fishermen who lived and worked in the area. Had they seen anything suspicious? Had they heard of anyone finding a body on the riverbank? Any leads? Everyone I asked simply shook their heads.

The Darkest Days

For weeks and months, I relived the night of my father's murder over and over, always with great distress. In the middle of the day, I would have flashbacks that left me jumpy, irritated, and angry. I had trouble concentrating. I had difficulty sleeping, frequently waking in the middle of the night from vivid nightmares, sweating profusely.

I carried tremendous guilt. I blamed myself for my father's death and felt anger and shame. I felt foolish to have trusted people who had turned out to be murderers. And I felt that I could no longer trust anyone. The entire world seemed completely, utterly dangerous. I avoided seeing Huong or even going near her house.

I knew I had a mental health problem, though I couldn't pinpoint exactly what it was. Was it psychological, or psychiatric, or both? I knew I needed help. But where could I turn? Not to a hospital run by the Communists. I didn't think they even recognized mental health issues.

With no other way to seek support, I turned to religion and Buddhist philosophy. I approached an elderly Buddhist monk I had met when I worked at Mrs. Hoang's print shop and told him that I needed confidential help. Sensing that I had something important to share, he instructed me to come meet him.

On a Sunday evening, I arrived at his small, simple pagoda. There I recounted for the monk our awful, tragic night on the river. I told him that my father had been an honorable, upstanding man.

I couldn't understand, I told him, why the men had murdered my father. Or why they had tried to kill me with the boat propeller and left Thuy and me to drown—and then had come back and saved our lives.

The ninety-year-old monk explained Buddhism's central tenet of reincarnation. People are reborn after dying, he said, and the quality of their new life depends on how they lived in their previous life. It follows the law of cause and effect: for every event that occurs, he said, there will follow another event whose existence was caused by the first. This second event will be either good or bad—or very good or very bad—in accordance with its cause. The law of karma, he said, teaches that the responsibility for bad actions is borne by the person who committed them. The elderly monk explained that the two men accompanying Song were worrying about how murdering three people would affect their next lives, so they had returned to rescue us.

The monk also explained the idea of *oan hon*, "the unjudged spirit"— the spirit of person who was killed unjustly and unexpectedly. After my father was killed, the monk said, his *oan hon* possessed the power to do extraordinary things—such as making the murderer turn the boat back to rescue us. He assured me that having successfully saved my life and Thuy's, my father's spirit had moved on to Nirvana, the Buddhist place of peace and happiness.

I was not a deeply religious person, but I believed the monk and accepted his explanation without reservation. I asked if he would be willing to come to our home to perform a Buddhist memorial service for my father and to bless Thuy and me in accordance with Buddhist tradition. He agreed, and one evening I returned to the pagoda to pick up the monk and drove him on my motorcycle to our home. There, Thuy had prepared a shrine with a picture of Buddha and a portrait of my father. She had also bought flowers, fruits, incense, and candles, and she had cooked rice and a vegetarian dish as offerings.

The monk lit the candles and burned the incense. He recited Buddhist sutras for my father, punctuating them by striking a bronze bowl-shaped bell with a wooden mallet. The bell reverberated so loudly that a few curious neighbors, hearing the sound, came to the door and watched the ceremony from outside. After a while, realizing that the service was for my father, their longtime neighbor, the neighbors left. I knew that the local police had assigned at least one of them to monitor my activities and our home and to report on us to the police. The Communists always suspected that when a person who disappeared might have actually secretly joined the anti-Communist resistance force. Surely, the witnesses' reports about the memorial service for my father would only confirm to the police that my father was indeed dead.

Losing Uncle Tao

Under the Communists, tragedy never seemed far away. Less than a year after my father's murder, another death struck our family.

Thuy had an uncle, a physician we called Uncle Tao. He had been a father figure to Thuy and her siblings, particularly after their father's death eighteen years earlier, in 1959. Uncle Tao was a gentle, intellectual man who loved to read books and listen to classical music, and who delighted in treating his nephews and nieces to ice cream.

Like most doctors in South Vietnam, Uncle Tao had been drafted into the military and served in army medical facilities. During the war, he was a commissioned officer, a major, and ultimately ran the army hospital in Bac Lieu province in the Mekong Delta.

All of that changed after the Communists' victory, when the authorities ordered Uncle Tao to report for re-education in North Vietnam. Since he had been an officer, the Communists considered him dangerous, despite his medical training. Like everyone else in the re-education camps, he suffered from mistreatment and endured hard labor, hunger, and a lack of medical care.

After three long years, the Communists finally accepted his story that he had been drafted into the ARVN but had never actually fought against Communist forces, only performed surgeries to save the lives of wounded South Vietnamese soldiers. The Communists released Uncle Tao and instructed him to report to Bac Lieu's Communist government for "local supervision." Bac Lieu's local authorities assigned him to work in the general hospital, but not as a physician. Instead they forced him to do whatever he was instructed to do by the hospital's administrator, a northern Communist woman with minimal education and a reputation for treating personnel from South Vietnam harshly. Instead of utilizing Uncle Tao's medical training, she punished him by forcing him to work as an orderly and groundskeeper, cleaning toilets and sweeping floors.

In the end, the harsh treatment was simply too much for him. Uncle Tao had lost his dignity. No longer able to practice his profession or provide for his wife and three children, he lost the will to live. One evening, he swallowed a bottle of medicine and hanged himself.

Thuy was devastated. It was like losing her father all over again. And though I had met Uncle Tao only a few times, I loved him, too, and his death hit me hard as well. I considered the fate of my male relatives: my father had been murdered; now Uncle Tao was dead; and my uncle Bac was in a re-education camp in North Vietnam for an indeterminate term. In Vietnam's male-dominated society, the loss of so many men was wreaking havoc on countless families like ours.

At the same time, the economy was in a free fall. Inflation was running at 700 percent annually. Food production was dropping because of the nationalization of industries, the collectivization of farming, and the US economic embargo. People were starving. Vietnam faced international isolation for its invasion of Cambodia.

My once-beautiful country was on its way to becoming one of the poorest countries in the world.

Uncle Tao's death descended upon us like a curtain of darkness. Now I couldn't perceive even a fading ray of hope. Still, all I could think was, *I have to get the hell out of here.*

With few alternatives left and my confidence waning, I was willing to try just about anything. In December 1978, I sent a telegram to my sister Thao, who was still at Pacific University. I wrote it in Vietnamese: "Khiem wants to visit *Chu Sam*. Please send some money so I can travel."

Chu was Vietnamese for "uncle." I wasn't sure Thao would understand who "Uncle Sam" was, being new to America, but I intentionally made the message cryptic enough to make it past the Communist censors. I figured that with the combined efforts of Thao, Bobbi Nickels, and Paul Hebb, they might realize that I needed help.

I didn't have much hope that I would hear back, and I never did.

After years of struggling to survive Communism, enduring multiple tragedies, and repeatedly failing to find a way out, I was running low on money, morale, and confidence. I wondered: Should I give up? Should I resign myself to being stuck in Communist Vietnam forever?

Then I found inspiration from my time in America. I thought of Luke Jackson, Paul Newman's character in the movie *Cool Hand Luke*, and Henri "Papillon" Charrière, played by Steve McQueen in *Papillon,* a movie I had seen with Thuy in 1973. Both heroes were prisoners who repeatedly attempted escape and never lost hope. Each forged ahead until he achieved success. At this very moment, I was in a huge prison called "the Socialist Republic of Vietnam." Was I willing to choose between freedom and death? I remembered learning about the famous statement of the American patriot Patrick Henry at the Second Virginia Convention in 1775: "Give me liberty or give me death!"

Yes, I would accept only liberty or death. There was no other way.

The Chinese Connection

I had always thought of myself as a clear-minded and intelligent person, but it had become increasingly apparent to me that my stress and my desperation to escape Communism had clouded my judgment. There was one person in my life, however, whom I could still trust to be a clear and calm thinker: my mother. She always took the long view and repeatedly reminded all of us that she had seen many regimes and leaders come and go: French colonial rule, the Viet Minh's provisional government in the countryside, the Kingdom of Vietnam under the Nguyen dynasty, the constitutional monarchy under Emperor Bao Dai, the Republic of Vietnam under President Diem, General Big Minh, and numerous military coup leaders, the Thieu and Ky regime, and now the Communists.

She did, however, want to protect my youngest brother, Khoa, who at age nineteen was facing the very real possibility of being drafted into the military. Vietnam was in the midst of a violent conflict with Cambodia, and a high proportion of the soldiers who were sent there were killed. Cambodia, as the saying at the time went, was "Vietnam's Vietnam." Though my mother had no intention of leaving the country herself, she felt lucky that all of us had survived the Vietnam War, and she wanted to do everything she could to prevent Khoa from being sent to fight and die in the war in Cambodia.

In her years selling goods on the gray market, my mother had developed many close, trusting relationships with ethnic Chinese merchants who had been her colleagues. The entire reselling enterprise depended on an honor system: since everyone involved had to avoid attracting the attention of the police, the merchants and suppliers needed to develop relationships of trust.

The ethnic Chinese were under tremendous pressure from the Communist government for two reasons: first, many of them were quite wealthy, and the Communists were intent on confiscating their riches; and second, with China and Vietnam no longer allies, the Communist authorities suspected that many of the ethnic Chinese were actually foreign agents working against Vietnam. The government treated the ethnic Chinese as scapegoats, blaming them for everything from food shortages to rampant inflation. But after a time, Communist authorities began a semiofficial policy of accepting payoffs from the ethnic Chinese in exchange for allowing them to build boats and then looking the other way when those boats, loaded with refugees, headed for the open sea.

Through her gray market network, my mother made contact with a particular Chinese merchant, a very wealthy woman named Mrs. Dau. Mrs. Dau lived in Saigon, but her extended family was in Rach Gia, the port city I had visited with the pilot, Manh, about 258 kilometers west of Saigon. Her family was in the process of building a boat and preparing to depart from Rach Gia. Knowing that she could trust the family, my mother made an investment: she put up seven taels of gold to purchase a spot on a boat for Khoa and then waited for word that it was time for the boat to launch.

Finally, the moment came. Toward the end of 1978, Mrs. Dau sent word to my mother to bring Khoa to her house. Late one evening, I drove him on my Honda moped. "See you in the US!" I said as I sped off. Khoa spent the night there, then left with Mrs. Dau the next morning for Rach Gia. He stayed there for a few weeks, waiting with a crowd of others for the boat to head out to sea. During that time, my mother made a few trips from Saigon to Rach Gia to bring Khoa food to sustain him during the wait and then the sea passage. During one of her visits, word arrived that it was time for the boat to depart. My mother was ecstatic. Of course, she was heartbroken to part with her beloved son, but at least she finally had hope that he might have a future.

Recognizing the risks he faced—foreign news broadcasts reported that about half of those trying to escape didn't survive the journey—my mother prayed for Khoa daily, burning incense and uttering words of hope for his safe passage. We knew that he had departed, but there was no way to ascertain his fate yet. It wasn't uncommon for pirates to raid the boats, stealing from the passengers or even seizing the engines, leaving boats to drift unmoored through the South China Sea or the Gulf of Thailand. Having a signal mirror to get the attention of passing vessels was little help: What ship could take on two or three hundred starving refugees?

With more and more boatloads of Chinese leaving Vietnam's shores, rumors began circulating that the government, facing international criti-

cism, would soon crack down on ethnic Chinese emigration and halt the
semiofficial policy of allowing their boats to leave. My mother realized that
that meant it was now or never: if the rest of us were going to get out, we
had to act immediately.

Reunion with a Friend

One morning in 1978, I was riding my bicycle to work when I heard someone calling my name: "Khiem! Khiem!" I looked around and spotted someone calling me. Then I saw who it was: Chien, my elementary school friend who had been reported missing in action in Laos. I stopped, hopped off the bicycle, and shook his hand.

"I'm so happy to see you alive!" I told him.

We made plans for me to visit him at home that evening. There, Chien—thin, malnourished, and looking much older than his age—told me his story: he had joined the Airborne Division as an enlisted man. In 1971, his unit had been sent into southern Laos to cut off the Ho Chi Minh Trail, the logistical system North Vietnamese forces used to transport troops and ammunition to South Vietnam. Amid intense fighting, North Vietnamese forces had captured Chien's unit, marched them north on the Ho Chi Minh Trail, and held them prisoner in North Vietnam.

I asked Chien why he hadn't been part of the prisoner exchange after the 1973 Paris Peace Accords. He explained that the Americans had been focused on retrieving their own POWs. Since South Vietnam's government had always denied suffering military defeat in Laos, it hadn't made an effort to recover Vietnamese POWs who were captured there.

I also asked why he hadn't been released after the Communist victory in 1975. Chien explained that since the Communists had been focusing on the task of dealing with a million former South Vietnamese soldiers, releasing POWs like him hadn't been a high priority and might have created a security risk.

Chien asked about my studies in America. We reminisced for a while about our teachers and friends in elementary school. Looking around his house, I noticed that much of the furniture was missing—a sign that the family had been forced to sell their belongings for food.

As I headed home, I reflected on how lucky I had been compared to Chien. He had suffered for seven long years as a POW in North Vietnam. When he was finally released, he returned home quietly: no parades, no welcome ceremonies. That night, I told Thuy about him, and we decided to give him a few kilos of rice the next day. It was the least we could do for my old friend.

Leaving Home

When Mrs. Dau informed my mother that her family was building yet another boat, my mother did not hesitate to secure places for us. My mother's plan was to remain in Saigon along with my oldest sister, Binh. Of course, my sister Thao was already in Oregon, and now Khoa was gone. That left my brother Khoi, who was twenty, my sister Mai, eighteen, Thuy, and me. Somehow, my mother gathered enough gold to purchase places on a boat for Khoi and Mai, and I paid for Thuy and myself. Mrs. Dau secured official travel permits for all four of us, just as she had for Khoa. The documents identified us as ethnic Chinese citizens of Vietnam. That's how we would be able to pass.

Before we could board a boat, we faced a more immediate challenge: getting out of Saigon. Ever since the days just after my father's murder, when I had raised suspicions by admitting to police that his death had come during our effort to flee the country, the local police had been monitoring my movements. Security officers routinely dropped by our house in the evening to talk and to make sure I was home. I suspected that what they really wanted was to seize our home once we left. To avoid raising suspicions when we fled, I planned to leave most of our belongings in place.

Here was the irony: we were leaving and hoped we would never see this home again—that at last we were leaving Vietnam for good. But we ran the risk of being arrested and then being released. And then what? If the local Communist authorities took over our house and we didn't actually make it out of the country, we would be rendered homeless. (In fact, homelessness had skyrocketed in Saigon, in large part because of the intellectuals—engineers, doctors, bankers, and teachers—who had been sent to re-education camps and even prisons and then released and returned, only to discover that the authorities had confiscated their homes.) Thuy and I were also nearly out of money. But it was reassuring to know that my mother and sister Binh would be staying in their house, so we would always have a place to call home and food on the table, provided by my mother. That was our backup plan.

Early on the morning of March 18, 1979, I hopped on my Honda moped with Thuy behind me, as if we were both heading to work. Instead, we rode to Thuy's mother's house. There, one of Thuy's brothers used the moped to deliver Thuy and me to the Mekong interprovincial bus depot. Soon, my brother Khoi and sister Mai joined us there.

We had been told to look for a truck bearing the name Construction Company of Southern Vietnam. When the four of us approached a vehicle meeting that description, the driver greeted us and handed each of us travel documents bearing our names and identifying us as employees of that company on assignment in Kien Giang province, where Rach Gia was located. To keep ourselves concealed, the four of us slid beneath a green canvas stretched across the truck bed, sitting amid a load of bricks for the ride to Rach Gia.

When we arrived in Rach Gia, the truck dropped us near an open-air market, where a man from Mrs. Dau's organization greeted us. He led us to a house a few blocks away where about twenty others were lodging, passing time while they awaited the day when the boat would depart. Examining our surroundings, I saw clues that it wasn't the only house that was occupied. Nearly all of the neighboring homes were also teeming with people—young, old, families, individuals—eager to get out of the country. No doubt the local police were aware that scores—or hundreds—of outsiders were making their way to this small town, but they didn't intervene. Indeed, I saw police patrolling, armed with AK-47s, yet they took no action to arrest the newcomers.

The next morning, a small boat took about twenty of us to Tac Cau village, a dock area bursting with activity. As we made our way through the crowd, I spotted a familiar face: Quang, my friend from Berkeley! He was with his wife, Julie, and their two young children, trying to escape just as we were. Quang had earned a doctorate in mathematics from Berkeley. Julie was a pharmacist. And now all of us were engaged in a secret plan to escape. We simply made eye contact as we passed each other. None of us said a word.

The boat ride took about twenty minutes. We arrived at a house, the residence of a Chinese family. There, someone instructed us to find a space outside to set down our things and begin our wait. Behind the house, the four of us found a spot under a thatched-roof lean-to. That spot would become a temporary home for the four of us for days or even weeks while we waited for the moment when our boat was ready to hit the water. Our lives were in limbo, between the routines of work and family in Saigon and whatever lay ahead. Beneath that modest shelter, the four of us slept on the dirt, rising when the sun rose and going to sleep when it set.

Days passed, then weeks. We waited anxiously. Would the boat materialize? Would the government change its policy before our boat was ready? While we waited in limbo, my mother visited, having traveled by bus from Saigon to bring us food—pork in small, dry pieces, like bits of jerky—and even some mosquito netting to protect us. She also told us that local Communists had seized our house in Saigon the morning after we left. I missed our belongings, our furniture. She left after a week, and then Thuy's mother visited, also bringing food for the wait and the journey. She assured us that she would be praying every day for our safe passage across the sea. After another week, my mother-in-law left and my mother returned.

Finally, a week after that, the organizers announced that the time had come: the boat was ready. Soon, we would be on our way. They escorted our entire group to the boat, a flimsy fishing craft that looked like it might safely carry about fifty passengers. Uniformed police officers were standing around it, each holding an AK-47 rifle. One officer was counting the people as they arrived. Looking around, I took in the size of the crowd of people waiting to board the boat. It seemed to number in the hundreds. I couldn't imagine how so many people could possibly squeeze into that relatively small vessel.

"How are all these people going to fit on the boat?" I asked one of the men who seemed to be trying to keep order and direct people. He told me that it was difficult to control numbers of people. Some who had showed up had not paid the boat organizers directly —they had made payments to the police, who were insisting that those people be allowed onboard. Under duress, the organizers had to accept whomever the police sent. "Otherwise," the man said, "nobody goes." In other words, the police wouldn't let the boat depart without the passengers they had designated.

Slowly, we all boarded the boat: young, old, men, women, even some toddlers and babies, ethnic Chinese, Vietnamese pretending to be Chinese. Hundreds of us packed in, our bodies eventually covering every available surface on the deck and in the hold, the cramped space below decks where fishermen would have stored fish and ice. That was where Thuy, Khoi, Mai, and I found a place. We sat on the floor, and I looked up at rafters. The ceiling was so low that even a short person like me could not stand erect. The air was thick, hot, and sticky, and I was sweating from the moment we boarded.

Now on the boat time passed slowly as we waited in the heat and humidity, until finally, just after midnight, I heard the engine come to life, and slowly, the boat began to move. Sitting in the crowded and sticky hold, I sensed we were moving, though from where we were sitting, it was difficult to tell in what direction.

Thirty or so minutes after the engines first started, the motion of the boat became more turbulent; clearly, we were moving from the calm, protected waters of the bay onto the open sea. Suddenly, I heard a burst of gunfire from outside. At first I panicked, worried that gunshot holes in the hull could sink the boat with our journey barely started. But then word circulated from the top deck down: the noise had been policemen shooting their AK-47s into the air, not in attack but in celebration, sending a message to our boat's crew and passengers: *This is as far as we go. You're on your own now.* (They might have also added: *Good luck—and thanks for the gold.*)

I thought about all I had endured over the past five years: I had lost my career, lost my home, lost my father, lost my hope, and nearly lost my life. But at this moment, I felt optimistic. I had faith that I would have a chance to restart my career, purchase a new home, catch up on my lost years, and rebuild my life.

For the first time in a long time, I smiled.

My father, Tran Duy Tinh, in his early twenties, as a guerilla fighter with the Viet Minh, a national independence coalition founded by Ho Chi Minh, battling the French for Vietnam independence.

My father, Tran Duy Tinh (1928-1977).

*My mother, Nguyen Thi Noi
(1926–2017).*

*My family in Tay Ninh (1958): my
mother and father and (from left) my
sisters Thao and Binh and me.*

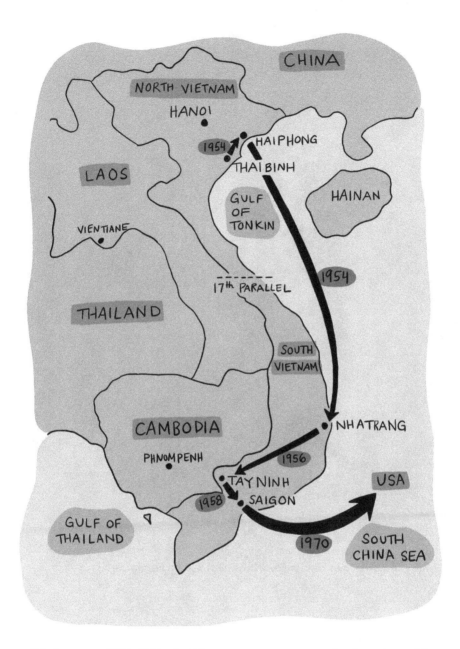

My journeys, 1954-1970. *In 1954, Vietnam was partitioned at the 17th parallel. The northern part became Communist North Vietnam and the southern part became pro-Western South Vietnam. My mother carried me from our village in Thai Binh to the port of Hai Phong to join my father on an American landing craft headed south. We disembarked at Nha Trang. In 1956, our family relocated to Tay Ninh, then, in 1958, to Saigon. In 1970, I traveled to the United States for college.* (Credit: Tim Tran and Alex Bell)

I earned this certificate in 1970 after completing nearly three months at Georgetown University studying English, civilization, and American institutions.

As a student at Georgetown in 1970.

Thuy and I enjoying our first snow at Pacific University in the winter of 1970.

With my Gamma Sigma brothers at Pacific University in 1970. I'm in the front row, second from the left, to the left of Art Wilcox, the faculty advisor. (Credit: Pacific University Yearbook, 1971)

Thuy and I in 1971 watching a pie-eating contest, one of many new experiences we enjoyed at Pacific University.

THE REGENTS OF THE

University of California

ON THE NOMINATION OF THE FACULTY OF THE
SCHOOL OF BUSINESS ADMINISTRATION
HAVE CONFERRED UPON

KHIEM MANH TRAN

THE DEGREE OF BACHELOR OF SCIENCE
WITH ALL THE RIGHTS AND PRIVILEGES THERETO PERTAINING

GIVEN AT BERKELEY
THIS FIFTEENTH DAY OF JUNE IN THE YEAR
NINETEEN HUNDRED AND SEVENTY-FOUR

GOVERNOR OF CALIFORNIA AND
PRESIDENT OF THE REGENTS

CHANCELLOR AT BERKELEY

PRESIDENT OF THE UNIVERSITY

DEAN OF THE SCHOOL

My diploma from the University of California, Berkeley, received in 1974.

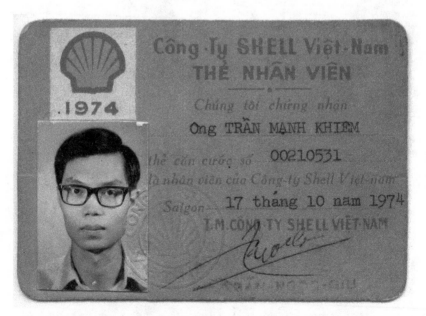

*I landed my first job working for Shell Vietnam in October, 1974. This was
my company identification card.*

TO : MR . PAUL HEBB
PACIFIC UNIVERSITY
OREGON

My sister Thao's letter (top) was miraculously delivered in 1975 from Wake Island to Forest Grove without a city name, street address, or zip code, courtesy of the American Red Cross and United States Postal Service. Simply addressed to "Mr. Paul Hebb, Pacific University, Oregon," it found its way into the right hands.

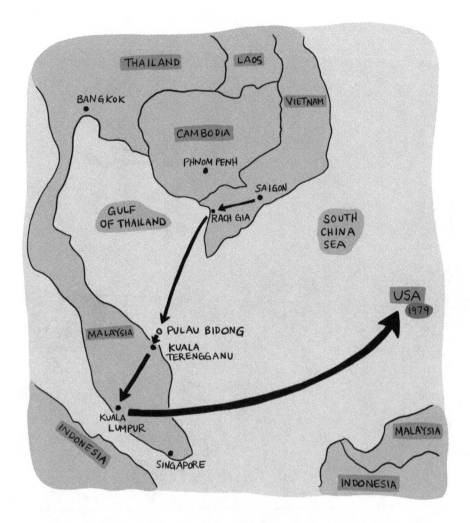

My journey, 1979. *After many failed attempts, I escaped successfully in 1979, moving from Saigon to Rach Gia, where I boarded a boat crossing the Gulf of Thailand to Malaysia, where I lived on the refugee island of Pulau Bidong. From there, I went to Kuala Terengganu, to Kuala Lumpur, and finally boarded a flight to the United States.* (Credit: Tim Tran and Alex Bell)

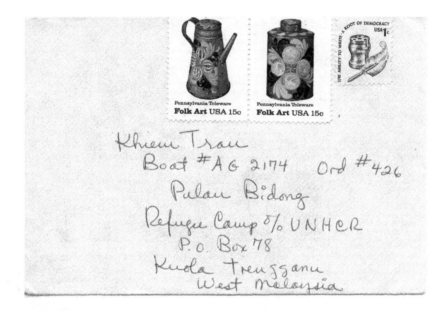

Khiem Trau
Boat #AG 2174   Ord #426
Pulau Bidong
Refugee Camp c/o UNHCR
P.O. Box 78
Kuala Trengganu
West Malaysia

This was my address on the refugee island of Pulau Bidong in Malaysia, 1979. Boat #AG2174 was the registration number of the vessel on which I arrived; UNHCR stands for the United Nations High Commission for Refugees; and Kuala Terengganu is the Malaysian administrative province of the island of Pulau Bidong. I received quite a few letters at this address.

Frankie Minnick, a member of the American delegation with which I worked on Pulau Bidong, created this drawing, of the team that interviewed refugees for resettlement in the United States. I interpreted primarily for Art Schoepfer (sixth from the right) and Bruce Beardsley (far right). Art worked for the US Agency for International Development (AID) for many years. Before I left the camp, he circled his name on the picture and wrote his Washington, D.C. mailing address on the back for me. Bruce gave me his business card, which listed his title: First Secretary, Chief of Consular Affairs, at the US Embassy in Copenhagen, Denmark.

This stove crafted from discarded food cans was my gift from "Big Fat Eight," a friend at the Pulau Bidong refugee camp, who used it each morning to brew tea he often shared with me. It now has a home in the Pacific University Archives.
(Credit: Robbie Bourland, Pacific University)

MR. TRAN MANH KHIEM is going
to be an interpreter in Kuala
Trengganu for a few days.

(K.B.TAN)

POLICE INSPECTOR.

4ᵗʰ SEPT 79

While working as a volunteer interpreter in the refugee camp at Pulau Bidong, I was asked to travel to Kuala Terengganu to interpret for the Malaysian court in a robbery trial involving a Vietnamese refugee. Since I had no passport or visa, this letter, signed by Police Inspector K.B. Tan, served as my travel document.

25th February, 1980

TO WHOM IT MAY CONCERN

Mr. Khiem Manh Tran was employed by Cong-Ty Shell Vietnam as a Senior Auditor reporting to the Head of Internal Audit Department, from 15th October, 1974, until 30th April, 1975, when the effective control of the Company by the Shell Group ceased.

Mr. Khiem Manh Tran took up his position upon his return from graduation in the U.S.A., at a time when the Company was operating under particularly difficult circumstances. Apart from the usual professional expertise a great deal of imagination and moral courage was required from our Auditors in the execution of their job under conditions of war and general deterioration of values.

In all essential respects Mr. Khiem Manh Tran came up to, or exceeded our expectations and when he was confirmed as a member of Middle Management at the end of his probationary period on 15th April, 1975, we had firm plans for Mr. Khiem Manh Tran to succeed the Head of Internal Audit Department by the end of that year.

I do not hesitate to recommend Mr. Khiem Manh Tran for the high level of his professional qualities, his capacity for work, and for his human qualities. My best personal wishes accompany him.

H. Haerry

Im grünen Hof 9
CH-8133 Esslingen
Switzerland

Applying for jobs in the United States in early 1980, I asked Dr. Haerry, the former finance manager of Shell Vietnam, for a letter of recommendation. He sent this wonderful letter from his office in Switzerland.

EMBASSY OF THE
UNITED STATES OF AMERICA

Copenhagen, Denmark

February 11, 1980

Mr. Khiem Manh Tran
2516 S. Baker Street, Apt.D
Santa Ana, California 92707

Dear Tran:

It was very good to receive your recent letter and to learn
that you are safe in the United States now. During the time
since my return to Copenhagen from the refugee camps of
Malaysia, I have often thought of the many activities we were
called upon to perform there, and the individuals like yourself
who contributed so generously of their time and expertise to
assist the American Delegation in the performance of its
functions.

During the time we worked together at Pulau Bidong Refugee
Camp, I had many opportunities to observe at first hand the
energy that you devoted to the many tasks you assumed. In
addition to your working as an interpreter for many of my
colleagues who did not speak Vietnamese, you also worked in the
camp as the press secretary of External Affairs Division of the
Camp Committee, and also taught English in your spare time. I
was especially pleased to work with you, in that you combined a
perceptive mind and a willingness to work with a very keen
sense of humor.

I'm certain that your industriousness and ability will immediately be recognized in the United States, and help you in
attaining success in your chosen field. Please feel free to
use me as a reference should any of your prospective employers
wish further comments on your abilities.

Best wishes,

Bruce A. Beardsley
Consul of the United States
of America

*I also asked Consul Bruce Beardsley, for whom I interpreted in Pulau Bidong, to
provide a reference letter. I was grateful for his kind words, which helped me land
job offers.*

My official portrait at Johnstone, after I was named Vice President of Finance in 1985.

My naturalization certificate; I became a US citizen in 1986.

One of my favorite activities was playing golf in charity tournaments like this one, which benefited Ronald McDonald House.

Golfing with my banker, First Interstate Bank vice president Dave Perry.

In May 1991, CFO, a magazine for top financial executives, published a cover story about my escape, my life, my philosophy, and my work. (Courtesy of CFO)

At a 2002 Johnstone event with my mentor, Johnstone founder and president John M. Shank (1918–2003).

At the 2017 dedication of the Tim & Cathy Tran Library at Pacific University, Cathy and I posed with a cake replica of the library.
(Credit: Adam Fein, Pacific University)

Delivering my remarks at the dedication ceremony for the Tim & Cathy Tran Library at Pacific University, October 6th, 2017.
(Credit: Adam Fein, Pacific University)

Cathy and me with (from left) Professor Emeritus George Evans, his wife Donna, and Bobbi Nickels, at the dedication for the Tim & Cathy Tran Library. (Credit: Adam Fein, Pacific University)

TIM & CATHY TRAN LIBRARY

In honor of
Khiem "Tim" '74 and Thuy "Cathy" Tran '74,
who found refuge and opportunity
at Pacific and in the United States
and who, in gratitude, have turned
their generosity to their alma mater,
President Lesley M. Hallick
and Pacific University
proudly dedicate
the Tim & Cathy Tran Library

— OCTOBER 6, 2017 —

The dedication plaque at the west entrance of the Tim & Cathy Tran Library. (Credit: Robbie Bourland, Pacific University)

Part Five

Voyage to Freedom

Finally at Sea

We sailed out of Rach Gia Bay on May 12, 1979. I knew exactly how long the journey to Malaysia should take because a couple of years earlier I had watched Manh, the pilot, chart the course across the Gulf of Thailand on the *National Geographic* map. If everything went well, it would be two and a half days.

If everything went well.

My heart was pounding in eager anticipation. For more than four years, I had spent nearly every waking hour focused on one goal: finding a way out of Communist Vietnam for myself and my family. Even my dreams had been about escaping. How to free myself and my family from Communist oppression had occupied my thoughts, my conversations, and my dreams. And now I had finally made it—at least, as far as the open sea.

As the waves tossed the boat, more than a few of the passengers became seasick. Some of those around us made it up the steep ladder to the deck quickly enough to vomit over the side of the boat, but others weren't fast enough to get to the rail, and the sound and stench permeated the cramped space. As for me, I was so excited and eager to be leaving that I was impervious to the motion, and the sound and smell of my seasick boatmates hardly affected me. All I could think about was freedom.

Of course, there were perils ahead. Listening to the BBC in recent years, I had heard many reports about the pirates who plied the waters off Vietnam, preying on boats like ours. In fact, an international group called *Médecins Sans Frontières* (Doctors Without Borders) had chartered a ship called *L'Île de Lumière* (The Island of Light) to provide aid to refugees who had fallen victim to pirates.

And then there were the more expected hazards of traveling at sea in a poorly constructed, overcrowded craft. We could hit inclement weather; our fuel might run out; our vessel could veer off course and end up floating, directionless, carried by the currents.

Nutrition was also a challenge. We had brought along enough food for a few days—mostly the dried meat my mother and Thuy's mother had brought us while we waited in Rach Gia. The crew also distributed rice and ramen occasionally—no meat or fish, and just enough to stave off hunger. The boat was also stocked with water, which was distributed in plastic bottles, though it was anyone's guess how long the supply would last. If the journey turned out to be longer than a few days, who knew how we could survive? Early on, a couple of the women, clearly not conscious of the limited water supply, used some of the water to brush their teeth. That drew harsh words from the crew and other passengers, who were angry to see their fellow passengers wasting survival supplies on personal grooming.

For the most part, the four of us—Khoi, Mai, Thuy, and I—stayed in our place inside the hold, not wanting to bother the people around us. For that many people to coexist in such cramped quarters was going to require self-awareness and restraint from all of us. Occasionally, when passengers had to relieve themselves, they would make their way through the dense crowd of people, climb the ladder up to the deck, and wend their way to a makeshift privy in the stern. After a few hours, when I felt the need, I ascended to relieve myself.

While I was on the deck, I started chatting with the boat's captain, Lai, who worked for Mrs. Dau and who told me he had served as an officer in the South Vietnamese navy. In addition to Lai, there was a skipper (whom I called Anh Hai, which meant "Brother Number 2") and two mechanics, who spent most of their time down below, attending to the engines. I told Lai that I had once charted the exact journey we were embarking on—from Rach Gia to Malaysia—for a trip that was later aborted. I told him what I recalled about the route I thought we should be taking.

"You're exactly right," Lai said, showing me the boat's heading on a nautical compass. When I told him that I spoke some English, he asked whether I could help if we made contact with a foreign ship.

Of course, I said, and told him that I had graduated from an American university.

"We may need your help," said Lai, impressed. I let him know where our family was situated in the hold so that he could find me, then descended again to rejoin my family.

The first day passed without incident, with most of us sitting quietly, almost meditating to pass the time and trying to focus on the positive. The boat's two large engines were operating continuously, though it was diffi-cult to know how fast the boat was moving through the water.

The second day, too, was relatively uneventful. There was little for us to do but keep to ourselves, thinking about the past and the wide-open future.

"They Want to Board Our Boat"

On the third day, I felt the engines slow down, and then, without warning, they stopped and the boat ceased its progress, drifting in the middle of the Gulf of Thailand. I climbed the ladder to see what was wrong. Looking out over the water, I spotted what appeared to be three ships. It was difficult to judge their size at first, but they didn't look like crafts that were coming to rescue us. They appeared to be three fishing boats. As they neared, I noticed that on all three of the vessels, something had been affixed to conceal the registration numbers that were painted on the sides of the boats.

I found Lai, the captain, looking through his binoculars at the three vessels.

"Who are they?" I asked.

"Thai fishermen," he said warily. "They want to board our boat."

"What for?" I asked.

Lai paused. "I'm afraid they're probably pirates," he said evenly. I noticed that he was trying to remove the wedding ring from his left hand, using a bit of saliva to loosen it from his finger.

"Why are you doing that?" I asked nervously.

"Well," he said, "if they can't get it off, they'll chop off my finger to get the ring."

I had a sinking feeling. I looked up again at the three approaching boats. "All three boats?" I asked. "They're *all* pirates?"

Lai nodded. While two of the boats stayed back, one of them drew closer to ours until one of the fishermen, a machete in his hand, leaped onto the deck of our boat, and then he ordered one of his mates to maneuver their boat close enough for them to tie a line and connect the boats.

Within minutes, nine other men jumped from the fishing boat onto the deck of our boat, each of them holding a machete in one hand and a plastic bucket in the other.

I didn't know what to think or expect. Without warning or introduction, they approached the passengers one at a time, gesturing with their sharp knives and barking orders in Thai, a language none of us could understand. One of the pirates confronted me and pointed his machete at my watch, a Seiko I had purchased six years earlier in Berkeley. I quickly took it off, handed it to him, and watched him toss it into his bucket, just another piece of booty.

I saw another one of the pirates confront a passenger and wave his machete at the man's waist. The man responded by emptying his pockets as quickly as he could. The pirate threw anything that looked like gold into his bucket, but any Vietnamese piasters he tossed aside.

Nobody on the boat wanted trouble. We all complied and gave the intruders what they demanded. All we wanted was to make our way to freedom—alive. The plundering went on for three hours, the ten men circulating through the packed deck and the covered area down below. They shouted in Thai to each other, and also to us, though none of us understood what they were saying. And then they shimmied back from our boat to theirs, untied the lines, and made off with their newfound loot.

Eager to put the encounter behind us, the mechanics almost immediately powered up the engines, and our boat began moving again. The vessel had been in motion for barely more than fifteen minutes when the second of the three boats approached us. I could see the crew, about the same number of surly-looking characters as on the first boat, all carrying machetes. One of them was also waving a gun. From our distance, it was difficult to discern whether it was a real gun or a toy, but he was pointing it at our boat. A few bullets in the hull could easily have sunk our boat, there in the middle of the sea, so our crew again turned off the engines in an effort to comply and avoid a conflict.

It was already late afternoon and the sun hung low in the sky. The fishermen's boat pulled close to ours and then they threw a rope to our deck, again hitching the two vessels. We all waited, nervous and silent, for them to board. But they left us waiting. Perhaps the men didn't want to start the job in fading light, preferring a time when they had daylight to aid their search for every last item of value. Especially in the lower quarters, they would need as much light as possible.

Tethered to the pirates' boat, ours could not proceed. So we waited, our boat floating in the open sea. I didn't sleep that night. Few of us did. Many passengers made whatever effort they could to hide whatever valuables they had been able to conceal from the previous group of pirates. Others just lay awake, dreading what the morning might bring. Some of the young women and teenage girls moved from the top deck down to our level, fearing what the armed and machete-wielding men might do to them. Our boat, previously top-heavy, became bottom-heavy.

When the sun rose, the boat was still tied to ours, but I was relieved to see that the other two vessels were out of sight. The eight or nine marauders, a crew even more menacing than the first, clambered aboard our boat. Wielding machetes and hunting knives, they behaved just as the previous day's raiders had, shouting at us passengers in Thai and gesturing threateningly with their blades. Knowing the other pirates had beaten them to much of the loot, they searched the boat's nooks and crannies, turning up crinkled dollar bills and hidden jewels. They found gold that had been concealed in bags of rice, in fuel tanks—almost anywhere.

Poking at a pile of dirty clothing with his machete, one of the pirates turned up an aluminum can of baby formula. He shouted in Thai, obviously trying to identify whose it was. When a young mother waved, claiming it as hers, he demanded that she hand it over to him. Then he opened it, revealing its contents: not formula but a hidden cache of diamonds. Rather than carrying bills or gold bars, this obviously well-to-do woman had condensed her family's wealth into diamonds.

And now her riches were gone, newly the possession of the pirate, who retired back to his boat, satisfied, while his comrades continued to plunder. The first group had focused mostly on the deck, largely avoiding the hold, which was crowded, putrid, and dark. But that didn't stop this group. The ruthless men filled their buckets with what the previous group had overlooked.

By noon, they had completed their ransacking. Their buckets overflowing, they stopped, apparently satisfied with their booty, scampered back to their own boat, pulled the line back in, and sailed off. Almost immediately, our mechanics revved the engines again. Temporarily relieved, I hoped that meant we could resume our journey. We were losing time, and we were all desperate to get to Malaysia.

That hope proved short-lived. Two hours after we started moving, the third fishing boat reappeared. Just as the second boat had done, it pulled up alongside our vessel. Along with my fellow passengers, I looked over the rail at the figures of the eight or ten men onboard this latest boat, trying to size them up and ascertain their intent. A couple of the men gestured with their arms, signaling for our boat to stop. Again the mechanics idled the engine, and a few of the men from the other boat used a rope to lash their craft to ours. Like the second group, this one didn't immediately jump onto our boat but waited as the light faded, leaving us with another night of floating and dread.

The next morning started as the previous one had: the group of pirates, armed with machetes and other knives, and one of them armed with a pistol, climbed onto our boat. Not finding much loot immediately—the first two groups had plundered all of the obvious and most of the hidden things—the intruders quickly grew frustrated.

That was when, for the first time, one of the pirates became violent. I was in the pilothouse when a commotion began. One of the men had grabbed a passenger, a girl in her late teens, and held a knife to her throat. He pulled her to one end of the boat, behind some crates, and began sexually assaulting her. I heard her screaming. Shocked as we all were, there was little that anyone could do: the intruders were armed with knives and a gun. Some of the older women closed their eyes and held their hands together in prayer.

Then, before anyone could intervene, I heard shouts in Vietnamese: "She jumped overboard!" "She jumped!" Indeed, the girl had pried herself free from the Thai intruder and, humiliated, mortified, and violated, thrown herself into the ocean.

Realizing what had happened, Lai, who was also in the pilothouse, began shouting directions toward the direction where the girl had been. "Throw her an empty jug!" he yelled to the crowd. "Throw her a jug!"

Somebody grabbed one of the empty plastic water containers and tossed it toward the girl, who was struggling on the surface of the water. Another person threw a second empty jug in her direction. I watched the girl treading water, the two jugs floating within a few meters of her. We all watched, waiting for her to swim toward the floating jugs so she could grab one of them and we could toss her a line.

She didn't grab a jug. She didn't swim toward the boat. Instead, she began swimming away from the boat. Within a minute or two, the girl disappeared behind a wave. The two empty jugs continued to bob in the water, but the young woman was nowhere to be seen. We all watched in agony as this girl, who must have boarded at Rach Gia with the same mix of anxiety and hope we had all felt, ended her own life, there in the middle of the Gulf of Thailand.

No one knew what to do, or how to respond. A few of the older women fell into silent prayer—Catholic prayers, Buddhist prayers. Pleading for the girl's life.

The rapist and his mates continued their plunder, making their way through the crowded deck and hold with their knives and buckets, just as the previous groups had. Finally, satisfied with their loot, they climbed back into their own boat, detaching the line and sailing away.

With that, our boat's engines came to life again, and we resumed our course through the water. Looking around at the faces of my fellow passengers, it was clear that events were taking a brutal toll. We had begun the journey with the relief and hope of finally escaping the ruthless Communist regime. But the events of the last forty-eight hours—the plundering, the breaks in our progress, and now the girl's death—were weighing heavily on all of us. Perhaps we could resume our journey. But would we ever recover from this trauma?

Hoping the worst was behind us, I made my way from the deck back down into the hold to be with Thuy, Khoi, and Mai. As cramped and uncomfortable as the lower space was, at least it felt a bit more protected from violence. The boat's progress continued, engines churning, for about six hours, and then I heard someone shouting: "Pirates!"

Within moments, somebody called down to the hold, "Khiem, we need you up here!"

Clambering up to the deck, I saw some of the alarmed passengers pointing off to one direction. There, approaching us, was a sight we all dreaded: yet another fishing vessel. The boat, slightly smaller than the others had been, pulled close, but this group of pirates didn't hesitate. One at a time, they climbed onto our boat—six or seven men, all carrying knives and plastic buckets, just like the previous groups. At least one of them wielded a pistol. They started checking our wrists for watches or jewelry, and, finding practically nothing, examined us passengers more closely.

After considerable searching, they had come up with only modest loot, filling their pails only about halfway. So they became more aggressive, slashing open bags of rice and ramen and dumping the food onto the floor.

When they found a few items hidden amid the dry goods—some American currency, jewelry the Chinese merchant's family might have hidden there for safekeeping—it encouraged the pirates to keep looking. They tossed whatever they found into their pails and kept tearing into the food supply, spilling much of the remaining rations underfoot.

Still not satisfied, the men plunged ahead, next going after the boat's potable water supply. When the men found transparent jugs, they would lift them to the light, searching for anything hidden inside, then put them back down. When the containers were opaque, they carelessly dumped out the precious water. There was nothing any of us could do to stop them; the men were armed—and increasingly angry. But it was difficult to watch, knowing that we had already been at sea longer than I'd expected because the repeated attacks had severely slowed our progress. Dumped-out rice, I figured, we could regather, store, and eat. But spilled water? It was simply lost.

This fourth group lingered onboard longer than any of the previous three groups of pirates, searching more aggressively. They were less belligerent toward individuals, but in attacking the water supply, they perhaps did the most damage to our quickly fading hope of making it to Malaysia alive. Eventually, though, the men decided they had done enough damage. They returned to their own boat, separated it from ours, turned on their engine, and headed off.

Yet again, the mechanics powered up the engines, and the boat began moving again through the waves. Only three hours passed before it happened again: yet another boatload of pirates arrived and boarded our boat. By this time, most of us had moved beyond worry, beyond fear, beyond anxiety. We were numb. The men—armed, angry, impatient, frustrated—moved among us, looking for loot and finding practically nothing. Like the group before them, they broke into some of the food supply, recklessly spilling it. It was difficult to summon emotion. By now I was sure most of my boatmates felt the way I did: dazed, defeated, overwhelmed. I noticed many of the passengers simply closing their eyes and uttering silent prayers—to God, to Buddha, to the universe. The pirates interrupted some of them midprayer to order them to move so the pirates could search every corner of the boat for loot.

After a couple of hours, this group, the fifth, left our boat, boarded their own with whatever they had been able to take, and departed.

Our boat resumed its journey, made it four more hours, and then encountered a sixth crew of pirates. They boarded, searched, and found little.
What had been shocking and terrifying the first time and even the second
time had now become a sort of absurd routine. With nothing left to lose,
most of us put up no resistance, simply looking on as the men struggled to
find things worth taking, observing these depraved and appalling characters
until, like the others, they departed, leaving us to float.

The boat started moving again, but it was difficult not to wonder: *How
many more? How many more attacks? How many more groups? How much more can
we take?* The last three had ripped through our food and, worse, most of our
potable water supply.

At least a dozen of the boat's passengers were quite elderly. Some of
them were rapidly losing energy and strength. These were clearly wealthy
people who had lived in villas and enjoyed the care of domestic servants. In
Vietnamese culture, we revered the elderly and respected their wisdom. So
all of us were conscious of the fragile condition of these older individuals,
and we all wanted to help them.

Lai, concerned about dehydration, tried to issue an order. He held up a
cup the size of an ordinary coffee cup.

"Unfortunately, we're running out of water, and we still have a long
journey ahead," he said. "Each person can have no more than one cup of
water a day. That's all. It's the only way we can survive!"

No one argued.

We had no sign that we were anywhere close to our destination. Our
chances of surviving the journey were fading quickly. We could last without food, but how could this mass of humanity last with such a meager supply of water?

And then there was the lingering, unspoken question of how much we
could take. If another group of pirates arrived and found practically nothing, would they take out their anger on us? Would more girls and women
become victims? Would we face more violence against the women on the
boat? Against all of us?

Sure enough, our worst fears were realized: four hours after the sixth
group of pirates fled, a seventh group arrived. Like the previous groups,
these pirates threw a line to our boat and one of them threatened us with a
pistol. Like the previous groups, they boarded carrying machetes and plas-

tic pails. Like the previous two groups, they destroyed whatever food they found and intentionally damaged water containers. They ransacked whatever they could. They pried open water jugs and threw them overboard while we looked on, helpless.

Then this group did something none of the others had attempted: some of the marauders climbed to the area where the engines were and opened one of the containers of diesel fuel. There, they found some hidden valuables the boat's mechanic had probably hidden there. Encouraged by that, they opened another, still looking. In the process, they spilled some of the precious fuel we needed to make it to the Malaysian shore. Watching, I became more worried than ever that we would all die at sea. It was more and more difficult to imagine how we would survive this.

Even with the few things they discovered under the caps of the fuel jugs, the seventh group of pirates wasn't finding much to plunder. The previous groups had stripped us of so much that there was very little of value left. I watched as they talked among themselves in Thai, apparently coming up with a new plan.

Dispersing again, they began accosting anyone wearing eyeglasses, raising a machete to each passenger's face and shouting in Thai, making it clear they wanted the glasses. One of the men confronted me and pointed his knife at my waist, signaling for me to take off my pants. I looked down. I was wearing my Levi's blue jeans, the pair my sister Thao had sent in one of her care packages from Oregon. They had become my most beloved piece of clothing, a reminder of my sister and my time in college. Sensing my hesitation, the pirate held his knife to my throat, and I quickly unbuttoned the jeans, pulled them off, and handed them over. Still holding the knife up, he reached with his other hand and grabbed my eyeglasses—the gold-rimmed prescription glasses I had acquired five years earlier in Forest Grove. He swiftly dropped the jeans and glasses into his bucket and moved on, leaving me in my underwear with fuzzy vision. I could make out the outlines of people and objects, but everything else was suddenly blurry, and I felt more vulnerable than ever. Slowly and carefully, I made my way down to the cramped quarters in the hold and put on my only spare pair of pants.

Other pirates were robbing other passengers of their jeans, though they seemed less interested in other clothing. Of course, the previous six groups of pirates had taken so much from us that by the time this group had boarded our boat, there was almost nothing left to seize. That clearly frustrated them.

Having humiliated us, taken our glasses and denim jeans, and wreaked destruction on what little we had to keep us alive, they departed, leaving us to float in the sea. The crew immediately tried to start the engine. But this time it failed. They tried again. Nothing.

My heart sank. Was this the end? The pirates had taken nearly everything: money, jewelry, gold, diamonds, food, water, even my eyeglasses and pants. Our only hope was to make it to land soon, and now that, too, seemed hopeless. Now they had apparently done enough damage to the fuel or the engines that our crew had no way to coax the boat back into action.

The late-May sun was beating down. We had practically no water. Without my glasses, I couldn't see clearly farther than a few feet. I could feel the motion of the waves, carrying the boat up and down, but we were not moving.

The two mechanics frantically tinkered with the engines, the fuel tanks, and the lines connecting them, all damaged by the pirates. Minutes ticked by.

Still nothing. Perhaps this was where our journey would end.

And then, against all odds, I heard one of the engines sputter to life.

Ghost Ship

The boat began to move. With the fuel supply low and only one of the two engines functional, the mechanics kept the engine operating at a low hum—enough for the boat to make steady progress, but at a level that would conserve what little fuel we had. Somehow, the pilot's compass had survived all of the attacks, and he was able to steer the boat in the correct direction, toward the coast of Malaysia.

How much further did we have to go? Nobody knew. We were moving, but it was clear that we had only a slim chance of making it to the Malaysian coast. Fuel was low, and even if the boat made it, many of us might easily die of starvation or dehydration before we reached land. Our only option was to lie back and try to conserve energy. I avoided exertion, trying not to do anything that would make me thirstier.

Our boat began to feel like a ghost ship. Everyone had fallen silent, resigned to the fact that we might not make it. Some moved their lips in prayer. All of us knew that we might well be facing our deaths there on the sea—that we might be close to the end.

I did not resist that thought. I had no regrets and no doubts that we had made the right decision in leaving the oppression and hopelessness of Communist-controlled Vietnam. If I perished in the attempt, so be it. At least I had tried. Thuy and I exchanged looks but few words. We each knew what the other was thinking and feeling. The same was true with my brother and sister. There were no words. Only silence. I ascended and stood in the pilothouse, trying to help with navigation. I looked around at the tightly packed deck: men, women, old, young, sitting and lying in almost complete stillness and silence.

And then a single voice broke the silence.

"I see a mountain!" someone shouted in Vietnamese. The man's voice was weak but loud enough to stir many of the passengers from their death-like trances. "I see land! Over there!"

The pilot instinctively reached for his binoculars, forgetting that one of the pirates had made off with them. Instead, along with everyone else, he squinted, trying to make out the outline of a ridge. Within minutes, more of the passengers could make out the land as our boat continued to move slowly in that direction.

"Let's move!" "Let's get there!" people were shouting, suddenly revived. Nearly everyone was urging the pilot to proceed toward the land mass as quickly as possible.

Amid the urgent calls to speed ahead, I sounded the one cautionary note. From listening for months to BBC broadcasts, I knew that Malaysia had been battling a Communist insurgency known as the Malayan National Liberation Army since 1968. The country's authorities were wary of refugees from Communist countries, fearing that the boats might be filled with Communist spies posing as refugees in order to infiltrate their country. If the Malaysian coast guard spotted our boat, I feared that rather than helping us get to shore, they might actually tow us further out into the ocean.

"The best thing is for us to stay out here and avoid being noticed," I told Lai. "And then after dark, when they can't see us, we can head in and storm the beach."

Lai agreed, and he explained to the other passengers that we would all be safer if we made landfall after dark. He ordered the mechanics to idle the one engine that was still working. It was afternoon, and five hours passed before the sun set. As we waited eagerly, nobody complained about thirst or lack of water. Finally, we had a sense of hope.

And then, in the midst of this eager collective anticipation, another tragedy struck. An elderly Chinese woman who was traveling with her family simply couldn't hold on any longer. Even for the healthiest of us, the conditions were difficult: hot sun, minimal food, no water, barely any room to move about. The elderly were particularly vulnerable, and this woman, sitting with her family in the lower part of the boat, had reached her physical limits. Here, within sight of the Malaysian shore, her body gave up, and she died.

Lai tried to convince her family that it would be best for all to bury the woman at sea, but they strenuously objected. Her son lashed out at the pilot: "It's your fault. She didn't have enough water or food! You're responsible for her death!" He and his family would not relent. The confrontation grew tense, with the son shouting at Lai: "I'll *kill* you if you try to throw my mother's body in the ocean!"

I understood that they were simply trying to follow Chinese tradition. They wanted to give the matriarch a proper burial. Amid the eager anticipation of reaching Malaysia, the death reminded us all of our mortality—of the fate that could have befallen any and all of us—and also added to the tension we were already feeling on the boat.

With darkness descending, the pilot pointed the boat toward land, and, running the only working engine, we slowly moved forward. For the first time in a few days, I felt my adrenaline rushing again. I felt confident we would make it to shore. But with my excitement came concern about what would happen if the Malaysian coast guard or police intercepted our boat. Would they really tow us back out to sea? We were so low on fuel and every other resource that I feared none of us would survive that. I had an idea about how to prevent that fate.

"When we get close, rev the engine at full power," I told Lai, who was at the helm, "and run the boat into the rocks."

"Why?" he asked.

"We need to destroy this boat," I told him, "so there's no way for them to tow us back out to sea."

He nodded. "That makes sense," Lai said with a wry smile. "I don't know what you were doing before this, but you make a lot of sense."

I smiled. "When we get to Malaysia, we can have a talk over tea," I said. "But now let's rev it at one hundred percent power."

The noise of the engine grew thunderous as we sped toward the coast. The pilot shouted to tell the passengers the plan and warn them to brace themselves for the impact. As we approached the beach, we neared some tall rocks in the shallow waters just offshore. The mechanics revved the engine to full throttle and—*BOOM!*—slammed into the rocks, badly damaging the hull, but not destroying it. At my suggestion, the pilot shouted to the passengers in Vietnamese and then in Chinese: "Please! Anybody who is able, help us destroy the boat! We need to sink it, to make it impossible for them to tow us back out to sea!"

There, in the shallow waters off the Malaysian coast, the women, children, and older passengers slogged through the seawater toward the beach. Meanwhile, we men and the older boys used whatever we could—our bare hands, chunks of wood, any piece of metal we could pry from the boat—to hack away at the hull, trying to inflict enough damage to make the boat worthless as a seagoing vessel. We kept at it for two hours, working in the dark until we had completely dismantled the flimsy craft that had carried us across the Gulf of Thailand. What was left of the craft was now so damaged that it quickly took on seawater and gradually sank, the bulk of it resting on the sandy bottom.

With the boat disposed of, the rest of us made our way through the shallow water toward the beach. The last people in our progression were the relatives of the Chinese grandmother who had died. Amid the elation and celebration of our arrival, they solemnly carried her body, treating it with care, love, and respect.

Watching them, I thought of my father, who had been denied that kind of respect in his death—who never got the proper burial he deserved. I had lost him in the last of my four unsuccessful attempts to get out of Vietnam. Now I had succeeded. I had found a way out, but it didn't seem right that we were here without him—that Khoi and Mai and Thuy and I had made it, but my father never got the chance to leave. As the family carrying the Chinese woman's body passed me, I stood erect, bowed my head, and said a silent prayer meant for the grandmother: "If you happen to meet my dad," I whispered, "please tell him that his son is always thinking about him."

Slowly we all made our way from the wreckage of the boat onto the sandy beach. I worried that some of the passengers might stray from the group and raise the suspicions of any Malaysian authorities who might be watching. The pilot cautioned the group to stay together for our safety, and we did, moving as one unit, a few hundred bedraggled souls on a strange and unknown beach.

Part Six

The Refugee Island
of Pulau Bidong

"Does Anyone Here Speak English?"

We had no idea where exactly we were, though we assumed it was Malaysia. In the darkness, I didn't see any lights, vehicles, or buildings. Our group waited on the beach, exhausted and spent from our journey.

Then, within an hour, I spotted the headlights of a vehicle approaching from out in the distance. Soon it became clear that I was actually seeing multiple vehicles: a police jeep accompanying two trucks. The vehicles stopped nearby, and a few uniformed men carrying rifles approached our group in the darkness. Without making contact and without explanation, they lit four campfires, forming the corners of a square around us. The fires provided enough light that they could see our group. Then the police officers spread barbed wire in a circle around us, completely surrounding us, so that none of us could escape. As the hours passed, these men stood watch nearby. We didn't interact with them. We still hadn't found water or food. And we didn't ask. Clearly, the job of these men wasn't to help us or feed us but rather to keep an eye on us. To them, we were potential Communist infiltrators, and their task was to prevent us from penetrating their society.

We were all completely exhausted from the journey, particularly from the last few days and the repeated pirate attacks. Most of the people in our group simply lay in the sand, sleeping—or trying to.

At dawn, I stood with Lai, the boat's pilot. For the first time, we could both see our entire party. Surveying the hundreds of people spread across the sand, he shook his head. "I can't believe that small boat could carry this many people," Lai said. Indeed, it seemed impossible, but it was true. More than ever, I felt grateful that we had somehow, miraculously, made it across the turbulent waters and, against all odds, reached this shore. Even aside from the pirates, so many things could have foiled our mission—bad weather, a leak, a mechanical engine failure, or just poor navigation—and yet here we were.

The sun rose and the fires died down. Suddenly I saw another vehicle approaching from a distance. It appeared to be a white SUV. When the vehicle got close to our group, it stopped just outside the barbed wire circle.

There was a blue United Nations emblem on the side of the vehicle and the letters UNHCR (for United Nations High Commissioner for Refugees). I turned to Lai. "These are representatives of the United Nations," I told him. "They're here to help us as refugees."

Two men stepped out of the vehicle. The first was a Caucasian man. He was followed by a Malaysian man in uniform who was obviously being deferential to the Caucasian man. Without my glasses, it was difficult to tell, but I assumed that the second man was a bodyguard, a liaison, or an interpreter. As the two of them approached us, the Malaysian police who had spread the barbed wire carefully pulled some of the wire aside to allow the two men to step inside the circle. All of us gathered around, and the Caucasian man addressed the group and told us his name. "I represent the United Nations High Commissioner for Refugees," he said in English, with an accent that sounded British or perhaps Australian. "Does anyone here speak English?"

I raised my hand. So did two others.

The UN official pointed to one of the others who had identified himself. "What are your credentials?" he asked.

The man answered tentatively: "I worked as an interpreter for the US Army."

The official pointed at the second man. "I was a high school English teacher," the man said.

Finally, the Caucasian man pointed at me, and I spoke up. "Khiem Tran," I said with a smile. "University of California, Berkeley! Class of 1974!"

He smiled and nodded slowly, taking in my answer—probably not what he had expected to hear from someone in this bedraggled collection of humanity on a beach in Malaysia. He gestured for me to approach. I did, and he began asking me questions.

"Where did your boat come from?"

"Rach Gia, Vietnam," I told him. He jotted my answer on a piece of paper.

"What was the date of departure?"

"May twelfth." It was now May twentieth.

He asked for the boat's registration number, and I told him: AG2174. AG stood for An Giang, a Vietnamese province on the Mekong Delta near Rach Gia, where we had started the journey.

"How many of you are there?"

"Three hundred, maybe three hundred fifty."

He asked about the ethnic makeup of our group. I told him we were probably eighty percent Chinese, twenty percent Vietnamese. He nodded; obviously he had encountered many, many vessels like ours.

"Was this a government-sanctioned voyage?"

I told him it was semi-sanctioned, that the government had given us permission to go.

As he listened, the Caucasian man nodded. He knew exactly what to ask and understood my answers.

"Any events on the journey?"

I told him about the seven groups of Thai fishermen who had attacked us.

He nodded. "Anyone injured or deceased?"

I pointed to the family with the elderly Chinese lady, whose body now lay on the beach, a white piece of cloth draped over her face. And I told him about the teenage girl who had committed suicide after the pirate had violated her.

The questions continued. As we spoke, a large van pulled up and someone brought cups of coffee for the Malaysian police officers and the UN official. I hadn't eaten in three days and had drunk practically no water since the pirates had destroyed our water supply. I stared at the coffee but said nothing, aware that I wasn't in a position to ask, but the UN official noticed and understood. He gestured for one of the police officers to bring me a cup. Moments later, the officer handed a cup of coffee to the UN official, who passed it along to me.

I took a sip. Coffee had never tasted so good in my life. I savored every sip.

A short time later, another UN truck arrived, towing a drab olive-colored two-wheel trailer full of drinking water. People from our group lined up, filled cups from the spigot, and distributed the cups among themselves. Some used their own cups and then shared with others, passing the cups around to make sure everyone had at least a sip. The water was revitalizing, renewing our spirits along with our bodies. We had suffered together, we had worried together, and together we had questioned whether this day would come. And now we were collectively revived. People savored their first sips, smiling and offering huge sighs of relief.

Watching this scene play out, just a day after I had all but given up, I felt reborn. I felt grateful to be alive.

Along with the water, the UN representatives distributed small sandwiches—minced chicken with ketchup on thick baguette slices—and we all ate what they gave us.

While everyone ate, the UNHCR official explained to me what would happen next: they were arranging for transportation to take all of us to a refugee camp. With so many refugees like us arriving on Malaysia's shores, the country's authorities were particularly wary about security, he explained, so the sooner they could get us to a refugee camp, the better.

Next, a convoy of military flatbed trucks arrived, and the police officers ordered our group to form a single line leading to the trucks. Apparently, though, they wanted to assert some kind of authority over us before we climbed in. An officer pulled out a bamboo cane, and before each person hopped up onto the bed of the truck, the policeman delivered a quick slap to the back with the cane. He struck every adult: Thuy, my sister and brother, men, women, elderly people. I took mine just as everyone else did. The officer didn't strike me hard enough to cause sharp pain, but it wasn't a light tap, either. It seemed that he was trying to send a message: *You're in our country now, and we're in charge—don't cause any trouble.*

The officer skipped hitting only one passenger, a man named Ali, whose complexion was slightly darker than the average Vietnamese or Chinese person's and who wore a sarong instead of a shirt and pants. Perhaps the policeman assumed Ali was Malaysian and Muslim and therefore treated him with slightly more respect than the rest of us.

Once all three hundred of us were on the trucks, the drivers revved the engines and drove us up the coast. They stopped after about an hour in a town called Kuala Terengganu, where we all piled off. The authorities led us to a landing, where they told us to wait. After some time, a boat arrived, and the police instructed us to board. Together with Thuy, Khoi, and Mai, I got on. The boat was about the same size as the one we had spent the last week on, but it was in much better condition, and only about seventy-five of us were aboard, about a quarter of the number who had crammed onto our vessel in Vietnam. The boat pulled out from the dock and headed to sea. Our destination quickly came into view: it was an island covering about a square kilometer, about twenty-eight kilometers off the Malaysian coast. This would be the next stop in my journey, a refugee camp called Pulau Bidong.

Isle of Refugees

I didn't know what to expect, but I fully accepted that this would be our home for the near future. I felt that some higher power had watched over my family and me to get us to this place without our boat capsizing, without falling victim to the bands of pirates. Arriving at this unknown, unexpected place, I felt elated.

As we neared, I could see a makeshift jetty and huge crowds of people teeming on the beach. After stepping off the boat, we entered a crude structure with a corrugated metal roof. Surveying my surroundings, I noticed some makeshift tables and benches where Vietnamese workers were processing the newly arrived refugees. We all formed lines and waited for our turn to answer questions from the registration workers.

When our moment came, the Vietnamese registrar asked my family and me a series of questions: name, date of birth, birthplace, address in Vietnam. As I answered each question, he wrote my answer on a page in a notebook. He asked about my education, which languages I spoke, and my occupation—both before and after the Communist takeover of Vietnam. His final question: "Where do you hope to settle after you leave Malaysia?" I listed my top three choices in order of preference: the United States, Canada, and Australia.

When I mentioned that I had gone to college in the United States and that I spoke fluent English, the worker took keen interest. "We have a great need for interpreters here," he told me, "particularly English speakers." As it turned out, Thuy and I weren't the only ones from our boat who had language skills. One woman I hadn't spoken to during the sea voyage had gone to Lycée Marie Curie, one of Saigon's best French secondary schools, and spoke fluent French. And an ethnic Chinese woman was fluent in both Cantonese and Vietnamese and also spoke some English.

The registration staff also explained that we would be able to receive mail using our boat's registration number, AG2174, and its "order number," 426. That meant ours was the 426th boatload of people to arrive at Pulau Bidong from Vietnam. More than four hundred boats! It was no wonder the island was so crowded with Vietnamese and ethnic Chinese refugees!

I soon learned that the registrars weren't collecting these details simply for the sake of having information. With some thirty thousand people, Pulau Bidong was essentially a small city, one that required every person's efforts in order to function. The camp's management team collected our information and recruited refugees for various roles. Those who were trained physicians or nurses, for instance, were put to work in the sick bay; mechanical engineers were assigned to construction; refugees who had served as military police for South Vietnam joined the security team. The camp had a fire brigade—and even a crew that made caskets. Occasionally a voice would come over the loudspeaker in the central area of the camp asking the carpentry group to report to its location. We all knew what that meant.

Soon after I arrived, the head of the interpretation staff, a Vietnamese refugee named Dich, sought me out and introduced himself.

"I'm glad you made it here safely," Dich said warmly. He asked me a few questions about my family, and then the conversation turned to work. He told me he could use an interpreter with knowledge of English and Vietnamese. He explained that the job wouldn't pay, but it was a way of helping my fellow refugees. Dich also oversaw the maintenance of refugees' registration files, with support from a group of file administrators. These were refugees who were not fluent enough to be interpreters but had some proficiency in reading English or French and Vietnamese. The team helped maintain and update the files on each refugee family unit and prepared the files for the delegations representing the various countries to which refugees were applying for refugee status. But with my command of English, he said, I would be most useful as an interpreter.

"In fact," he said, "we could use you as soon as tomorrow." Dich explained that a delegation from Australia would be arriving the next morning around 10 a.m. to interview refugees who had expressed interest in applying to resettle there.

"Sure thing!" I said. "I just need to find a place to stay tonight." I tentatively nodded at a nearby bench, figuring I could sleep there if I couldn't come up with something better. The area had a roof, after all, and I didn't know where else I might land.

Meanwhile, the interpretation department had also discovered Thuy, whose English was as good as mine. She, too, agreed to work as an English interpreter.

With such large numbers of people in such a small and confined space, the biggest challenge was figuring out where we would live. Arriving at Pulau Bidong wasn't like coming to a settled community with existing structures where we could move in. Everyone there built his or her own tent. That meant we were on our own—even that first night—to find a place to sleep.

But where to begin? The four of us decided to start by looking for familiar faces. I had known a lot of people in Saigon through my high school and various networks, so I hoped I could find somebody I knew who might be willing to take us in. I told Thuy and my brother and sister to do the same thing: look for familiar faces from home.

From the jetty and the registration area, we walked along a trail up the island's slope. The higher we ascended, the denser the tropical rain forest became. The four of us were surveying the makeshift structures and the thousands of faces when I heard my brother Khoi shout something.

"Khoa!"

Amid hundreds of unfamiliar faces, he had spotted our brother, Khoa, who had left Vietnam on a boat my mother had arranged a few months before the rest of us. Somehow, against all odds, all of us had survived and ended up on the same island, in the same refugee camp.

Khoa's hair had grown long—he probably hadn't had a haircut since he left Saigon. We all embraced. I felt stunned and overwhelmed. We asked Khoa about his journey from Vietnam, and he described a voyage that sounded very much like ours: multiple pirate attacks, near dehydration, desperation, and then the joy of landing in Malaysia and arriving at Pulau Bidong.

Along the way, he had befriended two other men traveling solo. Here on the slopes of Pulau Bidong, the three of them had built a shelter they were sharing, using a borrowed saw to fell trees for the structure. With new refugees constantly arriving, the areas close to the water were crowded. The later refugees arrived, the higher up the slope they placed their shelters. Khoa and his boatmates had placed theirs on the hillside about halfway be-

tween the waterline and the island's peak. He led the four of us to see the
shelter: an improvised platform under the shelter of a plastic tarp that Khoa
and his friends had managed to purchase—or maybe inherit from refugees
who were moving on from the island.

The quarters were too small for all of us, so we got to work cutting
more tree branches to extend the sleeping platform so it would accommo-
date seven. What we created wasn't perfect or even very comfortable, but
it would work. And in any case, we were grateful to be alive and together.

The next morning, as promised, I showed up to meet the delegation from
Australia at the administration area, basically a collection of makeshift tables on a dirt floor under a corrugated metal roof. The head of the interpreting department introduced me to the head of the delegation, who
greeted me warmly.

"What part of Australia are you from?" I asked.

"Sydney," he told me.

"I've heard that's a beautiful city," I said.

He asked where I had learned English.

"I went to college in the United States," I told him. "I graduated from
Berkeley."

"Oh, that's a good school!" he said. Speaking to someone in English
gave me an immediate sense of comfort. I was in my element.

The purpose of the Australian group's visit was to screen refugees to
decide whether they were suitable for emigration to Australia. I sat beside the Australian interviewers on one side of the table, and one group of
refugees at a time (usually a family) would approach and sit opposite us. The
representative would ask a question in English, and I would translate it into
Vietnamese, then translate the refugee's answer from Vietnamese to English for the Australian representative. The questions were routine: name,
date of birth, place of birth. How many in your family? What kind of work
did you do before the war? How many people accompanied you here?

The Australians interviewed one family at a time, usually directing the
questions to the father or husband while the rest of the family sat listening.
Parents were usually careful to ask their young children to be on their best

behavior during the interview. They wanted to make a good impression in the hopes of improving their chances.

One after another, the families arrived for their appointments. I listened to the questions and answers and did my best to make both sides feel understood. For the first time in years, I felt useful and engaged in my work. Not only had I survived the treacherous journey across the Gulf of Thailand, but I had also landed in a place where I was needed for my intellect—where my life experience was allowing me to help people.

Team Player

Within days of my arrival, I was part of a team, one that was engaged every day in the essential work of determining the future opportunities of the tens of thousands of refugees for whom Pulau Bidong was a temporary home.

My work interpreting for the interviewing teams kept me busy. Almost every morning around ten o'clock, a boat from Terengganu would arrive with that day's interviewing team. If the team represented an English-speaking country, they usually employed my services.

I worked most often with the American delegation, since the United States was by far the most popular destination of choice for Pulau Bidong's refugees. The Australian delegation might visit once every three weeks, but the American group came at least weekly. I interpreted for the US team so frequently that they came to treat me not as a subordinate but as a colleague. Certainly, they were there to do a job, but these were kind and educated people, and working with them was a pleasure.

Not that they were pushovers. Arthur Schoepfer, a tall, lean man in his late thirties who was one of the US team's leaders, had a reputation as tough and demanding. The refugees who would watch the interviews from the perimeter of the administrative area nicknamed him "The Tough One." On one visit, Dich, the interpretation division head, had assigned him an interpreter at random, and Arthur was unhappy with the interpreter's work—apparently the interpretation had been sloppy and unhelpful. At the midday break, I saw Arthur approach Dich and—speaking sternly but quietly, to avoid being heard—demand that he be assigned a different interpreter. That's when the team head turned to me.

"Khiem, we have a problem," he said. "Would you mind switching and working the rest of the day with Arthur?"

"No problem," I said. When I approached Arthur, he shook my hand and wasted no time. "Let's get to work!" he said. I spent that afternoon as Arthur's interpreter and learned that his reputation was accurate: he was serious, rarely smiling and never making small talk. He was tough and demanding—but also thorough and smart.

At the end of the day, he shook my hand again. "Thank you for doing a great job," he said.

I felt relieved—even more so later, when Dich, the department head, approached me. "Art was very pleased with your work," he said. "Going forward, he wants to have you as his interpreter whenever he's here."

I was delighted, and Arthur and I quickly developed a close working relationship, passing the long days filled with interviews by sharing jokes and observations. I also grew to understand Art's reputation in the camp: the refugees thought he was so tough that if it turned out he was your interviewer, you stood little chance of being admitted to the United States. They gathered around and watched his body language and facial expressions, intimidated by his very presence.

In contrast, the woman for whom Thuy was interpreting, Anita Lee, was much less threatening. The only African American in the American delegation, she had a kind manner and always seemed to be smiling. When she interviewed refugees, they felt that they had far greater odds of obtaining approval to go to America.

Then there was Bruce Beardsley. Bruce struck me as a gentleman and an intellectual. He had significant experience working as a diplomat and a calm and gentle presence. Bruce conducted his interviews with professionalism and intelligence.

One morning, as the American delegation showed up, I noticed that Bruce was immaculately dressed—in trousers and a nicely pressed shirt—while the rest of his colleagues were in casual wear. "Good morning, Bruce," I said to him. "You look very nice today. You win the 'best dressed' title on Pulau Bidong!" We all laughed, Bruce and Arthur the hardest of all.

★ ★ ★ ★ ★

As an interpreter, I became part of a well-organized system that sifted through Pulau Bidong's thousands of refugees and determined their ultimate fate. It was no small job. With nearly thirty thousand refugees on the island, more arriving daily, and teams from a different country showing up practically every day to interview, there was no end to the details we had to manage.

The camp administration used an approach I knew from accounting:

FIFO, or "first in, first out." The earlier refugees had arrived, the sooner they were interviewed and processed. If the family's first choice was the United States, the US delegation would meet them first. When one country rejected a family's application—at least for the time being—the next on their list would interview them.

I learned that different countries had different priorities in choosing refugees. Greece was looking for people with skills such as housekeeping, cleaning, and driving. If a particular refugee had experience as a cook, Greece might give that person's application priority. Switzerland had a reputation for being accommodating and welcoming to people who were sick or disabled. The country saw its role as humanitarian, providing medical care and a welcoming home to those in extreme need.

Canada wanted immigrants who were educated or who had money in bank accounts, so if an ethnic Chinese family happened to have money in a French bank, that increased the odds that Canada would offer to take in the family.

Other countries had clear preferences that weren't official policy but that I observed through experience. For example, Australia's delegation consistently showed a preference for good-looking, single young women. One day I was interpreting for the visiting Australian team when they interviewed a family—mother, father, two sons, and one attractive daughter. The team approved the daughter to settle in Australia but rejected the rest of the family. (Not wanting to go without her family, she declined the offer and opted to wait until the whole family could be placed.)

As for the United States, its top priority was bringing in refugees with family connections in America. In my case, the fact that my sister Thao was living in the United States weighed far more heavily than my diploma from Berkeley or my fluent English.

Sometimes the mix of refugees' skills and various countries' needs and priorities made the process unpredictable. When it came time for Dich, the head of the interpretation team, to be interviewed himself, it turned out that although he was fluent in English, he did not have relatives in the United States, nor had he gone to school there, nor had he ever worked with the US military. He didn't want to be a cook or driver, so Greece wasn't an appealing option for him. He wasn't an attractive woman, so Australia wouldn't take him. After the British team interviewed him, they offered him settlement in the United Kingdom, so he was bound for London.

Even with the many countries' delegations constantly passing through Pulau Bidong, many refugees were repeatedly rejected. The camp administration had an expression for these individuals and families. Anyone who was rejected three times went into a file nicknamed "garbage," a term concocted by refugees who had themselves been rejected multiple times.

Some of these people had been waiting for years to find a way off the island. One particular ethnic Chinese man told me that he had built a boat that had delivered hundreds of people from Vietnam, but he and his family had been waiting for three years for a country to take them in. "We helped a lot of people escape, and they've all come and gone," he told me. "And we're still here."

To offer reassurance, I reminded him of the line that we had all heard often in the refugee camp. "Just be patient," I said. "The Americans have promised to pick up all the 'garbage.'"

Indeed, that was many people's last hope: that no matter who else rejected them, the United States would take them in. I once asked Bruce Beardsley, my colleague on the American team, to explain what might motivate the US to do that. "I really appreciate the fact that America will interview refugees who have been here for years," I said, "but could you explain the logic behind that?"

Bruce explained that South Vietnam and the United States had been allies, fighting Communism together. "In a sense, we reneged on our promise to help you because of the political climate in our country," he said. "So we feel a moral obligation to provide settlement for Vietnamese refugees who might be rejected by the rest of the world."

Still, the wait could weigh heavily on people like the Chinese boatbuilder who had been waiting for a full three years. They lived from day to day, waiting hopefully and patiently for their chance. Once in a while, the US delegation would look at the "garbage" file and offer those families another interview. That was cause for celebration. It meant their wait was over. America was fulfilling its promise to pick up all the "garbage."

Since I worked so closely with the US delegation, I gained a reputation among the refugees as a knowledgeable expert on resettlement in America. Refugees often asked me for advice on how they might convince America to accept them. The truth was that there was no particular secret. The process was quite transparent. My best advice was to be honest—not to claim or pretend to be anything they weren't. Not only did dishonesty not pay, but it could also permanently end the possibility of gaining admittance to the United States.

I learned the hazards of dishonesty after sitting in on an interview conducted by an older gentleman in the American delegation, whom I'll call Tom. The refugee being interviewed made a remarkable claim: that back in Vietnam, he had once come across a shallow grave that contained the remains of an American soldier.

Of course, that caught Tom's attention immediately. It was well known that it was America's top priority to locate GIs who were missing in action or prisoners of war. As the man spoke, Tom gave me a serious look. "Khiem, we have a critical situation here," he said under his breath. "Let's make sure we get it right."

Tom began firing questions at the man, and I translated. *Where was this grave? Where were you living at the time? When did you find the grave? How did you find the grave? How did you determine it was an American? Did you find the dog tags?*

Finally, the man became so confused and flustered by the barrage questions that he backed down from his claims. "Please," he said to me, "tell him I just made it up."

American authorities had trained their representatives in how to investigate the kinds of claims this man was making. Certainly, if the man's claims were true, they wanted to know. But Tom was able to zero in on the lies quickly. He wrote down in capital letters in the applicant's file: FRAUD. That notation probably put a permanent end to the man's chances of settling in the United States.

Sometimes the interviews could be downright comical. Once I was interpreting an interview with a man who had arrived at the session with his wife and three children. Suddenly, in the middle of the interview, a young, attractive woman appeared and approached me.

"I'm his second wife," she told me quietly in Vietnamese.

The American interviewer looked at me. "What did she say?" he asked.

"Well," I said, smiling, "she claims that she's this man's second wife."

The interviewer laughed. I laughed too. The situation got more awkward from there. The interviewer told me to ask the woman to wait nearby until the interview was over so we could question her. Then we went back to questioning the man. "Is it true that this is your second wife?" the interviewer asked him.

"No, she's not my wife," the man said. "She's my *girlfriend*."

I tried to be diplomatic. Instead of *girlfriend*, I used the word *mistress*. That provoked more laughter, so much and so loud that the interviewers and family at the next table all looked up to see what was going on. Considering the circumstances that so many of us had endured in order to escape Communist Vietnam, it was difficult to believe that this man had managed to do so not only with his entire family but with his mistress as well!

As in that instance, the interviews could produce a particular kind of black humor—humor that helped me forge a strong friendship with Arthur Schoepfer. One time, interviewing a refugee who wanted to settle in the United States, he asked the man where his parents were. "They're both dead," the man explained. Any living brothers? "No." Sisters? "No." Any close relatives living outside Vietnam? "No." Any close relatives living inside Vietnam? The man shook his head.

Arthur turned to me. "He must be a very lonely person," he said. "No parents, no sisters, no brothers, no living relatives!"

"He's even lonelier than J. Edgar Hoover," I quipped. "At least Hoover had his mother!"

Arthur laughed hard at that. The refugees waiting nearby to be interviewed were probably delighted to see that Art, the supposedly tough interviewer, seemed to be in a good mood.

The Gift of Vision

Without my glasses, I had difficulty reading the refugee files that I needed to examine in my work as an interpreter. Whenever a colleague asked about my habit of holding a sheet of paper very close to my eyes to read it, I explained that I was nearsighted and that pirates had robbed me of my eyeglasses during our passage from Vietnam. Over time, I had become accustomed to this inconvenience.

One day a young man named Phuoc, who had worked for some time in the file administration group, sought me out for some advice, and I suggested we meet in the camp library. When Phuoc arrived, I was reading a magazine, holding the page at close range. Phuoc told me that back in Saigon, he had been studying at the School of Education, hoping to become an English teacher after graduation. He could read and write English well, but not well enough to serve as an interpreter. Knowing that I had graduated from an American university, Phuoc asked me whether I thought that it still made sense for him to seek work teaching English in America.

"Since English is our second language," I told him, "teaching English to American students who are native English speakers might be challenging." If he really wanted to teach, I suggested, he might want to study to be a math teacher. I told him how fulfilling my Upward Bound job had been.

Phuoc thanked me for the advice and then asked another question. "I noticed how close you hold the reading material," he said. "Why do you do that?"

"I used to have glasses," I said, "but pirates took them." He asked if my prescription was strong, and I told him it was only about negative two diopters. "I hold the page closer when reading so that my eyes won't tire so easily."

Phuoc took off the glasses he was wearing and handed them to me. "These are only minus one point two five diopters. Do they make your reading easier?"

I tried them on and glanced at a page. The letters looked much clearer. "Quite comfortable!" I said, returning the glasses.

A few weeks later, I realized that I hadn't seen Phuoc for some time in the interpretation area. I asked around and learned that he had left the camp. I felt disappointed that he hadn't said goodbye. Later, I dropped in on the camp library, where I found an envelope addressed to me. I opened it to discover a surprise: Phuoc's eyeglasses and a note:

Dear Brother Khiem,

I had to get on the boat to Terengganu early this morning and was not able to say goodbye to you. Please accept this pair of glasses because you need them to do an important job here. I'll get a new pair when I arrive in the US. Thank you for your advice. I think I will study to be a math teacher.

Sincerely,

Phuoc

I put on the pair of glasses and picked up a newspaper someone had left. The words were clear and much easier to read. I wished I could have thanked Phuoc in person.

"Nobody Here Thinks This Is Terrible"

The only thing that pulled me away from my work as an interpreter was a visit from an important dignitary. Knowing my background as a Berkeley graduate and former Shell executive, the camp's administration had quickly identified me as someone who would be useful beyond my day-to-day work as an interpreter for refugee-resettlement interviews. The other interpreters had a functional mastery of English, but my life experience gave me more understanding of both the nuances of the language and the subtleties of American politics and media. Because of that, soon after I arrived at Pulau Bidong, the administration designated me the camp's unofficial press secretary.

In that role, the camp government assigned me to accompany any English-speaking politician, reporter, or other prominent individual who visited the island. One guest was a Democratic congressman from New York, Representative Stephen Solarz. He arrived at Pulau Bidong by Malaysian Air Force helicopter, accompanied by an entourage of aides, journalists, and photographers. I gave the congressman a briefing about the camp, telling him how many refugees lived there, the ethnic makeup (60 percent ethnic Chinese, 30 percent Vietnamese, and 10 percent a mix of Filipinos and others), from where they had come (mostly southern Vietnam, departing from the Mekong Delta), and how the camp's governing structures functioned. I took him on a walking tour, showing him the various facilities refugees had built: the sick bay, a Buddhist pagoda, a Catholic church. I even walked Representative Solarz and his entourage up the hill to the hut I shared with my family and my brother Khoa's friends.

"These are just *terrible* living conditions," Representative Solarz said, shaking his head.

"No, sir, nobody here thinks this is terrible," I assured him. "We are all very happy that we made it here." It was true. What everyone at Pulau Bidong had in common was that we had all experienced traumatic escapes. Every journey was different—the weather, the encounters with pirates, how rough the seas were, how much time the voyage took—but we had all experienced trauma. We knew that the worst was over, and for all of us, the priority now was to recover, maintain good health, and prepare ourselves for the future. We were all grateful to be alive. And we understood that this island wasn't a permanent home, just a stopover on the way to something better.

"How's the food?" he asked.

I admitted that the cuisine could have been better. Most of what we ate came in cans, and if a can was labeled "chicken," the contents weren't thighs or legs but rather a bit of broth and maybe part of a chicken's neck. A container of "sardines" wasn't sardines but some unidentifiable fish species. But we could live with it, I told him. This wasn't a life sentence—just a temporary stopover.

"Any fresh fruits and vegetables?" he asked.

Only for those who foraged in the island's forests, I told him.

Representative Solarz asked where I hoped to settle eventually. I told him that I hadn't been approved yet, but I hoped to move to the United States—to Oregon, where my sister was living—and that I looked forward to becoming a citizen after five years so I could vote in elections. "Too bad it will probably be Oregon and not New York," I said, "or I would vote for you!" That made him laugh.

I mentioned to Representative Solarz that I had known Les AuCoin, the Pacific University alumnus for whom I had once campaigned when he was running for the Oregon legislature. Les was now a member of the US Congress. Representative Solarz pointed out that Representative AuCoin and he had been elected to Congress in the same year, 1974. I asked him if he would say hello to Representative AuCoin for me.

"I'd be happy to," he replied.

I posed for pictures with Representative Solarz and the rest of his party on the helicopter pad, and then they all boarded and took off.

When I got back to work, Arthur Schoepfer needled me for standing him up. "What?" he said, joking. "You think I'm less important than a member of the United States Congress?"

"Well," I said with a grin, "I just go where I'm told."

After that, I felt that my status had changed at the camp. When I had boarded the boat in Rach Gia, I had been undercover, pretending to be an ethnic Chinese person. When I had stepped up on the beach and told the UN representative that I was a Berkeley graduate, my boatmates had probably been at least surprised, if not impressed (though few could understand the English conversation). And now, during Representative Solarz's visit, crowds of my fellow refugees had seen me walking side by side with an American politician and his aides, pointing out the sights and offering a running commentary as a throng of photographers and refugees trailed along.

After that, as I walked around the camp, people started greeting me with *"Kinh chao ong"* ("Greetings, sir, with respect"). I would reply in kind: *"Kinh chao ong."* Many of the other refugees had learned my name because they heard it frequently on the loudspeakers that blasted announcements throughout the camp's central area: "Paging Mr. Tran Manh Khiem. Please report to the administration area to meet the American delegation." As I answered the pages, rushing from one place to another, more and more people would offer a respectful greeting as they saw me pass.

It made me feel important, but more than that, I felt fulfilled, even happy. I felt useful, just as I had in my early days at Shell in Saigon and, before that, during my summers teaching at Upward Bound. The work was fulfilling, I was tapping into my skills and interests, I was learning on the job, and I had the opportunity to interact with fascinating and kind people almost every day.

Meet the Press

Some of the most interesting people I encountered were the journalists I met in my role as Pulau Bidong's press secretary. A reporter and photographer from *Life* magazine interviewed me and shot photographs of me. A crew from the Canadian Broadcasting Corporation filmed an interview with me. I even spoke to a writer from *Der Spiegel*, the German newsmagazine. (He interviewed me in English, but I knew enough to end the session with *"Auf Wiedersehen!"*)

It turned out that because of the timing of our arrival, I had missed one of the biggest media visits. Ed Bradley and a crew from CBS's *60 Minutes* had visited Pulau Bidong just a couple of weeks before I arrived to shoot a segment on the refugees from Vietnam, a group the American media had come to refer to with a new term: "boat people." During my stay, I did assist reporters from *Time*, *Newsweek*, the *Los Angeles Times*, and the *Washington Post*, and a host of international reporters from a range of media outlets, including *Paris Match* and the BBC.

Whenever a journalist visited, my job was to greet the person at the jetty around nine in the morning, when the boat arrived from Terengganu. The boat was easily recognizable for its two flags: the Malaysian flag and the UNHCR flag. I could usually recognize the reporters because most of them wore the same kind of shirt, with lots of pockets, and they carried cameras and other accoutrements. I would introduce myself as their guide for the day.

Most of the journalists were immediately struck by the population of the camp, the throngs of refugees who were sharing space on this small, previously uninhabited island. The journalists were usually very kind. I took one reporter on a long walking tour of the camp that ended with a long hike up to the hut where I lived.

"Can we sit down and have some lunch?" he asked.

"Sure," I said.

He reached into his backpack and pulled out a bag of fried chicken that he had probably purchased in Kuala Terengganu. "We can share," he said.

I shook my head. "I already ate," I said, "and there's only enough for one person." Then I saw the golden-brown pieces of chicken and took in the aroma, which reminded me of the "finger-lickin' good" Kentucky Fried Chicken I had enjoyed years earlier in the United States. The reporter seemed to notice.

"Come on," he said. "At least try one piece."

I accepted and took a drumstick. It was the best piece of chicken I had tasted in a long time. I chewed slowly and savored every morsel. It was a welcome break from the canned rations I'd been eating for months.

While some kindnesses like the chicken were simply offered, there were two favors I did ask of the journalists and others I chaperoned through the camp. I often asked them to take letters I had written, knowing that if a visitor brought an envelope back to the US and mailed it from a post office with US postage, it had a better chance of getting to its destination than if I asked a departing refugee—who might not have the cash for postage—to mail it.

I also made requests for reading material. Any time English-speaking people visited, I asked whether they had any English magazines or books with them. Most people were carrying some kind of reading material—a paperback novel or maybe a copy of *Time* magazine they had brought for the flight. I explained that we had few English books on Pulau Bidong, so if they could leave a book or magazine, many people there would appreciate the gesture. Most visitors were willing to part with at least a couple of books.

Gathering pieces of literature in that way, I helped to augment a small existing library, ultimately building it to a couple of hundred titles. After one of the interpreters left the refugee camp, we converted his hut, just a few minutes from the interviewing area, into a sort of library. It became a gathering place for well-educated speakers of English and French (we also collected French books). It was a far cry from the Pacific University library or the Abraham Lincoln Library in Saigon, but being surrounded by books—and readers—reminded me of those significant places from my past and gave me a warm and familiar feeling.

Life, Death, and the Outside World

One thing that surprised every visiting reporter was the number of doctors on Pulau Bidong. There were more than eight hundred! Communist Vietnam was an awful place for medical professionals, well-educated people who, after the Communist takeover, found themselves working for people with perhaps fifth-grade educations who had spent decades away from civilization. It was no wonder so many medical professionals had risked everything to find a new life.

In the camp, though, the doctors had little access to medical instruments or medications. With no antibiotics available, an untreated infection could lead to complications or even death. In addition to the sick bay, Pulau Bidong had a cemetery with no small number of graves. I often heard of new boatloads that arrived with the bodies of elderly people or infants who had died on the journey—just as had happened in our boat. In one tragic freak accident on the island, a coconut dropped from a tree and killed a refugee.

For the most extreme medical cases, the camp's administration would summon help from *Médecins Sans Frontières* (Doctors Without Borders), the nongovernmental organization that provided health care on their ship, *L'Île de Lumière* (The Island of Light). On one occasion, Dich, the department head, asked me to take the tender to the ship to interpret for a French surgeon working on the ship. I demurred, insisting that my French was very weak. Still, he convinced me to go, assuring me that the surgeon spoke English. Before the surgery, the French doctor asked detailed questions of his Vietnamese patient and I interpreted in English for him. After the hour-long operation, the doctor took me to the ship's dining area, where I enjoyed a *café au lait* and a warm *croissant*. Heaven!

I was able to leave the island just one other time. I was recruited to interpret for a courtroom trial on the mainland in Kuala Terengganu. The Malaysian court was holding a trial for a Vietnamese man who stood accused of committing a robbery at sea. The court needed an interpreter to translate Vietnamese to English for the judge, the defense team, and the prosecution, and from English to Vietnamese for the defendant. Before I left, I received a handwritten note that served as my travel document:

"*Mr. TRAN MANH KHIEM will be an interpreter in Kuala Terengganu for a few days. K. B. TAN, Police Inspector.*"

When I arrived by boat in Kuala Terengganu, a police jeep picked me up and the officer invited me to sit in the front seat, which made the ride far more comfortable than my last road trip, in the crowded bed of a military truck. The driver brought me to a hotel, where I checked in to my own room (paid for by the court), and then I visited the hotel restaurant, where a waiter brought me lunch.

"Would you like a beer, sir?" he asked.

I hesitated. I knew that alcohol was generally prohibited for Muslims in Malaysia. But I was in a Chinese restaurant in a Chinese section of the city, and the idea of drinking a beer was certainly appealing. "Sure!" I said. And he brought me one. There I sat, a refugee in a hotel restaurant, savoring a bottle of beer. The taste immediately brought me back to my days of enjoying six-packs with my Gamma Sigma fraternity brothers at Pacific University. That night, I slept in a real bed, luxuriating in the comfort after my many months on our makeshift bed on the uneven floor of our hut.

The next morning, in court, the judge swore me in and asked my credentials. I told him I had graduated from the University of California, Berkeley.

"What was your major?" he asked.

"Finance and accounting, Your Honor!" I said. (Unsure whether to address this judge as "Your Honor" or "my lord," I followed the American practice.)

"Did you study law?" he asked.

"Yes, the Legal Aspects of Business course, sir!" I answered.

"Good enough," he said, and the trial proceeded.

I never learned the verdict, but what I never forgot from that visit was the taste of the beer, the Chinese cuisine, and the wonderful, luxurious bed. What a difference from my life on Pulau Bidong!

Big Fat Eight

One of the closest neighbors to the hut I shared with my family was an ethnic Chinese man named *Tam Map*, who was at Pulau Bidong with his wife, who spoke little Vietnamese, and their young son and daughter. His name, roughly translated, meant "big fat eight." My impression was that he had been very wealthy in Vietnam—and apparently very well fed. And he must have been the eighth child in his family, so to everyone who knew him in Pulau Bidong, this obese Chinese man was just Big Fat Eight.

Big Fat Eight had a talent with his hands: he could make or repair practically anything. One time, he discovered a termite mound up the hill from our shacks. He noticed that because of the termite activity, the soil had an unusual quality, so he brought some of the clay home and used it to construct a brick oven. That showed remarkable ingenuity. Big Fat Eight would fire up his homemade oven every morning and bake bread that he then sold in the camp's market. He also fashioned a small stove out of one of the cans from the food rations the UNCHR distributed to refugees. For fuel, he used the fish oil that came in the mislabeled cans of sardines. It was an ingenious invention.

Big Fat Eight asked me to tutor his young son and daughter in English, and he paid me by serving me tea. Most mornings, before I headed to the central area to work as an interpreter, I would stop by Big Fat Eight's hut and he would boil water on the little stove and brew us a cup of tea. We would sit together and savor those quiet moments.

Big Fat Eight respected me for the work I was doing, and he revered intellectuals, but unfortunately, he had difficulty with the emigration process. He had no relatives in the United States or anywhere else besides Communist China, and he didn't want to settle there. He had been going through the process of interviewing with delegations from three different countries, but all three had rejected him. Of course, that made him part of the "garbage" group.

One day, Big Fat Eight tracked me down to share some news: he had heard that a delegation from the Netherlands would be interviewing refugees and had expressed a particular interest in candidates who were willing and able to perform manual labor.

"Should I apply to go to Holland?" he asked.

"You know you're in the 'garbage' group, right?" I asked.

"Yeah," he said.

"It might take two or three years before the Americans take all of the 'garbage,'" I reminded him. "Do you think you can wait that long?"

"I've already waited three years," he said. "I don't want my kids to have to wait another three years."

I knew enough about Holland to know that Amsterdam had a Chinese population, which would help Big Fat Eight to make social connections and find work. I advised him to apply. "The worst that can happen is that they'll reject you," I said, "and you can go back to waiting for the Americans."

He applied, and the Dutch delegation accepted Big Fat Eight, his wife, and their two children. On their last morning in Pulau Bidong, we shared a cup of tea as we had every day. As we sat together, he handed me the stove he had crafted from the food-ration cans and some of the leftover tea leaves.

"I won't need this in Holland," he said, "but you'll need it here. Why don't you keep it?"

Moved by the gesture, I thanked him. We said our farewells, and I carried the stove back to my hut.

Unaccompanied Minors

If there was one group of people who got special treatment on Pulau Bidong, it was the children who weren't accompanied by their parents. Many Vietnamese parents could not afford to pay for their entire families to escape the country. But they knew that as the offspring of South Vietnamese parents, their children had no real future in Communist Vietnam. If the parents could scrape together enough money or gold, they would pay for their children to travel independently on the boats sailing to freedom. These mothers and fathers were making a remarkable sacrifice. They were willing to bear the tremendous hardship of life under Communist oppression, but they wanted their children to have lives of opportunity. So the camp was full of teenagers who had made the way across the Gulf of Thailand on their own, without their parents.

When these young people arrived at Pulau Bidong and told the registration staff that they were on their own, the staff placed their names on a special "unaccompanied minors" list. When a visiting delegation selected a family for settlement, they often placed an unaccompanied minor bound for the same country with the family. If a family was settling in California, for example, and the minor had relatives there, the American delegation might make the match. Most families were happy to offer help and connect these children with their relatives scattered around the world.

I knew one fourteen-year-old boy, for example, whose mother had secured a place for him on a boat to escape Vietnam. He had memorized the address and phone number of his brother, who was living in Montana. He gave that information to the UNHCR and the American Red Cross verified it, so he was given priority to interview with the US delegation, which placed him with a family heading to the US.

Of course, there were also plenty of children attached to their own families. In many cases, Vietnamese parents wouldn't have made the treacherous journey at all except for the chance to give their children a better life than they could have had in Vietnam. The camp ran a small, one-room school for them, and some also spent time gathering vegetables or bamboo in the wild reaches of the island. For younger children, there were play-groups and gatherings to sing or study English. The camp did its best to keep them occupied.

America Bound

Finally, in late August, about four months after our arrival, the time came for my own family to be interviewed to settle in the United States. To avoid a conflict of interest, the team didn't assign Bruce Beardsley or Arthur Schoepfer, who had become my close friends, to interview us. It didn't matter to me—all of the American interviewers were kind and compassionate people, including the one who was assigned for our interview, Anita Lee, an interviewer for whom Thuy had interpreted often. I had also worked for Anita, and she even had a nickname for me: Berkeley Man.

As the five of us sat there, Anita flipped through my file, which was considerably thicker than practically any file I had seen in my many days of sitting in on placement interviews. I was surprised to learn of some of the contents. One page was a letter on my behalf from Bob Packwood, a United States senator from Oregon, addressed to Robert Hopkins Miller, the US ambassador to Malaysia. Another was a letter from Oregon's other senator, Mark Hatfield. And there was one from Congressman Les AuCoin, whom, of course, I knew personally.

Anita held it up, read it silently, and then looked up at me.

"You know an *American congressman*?" she asked.

"Well, yeah," I replied humbly. "I worked on his campaign when I was a student in the US."

I'd had no idea the letters would be in my file. I could only guess that my sister Thao and my friends in Oregon—Bobbi Nickels, Paul Hebb, and others—had been busy advocating on my behalf. In fact, one of the letters in the file was from Paul. Another was a handwritten note from Arthur Schoepfer. Anita looked over Arthur's note, nodded again, then looked over toward where Arthur was conducting his own interview at a nearby table.

As she concluded the interview, Anita didn't wait to give us the news. "Khiem," she said, "you and your family are going to America!" We all smiled at each other, happy to have the official news. She told us that the administration would alert us when a boat was available to transport us.

In the meantime, I got to work preparing to turn over my duties to other refugees. The camp administrator asked me to arrange for a couple of other interpreters to shadow me for the rest of my time as press secretary, so they could learn the job.

"Just understand, they aren't American college graduates, but they'll do okay," he said.

I found Arthur Schoepfer and informed him that my family had been approved and that the camp would probably assign a different interpreter to him, unless he wanted me to stick with him until my departure.

He shook his head. "Khiem, you've done a lot for us, and a lot for the camp," he said. "Just take the time to get yourself ready to leave." He handed me a card with his contact information at the USAID office in Washington, DC. "Keep in touch," he said. And we parted.

A couple of days later, I said goodbye to Bruce Beardsley, and he, too, gave me his business card—from the US embassy in Denmark. In order to make sure that I would be able to reach him in the future if he changed positions, on the back of the card he wrote the address and phone number of his mother, who lived in Nevada.

Frank Minnick, another of the interviewers, presented me with a drawing he had sketched with caricatures of every member of the US delegation. Somehow, with a few strokes of the pen, he had captured the personalities and expressions of the colleagues with whom I had worked over the previous four months: Bruce, Art, Anita, and the rest. It was a keepsake I would never part with.

On September 10, 1979, our family reported to the jetty dock, the same place where we had arrived just over four months earlier. I was carrying a plastic bag with some mementos: scraps of paper with handwritten addresses, the drawing from Frank, and one other significant object—the small stove Big Fat Eight had crafted from food-ration cans. I didn't know exactly where I would be going, but I knew I never wanted to forget those mornings sipping tea in his hut.

As the UNHCR boat departed and motored toward the Malaysian coast, I turned and watched the island of Pulau Bidong shrink into the distance, reflecting on the people I had met and all that I had accomplished since I had arrived four months earlier—traumatized, exhausted, bewildered, but hopeful.

The boat took us to the small town of Marang, where we boarded a bus to nearby Kuala Terengganu. There we boarded a large bus for the seven-hour drive to Kuala Lumpur, the Malaysian capital, where we arrived at a refugee transit camp. There, we underwent medical examinations, had our photographs taken, secured our travel documents, and waited—along with hundreds of other refugees. We stayed there for nearly three weeks, until we finally had our paperwork and travel documents.

Finally, on September 29, we boarded buses for the Kuala Lumpur International Airport. The staff at the refugee center gave us the travel documents we would need to board the flight and enter the United States. At the airport, our family, along with about fifty other refugees, boarded a Malaysia Airlines flight bound for Tokyo.

As the aircraft ascended, I looked out the window and watched the Malaysian hills recede into the distance. I felt a great debt of gratitude toward the Malaysian government, the United Nations High Commission for Refugees, Doctors Without Borders, and the delegations from many countries that had collectively saved and sustained me and so many other refugees, enabling us to move on to promising futures.

Among the businessmen and various other travelers, anyone could have identified us as refugees. We were surely the worst-dressed passengers, most of us wearing simple, faded clothing, and we all had dark complexions from spending so many hours outside in the hot Malaysian sun. We were also thin. I weighed ninety-five pounds, down at least seventeen pounds from my normal weight. And after so much time in the warm, tropical climate both in Vietnam and Pulau Bidong, we were shivering in the chilly cabin of the jet until a kind stewardess brought us each a blanket to wrap around our bodies.

Besides feeling cold, I felt elated. Each step, each day, each hour was bringing me closer to my final goal of settling in the United States. After all of our efforts, the dangers we'd faced, the mishaps along the way, it was difficult to believe we were actually on our way. Sitting in my airline seat, I began daydreaming about what I would do when we arrived in the United States, what my future might hold for me.

The modern jet airplane was my first encounter with the latest aviation technology of 1979, after four years in Communist Vietnam (which was under economic embargo) followed by four months in the refugee camp.

I kept asking myself, "Is this real?" The stewardess brought the tray of food—chicken; never had an airplane meal tasted so good.

The flight landed in Tokyo, and I immediately felt as if I was on familiar ground. I had been in Tokyo twice before—once with the USAID group on my first trip to America in 1970, and once on the return journey to Saigon in 1974. That second time, I had experienced mixed feelings about leaving my friends in America and heading home to Saigon. This time, I felt nothing but gratitude, relief, and anticipation. Even just browsing at the airport shops and seeing some of the prices listed in dollars and yens filled me with excitement. I didn't have a penny, but I was thrilled to be back in civilized society, in a world where it was normal to see airport souvenir shops and snack bars.

Back in the USA

As the plane touched down at Seattle-Tacoma International Airport, I felt as if, at long last, I was truly coming home. I thought of the Beatles song "Back in the USSR" and applied my own words: "Back in the USA." Going through immigration at the airport, I led the way for our group of refugees.

"How many are in your group?" the agent asked.

"About twenty," I replied.

He looked at me, then at the rest of our group, smiled at me, and said seven beautiful words: "Welcome to the United States of America!"

"Thank you very much, sir!" I said, feeling my eyes well with tears.

"Do all of you have the same travel documents?" he asked, looking at the papers I had received in Kuala Lumpur.

"That's all we have." I smiled. He stamped my papers and waved me past.

After that, we split into smaller groups bound for various locations. One family was headed to Bozeman, Montana, and needed help finding the gate. I helped them along and made sure they connected with an airline employee when they got there.

At a newsstand, I looked at a newspaper on display and quickly perused it. It was the first current US periodical I had seen in years, but I didn't have the money to buy a copy. While we waited at the gate for our flight to Portland, I found another newspaper left by someone on a chair. I devoured every article, desperate to catch up on the news.

The five of us boarded an Alaska Airlines flight to Portland, and I sat in a window seat. I felt like I was watching an old familiar movie. Out the window, I saw sights that had become familiar during my Pacific University days: Mount St. Helens, the Columbia River, Mount Hood. There aren't words to describe the elation I felt touching down at the Portland airport.

It was September 30, 1979, five years since Paul Hebb had dropped me off at this very airport. Five years that felt like fifty.

Part Seven

Rebuilding My Life

"I Travel Light"

As we walked down the jetway in Portland, and almost immediately, I spotted an older, white-haired Vietnamese gentleman holding a sign bearing handwritten messages in English and Vietnamese: *WELCOME TRAN FAMILY / GIA DINH TRAN.*

I approached him. "I'm Khiem Tran," I said. He greeted me with a smile. The man was a driver for the US Catholic Conference (USCC), which was working to assist refugees in resettling in the United States. He had been assigned to pick us up. He asked if we had checked luggage, but I told him we had none—only the few things we were carrying. The five of us followed him out of the terminal and piled into his small station wagon. I immediately thought of my first ride from Portland International Airport, when Mr. Ken Meyer, Pacific University's dean of admissions, had picked up Thuy and me and then hosted us in his beautiful home. So much had happened since then.

I struck up a conversation with the driver, asking how long he had been working for the USCC. Four years, he said—since 1975. "You must have been lucky enough to escape Vietnam in 1975," I said.

"Well, if I hadn't, I would have been dead by now," he replied.

I asked why.

"I was an officer in the South Vietnamese army," he said.

I asked what rank. He told me he was a lieutenant general. I asked his name, and when he told me, I recognized it. He had been not just an officer but a three-star general—one of the top military leaders in the country. He had indeed been lucky to escape, since the Communists had forced any military man of his rank into a re-education camp—and many had never returned. Now this man who had been among my country's top military brass was working as a driver. It made me worry about my prospects.

I asked how the economy was doing. "Not good," he said. It was 1979. Jimmy Carter was president. Unemployment and inflation were both high, and Ronald Reagan, then running for president, had coined the term *misery index.*

Would I be able to find a job? For now, I put that concern in the back of my mind. After a drive of more than an hour, we arrived in Forest Grove. As we passed Pacific University, I pointed out to my brother and sister the campus sign, the dorms where I had lived, the classroom buildings.

Finally we arrived at an apartment building, where we were greeted by a small but enthusiastic crowd: my sister Thao; Bobbi Nickels, my old friend from Upward Bound who was now Thao's roommate; Paul Hebb, my Upward Bound boss; and Charlie Trombley, the dean of students. I hugged Thao and Bobbi and shook hands with Paul and Dean Trombley.

Dean Trombley was looking in the back of the station wagon, wanting to help. "Is there some luggage I can get?" he asked. Bobbi, too, wanted to help carry whatever we had with us.

But we had none. The only thing each of us had was a simple white plastic bag bearing the United Nations logo and the blue letters "UN-HCR."

Bobbi looked at me, puzzled. I shrugged, smiled, and held up my plastic bag. "I travel light," I said.

At that, Bobbi's eyes filled with tears.

My bag held only a few items: the drawing of the American delegation that Frank Minnick had given me, my travel documents, and the newspaper I'd picked up in Seattle. My brother Khoi was carrying the only other item I'd brought from Pulau Bidong, the little stove from Big Fat Eight.

Bobbi knew my sense of humor, but the truth was that the reunion was packed with emotion. I had been dreaming of this moment for years, and Bobbi had been working hard toward it, too.

Friends of Khiem

I soon learned just how much Bobbi had been doing on our behalf. Back in 1975, when the fall of Saigon was looming, Bobbi had taken the initiative to create a group she called Friends of Khiem, which had the singular goal of helping me to escape from Vietnam. Bobbi had started by appealing to a core group of my friends and then had reached out to a larger group: my classmates, my fraternity brothers, my peers from the Symphonia music group, my professors, our coworkers at Upward Bound, Captain Good's mother—virtually anyone who had heard of me during my years at Pacific. She'd mailed out letters asking for donations, and these kind people had contributed with remarkable generosity. Some had given five or ten dollars, some fifty or more. And it was all to help me buy my way out of Vietnam.

Bobbi had used some of the money she'd raised to pay for her own trip to Hong Kong, where she had an uncle. There, she'd tried to negotiate a spot for me on an oceangoing ship. Unfortunately those efforts had been unsuccessful, but years later, when she learned that my family and I had escaped the country and arrived at the refugee camp in Pulau Bidong, Bobbi used some of the funds to purchase medications and other supplies that she sent us there. She and Paul had also gone to great lengths to make contact with Oregon's US senators and congressional representatives, appealing to them to write the letters that had made it into my file in the refugee camp. Of course, being an exemplary administrator, Bobbi had kept careful records along the way, cataloging every donor, donation, and expenditure, and keeping a file with photocopies of every significant piece of correspondence.

I also learned the remarkable story of my sister Thao's journey to America, which had been quite difficult. She traveled in the ship's hot and crowded hold and ate only dried food and army rations. After a week on the open sea, the boat arrived at the US naval base at Subic Bay in the Philippines. There, she spent a month with others in a Red Cross tent village. From there, a US military transport plane delivered her to Wake Island, an unincorporated US territory in the western Pacific.

The US had established a refugee processing center on Wake Island as part of Operation New Life, the American effort to rescue and resettle South Vietnamese refugees after the Communist takeover. A Red Cross official there helped her search for family members who might have made it out of Vietnam—to no avail. Later, in an effort to help the refugees make contact with relatives or acquaintances in America, Red Cross representatives at the center distributed envelopes and paper and encouraged refugees to write letters. Of course, Thao didn't have any relatives in the United States, but she recalled the instructions that I had shared with the entire family: if we got separated, she should make contact with my friend Paul Hebb at Pacific University in Forest Grove.

Thao quickly wrote a letter apologizing for her poor English and explaining that she was the sister of Khiem Tran, had escaped Saigon, and was living in a refugee center on Wake Island. She folded the brief letter, slipped it into an envelope, and, writing in all capital letters, addressed it with all of the information she could remember:

TO: MR. PAUL HEBB
     PACIFIC UNIVERSITY
     OREGON

Hoping that would be enough, she handed the simple white envelope to a Red Cross worker and waited.

A few weeks later, in late June 1975, Paul Hebb was retrieving his mail from his Pacific University mailbox when he discovered an envelope addressed to him with a handwritten return address in Lawton, Oklahoma. Opening it, he found, folded inside, the Red Cross envelope and the letter from Thao. Apparently a Red Cross supporter in Oklahoma had helped deliver some of the refugees' letters to the postal service, and miraculously, without a street address, zip code, or even a city, Thao's letter had found its way to Paul.

Shocked and delighted, Paul immediately shared the letter with Bobbi Nickels. Without hesitating, Bobbi wrote back and told Thao that she and Paul would sponsor her in coming to America and settling in Forest Grove. It was Bobbi who set to work on the paperwork and made all of the arrangements to bring Thao from Wake Island to Oregon.

When typhoon season arrived at Wake Island, the Red Cross relocated Thao to Camp Pendleton, California. Then, in August 1975, more than three months after she had left Saigon, Thao flew from Los Angeles to Portland, where Paul Hebb and Bobbi Nickels greeted her at the airport.

Bobbi, still working at Upward Bound, invited Thao to share her apartment while Thao got acclimated. She also enrolled her in Upward Bound for tutoring in English and basic skills to prepare for college. A few months later, Thao gained admission to Pacific University and moved into a dormitory. Supported by scholarships and her work in the campus food service and at the library, Thao made her way through school, majoring in mathematics and enjoying the same rich and varied college experiences Thuy and I had benefited from.

Now, knowing that the rest of us were on our way, Bobbi had rented a two-bedroom apartment not far from where she and Thao were living, where we could stay when we arrived. Bobbi had shopped at garage sales and bought all the basics we needed to function: furniture, dishes, and pots and pans. The five of us moved into the apartment, and Thao joined us there. We settled into these temporary quarters with the men in one room and the women in the other. The space was tight, but it was luxurious compared to the hillside shack we had been sharing on Pulau Bidong. Here in Forest Grove, we had indoor plumbing, a refrigerator, and heating. Nobody was complaining.

Bobbi, who had taken over Upward Bound from Paul a couple of years earlier, didn't have any teaching jobs open at Upward Bound, but she offered me a part-time position as a math tutor—not in Forest Grove but at the library in downtown Portland. The pay wasn't great, but it was a start, so I accepted.

Every Saturday, I took the bus from Forest Grove to downtown Portland and walked to Multnomah County's Central Library, a grand, Georgian-style building. I met students in the lobby and then, after a couple of hours of tutoring, made my way to the periodical room, where I found the back issues of my beloved *Time* magazine. I hadn't read a current issue of *Time* in nearly five years, since February 1975, when, just before the fall of Saigon, the Abraham Lincoln Library had shut its doors. Not only had I missed the pleasure of reading the articles, but I had also missed five years of news. So after every tutoring session, I made my way through back issues of *Time* and caught up on what had happened in the world while I had been living under Communism and in the refugee camp: Jimmy Carter's victory over Gerald Ford in the 1976 presidential election; the 1979 accident at the Three Mile Island nuclear reactor; the Portland Trail Blazers' 1977 NBA championship; the Jonestown cult suicides; and so much more. I paid the closest attention to the stories that directly affected me: *Time*'s analyses of the fall of Saigon, the ascendance of Vietnam's Communist government, the slaughter in Cambodia, and the plight of the boat people.

Job Hunting

I also used those library visits for another purpose: perusing the want ads in the *Oregonian* in search of a job in Portland. I realized almost immediately, though, that it would be nearly impossible to hunt for a job from Forest Grove, which was about ninety minutes from Portland by bus, so I began looking into other housing options.

I got some help from a friend of my sister Thao, who was now going by the American name Laura. Laura had befriended a Vietnamese family, also refugees who had arrived in Forest Grove in 1975, around the time she did. The couple—his name was Dung, hers was Ha—was now living in a small house in a residential area of northeast Portland. When Dung came to visit Laura, I asked him for advice about securing an apartment in his area.

"You're welcome to stay with us while you look for work," Dung said.

At first I declined, not wanting to impose, but he insisted, and before long, Thuy and I had relocated to Dung and Ha's three-bedroom home near the Hollywood district. While we were staying there, Ha came across a job posting at her employer, a major bank in Portland, for a mail clerk position. Thuy applied and landed an interview. Since Thuy had a bachelor's degree, the interviewer offered her a job one step higher in the organization, as a credit limit control clerk. She accepted immediately, and in March 1980, with an income secured, Thuy and I began hunting for our own apartment.

We would have settled for a one-bedroom apartment or even a studio, but the first vacancy we came across was a compact two-bedroom about a block from Dung and Ha's home. I asked the property manager for an application and started filling it out on the spot. I had no problem with the initial information: name, birth date, current address. But after that, the task became more complicated: it asked for our last three addresses and last three jobs. I wrote down the information but knew that it might not matter. Then I wrote in all capital letters: REFUGEE FROM VIETNAM.

The leasing manager was a very pleasant man, but when he looked over the application, he simply shrugged.

"Unfortunately, I don't think I'm going to be able to verify most of this," he said.

"True," I acknowledged.

But then he came up with an offer. "If you can get someone to co-sign your application, providing that person has a job and salary, I'll rent the apartment to you," he said. He offered to hold the apartment for forty-eight hours while we tried to line up someone to cosign.

Returning to Dung and Ha's house, I called Steve, one of my close friends from Pacific, and explained the situation. I remembered Steve as a student at Pacific majoring in business administration. Math was not his strong suit, and I had helped him out when he was struggling in statistics, a course he needed to pass in order to graduate. At the time, I happened to be working as a grader in that class, so I offered to tutor him. Through our collective effort, Steve eventually earned a passing grade—and a diploma. Now, five years out of school, he had a decent job at a savings and loan association in downtown Portland, so I figured he would be in a solid position to help us out.

"I know it's a big favor," I said, "but would you co-sign the lease?"

Steve agreed without hesitation. As soon as he got off work that evening, he met me at the apartment. Together we visited the leasing manager, and Steve filled out the co-signer section of the application, writing down his last three addresses and last three jobs. He also filled in the space for salary, and I couldn't help but notice that Steve was making good money. Not only did that give me confidence that the leasing manager would approve our application, but it also gave me hope for my own job search. If my old friend could pull down that kind of paycheck, maybe I could land a decent job too! I felt encouraged.

Steve handed his application to the leasing manager, who looked over the paperwork.

"I'm happy to rent you the apartment," he said. "I'll need the first and last months' rent, plus a security deposit."

I had come up with cash to pay one month's rent of $275, but I hadn't realized that I would need additional funds. I paused, silent, not knowing what to do. I didn't want to admit to the manager that I didn't have the money. Before I could say anything, Steve stepped in.

"I've got it," he said, pulling out his checkbook.

I couldn't believe it. I didn't want Steve to pay my rent, but he hadn't hesitated to help. The leasing agent handed me the key to the first real home that Thuy and I would share in America. As Steve and I walked out, I tried to hand him the cash I had brought with me.

"No, Khiem, you need to keep it," he said. "When you make some money, you can pay me back."

I told him I would, and I silently promised myself that I would repay every penny. With interest.

Steve wasn't the only friend looking out for us. As soon as Thuy and I moved into the apartment, another set of friends surprised us with a different kind of help. My close friend Jim Remensperger's wife, Joanne, threw a party at their home and invited about six couples. Everyone who came brought housewares and furniture to help Thuy and me outfit our apartment. They had raided their parents' garages and attics for all kinds of stuff: mismatched dishes and glassware; cutlery; pots and pans; salt and pepper shakers. There were even two pairs of chopsticks: one for Thuy and one for me. Whatever their parents hadn't given away to Goodwill or the Salvation Army, they brought to the party for our new apartment.

The next morning, Thuy looked in her purse and discovered a wad of cash that hadn't been there before. Without telling us, our friends had each contributed some money, and the donations added up. One friend had given a hundred-dollar bill.

At the party, Jim introduced me to a friend of his, Ralph, who was working as an auditor for a Big Eight accounting firm. After hearing of my background, Ralph encouraged me to apply for work there. I followed up and somehow managed to land an interview. Ralph offered me some advice: I should wear my "Sunday best," specifically, a dark suit. Since I didn't have one, Ralph drove me to Lloyd Center, a shopping center in northeast Portland, where we made our way to the men's department at Sears. I chose a dark three-piece polyester suit, a tie, and two long-sleeved dress shirts—one white, one light blue. Ralph suggested a wool suit instead, but I look at the price tag and grimaced. What I wasn't expecting was that Ralph would insist on paying for the entire purchase. I took a mental note of the total and promised myself that I would one day pay him back.

When I saw Ralph and his wife Teresa along with the Remenspergers the weekend after the job interview for which I had purchased the suit, he asked how it had gone. I told him I felt good about it.

"Did you wear your Sunday best?" he asked.

"Yes," I told him. "I even wore my English Leather."

Everyone looked at me. *"What?"* Ralph asked.

I told him that I had seen the TV commercial for English Leather cologne, with a woman saying, "All my men wear English Leather—or they wear *nothing* at all." So I had worn my English Leather cologne, too.

They all broke out laughing, Jo and Teresa the loudest.

When Ralph took me to Sears, he suggested that I apply for a store credit card as a way to start building a credit history. I took home an application, filled it out, and dropped it in the mail. Before long, I received a letter from Sears rejecting my application. The reason? "Lack of credit history." The huge corporation didn't care that I had a bachelor's degree or that I had once worked as an executive at Shell. All they could see was what I *didn't* have. I couldn't blame Sears. Some credit clerk had been forced to follow Sears's guidelines and had made the decision accordingly. But the rejection didn't feel good, and it made me even more determined to prove myself.

A few months later, after Thuy made it past her probationary period at the bank, she applied for an employee Visa credit card. The bank approved her application! Finally, we were able to begin establishing our credit, and I felt eternally grateful to the bank. (In fact, I've held on to that card all these years and still use it on occasion even though it doesn't have a special rewards or rebate program. I'll never cancel it.)

Other friends and acquaintances extended themselves in other ways. I had told my friends about how one of the pirates had robbed me of my prescription eyeglasses on the journey to Malaysia. For months, I had been getting by with the much-weaker lenses my friend Phuoc had left for me on Pulau Bidong, but they were far from ideal. Fortunately, Pacific University had a school of optometry, and Dean Trombley arranged for me to have a free eye exam there. As it happened, Professor George Evans, who had taught me English and befriended Thuy and me in our first year at Pacific, was active in the Lions Club, which, among other projects, promoted the importance of vision. Professor Evans arranged for me to have my eyeglass prescription filled. I hadn't realized how much I had missed having clear vision until I had it again.

Being the recipient of my friends' generosity filled me with a mix of reactions. Mostly, I felt grateful to have such wonderful people in my life, individuals who didn't hesitate to extend themselves and meet our needs. After all we had been through, it felt good to be cared for, to experience such generosity and thoughtfulness. But part of me also felt determined to pay back every favor, every gesture, and every penny if I could. In some cases—such as the time the hundred-dollar bill showed up in Thuy's purse—the gifts were anonymous. But whenever I could, I wanted to know who had given to us and exactly how much, because I wanted to repay the debts—with interest.

"10-Key by Touch"

Again and again, I returned to the Central Library to peruse the want ads in the *Oregonian*, searching for any job that sounded relevant—mostly entry-level accounting positions. The ads were written in a compact style. Since the companies paid for the ads by the word, they tended to use abbreviations and acronyms to save money. I started noticing the same phrase in nearly every ad: "10-key by touch." Sitting in the library's reading room, scanning the columns of job listings, I kept seeing that phrase: "10-key by touch." I had no idea what it meant.

I started asking my friends, and finally one of them explained it. A "10-key" was a calculator with one key for each of the digits, zero through nine. "They want you to be able to use a calculator without looking at it," he told me. He explained that a job interviewer would probably give me a list of calculations and then watch to make sure I was able to enter them accurately by touch—without looking at the keys.

Fair enough. The problem was that I had never used one of these machines. After the fall of Saigon in 1975, the US had slapped a trade embargo on Vietnam that barred any kind of new technology from entering the country. In that period, digital calculators had become commonplace in the US, but I never saw one in Saigon—and certainly not in the refugee camp.

I didn't want to let that handicap make it difficult for me to land a job, so I decided to buy a machine and teach myself the skill. I couldn't afford a new calculator, so I went to a flea market and found a used adding machine with a tape ribbon. Over the next couple of weeks, I taught myself to use it, practicing for four or five hours each day until two things happened: my fingers were practically numb, and I had mastered the keys. From then on, the "10-key by touch" requirement wouldn't disqualify me from applying. Suddenly, new opportunities seemed to open up before me.

"A Perceptive Mind and a Willingness to Work"

Now I was ready to start applying for jobs, but I needed a résumé. Again, I used the Central Library and checked out a guide to writing résumés. I borrowed a friend's IBM typewriter and, pecking with my two index fingers, typed out my résumé.

I knew I would also benefit from letters of recommendation. Particularly because my background was atypical for someone applying for an accounting job, I knew that potential employers would value the testimony of reputable people I had worked for. Of course, with these people spread across the world, gathering reference letters would not be a simple matter.

The first person I pursued was Mr. Haerry, who had been the financial manager of Shell in Saigon. I hadn't had contact with Mr. Haerry since just before the fall of Saigon, when he was among the Shell executives who were evacuated by the British embassy. I didn't know where Mr. Haerry was at that point, but I assumed he was still part of the Shell organization, so I sent him a letter in care of Shell International Petroleum Company in London. I told him about my last few years—the difficult times under Communism, the treacherous escape by boat, the months at the refugee camp, and how I had landed back in Portland. And I asked him for two favors: Would he write me a letter of recommendation, and did he know of any potential opportunities for me with Shell in Houston?

Miraculously, the letter found its way to Mr. Haerry, and just weeks later, I received a return letter from him postmarked from Switzerland. He couldn't help with a Shell Houston job, but he did come through with a recommendation letter that captured not only my performance at Shell but also the unusual conditions under which I had worked:

> Mr. Khiem Manh Tran took up his position upon his return from graduation in the USA, at a time when the Company was operating under particularly difficult circumstances. Apart from the usual professional expertise a great deal of imagination and moral courage was required from our Auditors in the execution of their job under conditions of war and general deterioration of values.

In all essential respects Mr. Khiem Manh Tran came up to, or exceeded
our expectations and when he was confirmed as a member of Middle Man-
agement at the end of his probationary period on 15th April 1975, we had
firm plans for Mr. Khiem Manh Tran to succeed the Head of Internal Audit
Department by the end of that year.

I do not hesitate to recommend Mr. Khiem Manh Tran for the high
level of his professional qualities, his capacity for work, and for his human
qualities.

I knew, of course, that a bit of exaggeration was built into most recommendation letters, but I felt both moved and validated by his words, particularly the bittersweet confirmation that if history had gone differently, I
probably would have had a major promotion coming my way.

The second recommendation I sought was from Bruce Beardsley,
whom I'd worked with on the US resettlement delegation on Pulau
Bidong. When I had left the refugee camp, Bruce had given me his business
card from his posting as consul at the US embassy in Copenhagen. I wrote
him there, and he replied quickly with a glowing recommendation:

I was especially pleased to work with you, in that you combined a perceptive
mind and a willingness to work with a very keen sense of humor. I'm certain
that your industriousness and ability will immediately be recognized in the
United States and help you in attaining success in your chosen field.

Once I had received these letters of recommendation, I began mailing
the résumé with a cover letter. I knew that I was qualified for higher-level
jobs—after all, I had excelled as a Shell executive. But I also understood
that, given the five-year gap in my résumé, it might be difficult for employers to recognize my qualifications. So, to enhance my odds of receiving an
offer, I limited myself to applying for entry-level positions.

In my first round, I sent résumés to six employers, each with a letter
signed, "Sincerely, Khiem Manh Tran."

It didn't take long to hear back. All six replies arrived within a week,
and the letters were remarkably similar. "Thank you for your application,"
each said. *"Unfortunately, at this time we do not have a position that is appropriate*
for your qualifications."

They also had something else in common, the salutations: "Dear Ms. Tran," "Dear Mrs. Tran," or "Dear Miss Tran." Every one of the employers had assumed from my first name, Khiem, that I was a woman! Clearly, having a name that was so unfamiliar to most Americans would present a challenge in the job market.

So I changed my name.

I didn't give it much thought. When Thuy had started at US Bank, her colleagues found it so difficult to pronounce her name and spell it correctly that she started using the name Cathy, which her first English teacher had given her back in high school in Saigon. (The teacher had chosen a name that started with the letter *C* because Thuy was sitting in the third row and it's the third letter of the alphabet.)

Following her example, I changed my name from Khiem to Tim. Tim was the American male name that seemed closest to my own name. It rhymed with Khiem, but nobody would mistake it for a woman's name.

I retyped my résumé, changing only one detail: instead of Khiem Manh Tran, I was Timothy Tran.

Not long after that, on a visit to Thao and my other siblings in Forest Grove, I took a stroll around the Pacific University campus. There I bumped into Alice Hopkins, a Pacific administrator I had known as a student. When I filled her in on my job search, she asked if I had my résumé with me.

"Of course," I said.

Alice offered to photocopy it for me. I accepted her offer, and Alice took the page and returned a few minutes later with twenty copies. It was a nice gesture—I had so little money that the couple of dollars Alice had saved me made a big difference.

The next day, I mailed out the résumés with my new name, Timothy, to the same six employers that had rejected me, as well as to four more that had advertised positions.

And something remarkable happened: all six companies contacted me to invite me for interviews! Even better, the first company that interviewed me offered me a job.

I didn't accept it immediately (though I didn't reject it). By that time, I had other applications out, and I was waiting to hear responses. But it was clear to me that these companies had practiced discrimination. When they thought I was a woman, they didn't have any openings. When they thought I was a man, suddenly they opened the door. Given that, why would I want to work for any of them? The experience gave me a taste of the sexism that women in the workplace face all the time. To borrow a phrase President Clinton would make popular years later in his first presidential campaign: "Ladies of America, I feel your pain!"

Finding My Way to Johnstone

A few days after mailing my "Timothy Tran" resume, I got a phone call from one of the employers I had contacted most recently, a company called Johnstone Supply, which had posted an opening for a staff accountant. The caller asked about a few details from my résumé, then invited me to come for an interview. I accepted, and we set a date.

As it turned out, getting myself from home to Johnstone wasn't simple: I had to take a bus from our apartment in northeast Portland to downtown, then transfer to another bus to southeast Portland. The interview was in the midmorning, but I got an early start and arrived downtown around 9 a.m. Finding myself with a bit of extra time, I dropped in on my friend Steve at his workplace, a savings and loan in the heart of the city. While we sat chatting in his office, Steve handed me a book of bus passes for TriMet, the Portland area's transportation agency.

"Oh, you don't have to do that," I said.

But Steve knew that I didn't have a car. "Just keep them," he said. "You're going to be doing lots of interviews, so you'll need to get yourself around."

I accepted the book of tickets, and then I left Steve's office and found the place to catch the bus that would take me to Johnstone's office. I had the address written on a slip of paper: 2950 SE Stark. Nervous about the interview, I wanted to be sure not to miss the stop, so I watched the passing street signs carefully. Still, when I finally descended from the bus, I discovered that I was in the wrong place. Anxious about being late and making a bad impression, I peered up and down the street, not sure which way to go. I decided to walk into the building directly in front of me, and the first person I saw was a Catholic nun wearing a habit. I had walked into a convent.

"Excuse me, Sister," I said. "Could you give me some help?" I showed her the slip of paper with the address and asked if she could point me in the right direction. I told her I was trying to get to a job interview there. With great kindness and gentleness, she pointed me toward 2950 SE Stark. I thanked the nun, and as I headed toward the door, she called after me,

"God bless you. Good luck to you!"

I followed the nun's directions, walked down the street, and, to my great relief, found the address, a two-story redbrick office building. Looking up, I felt a surge of confidence and excitement. *I'm going to nail this interview,* I thought as I walked into the building. *I just know it.*

The interviewer was Myron Child, the company's controller. If I landed the job as staff accountant, I would be reporting directly to him. Myron was a gentleman—mild-mannered, informal, and friendly—and I immediately felt a rapport with him. Myron had reviewed my résumé. He had also read the letters of recommendation from Mr. Haerry at Shell and from Bruce Beardsley at the US embassy in Copenhagen. After we chatted for a while, Myron told me that he liked the idea of hiring me, but he had one serious reservation.

"You're obviously a very capable and hardworking person with a lot of integrity," he told me. "My only concern is that you might use this position as a stepping-stone to a better-paying, more prestigious job."

I gave Myron a long, serious look. "Sir," I said, "I'm a boat person. I just arrived here as a penniless refugee. All I want is a job so that I can use my education and training, and support myself and my wife. I cannot promise that I will stay with this company for the rest of my life. But right now, all I need is a job, and I pledge to you that if you give me one, I will do my best."

"Well," Myron said, "that's good enough for me."

He offered me the job, and at a salary that was considerably higher than the offer from the company that had made me an offer as Tim but not as Khiem. I accepted, we shook hands, and he told me I could start the following Monday—March 17, 1980.

I walked out onto Stark Street, excited to launch my career and knowing that I couldn't have done so without the help of Ralph, who had bought me the outfit; Alice, who had copied my résumé; Steve, who'd given me bus passes; and the very kind nun who gave me her blessing.

A few weeks later, both Cathy and I received our paychecks. That weekend, we wanted to celebrate the fact that we had both earned some money, so we went to the best fast-food restaurant we could afford: Skippers Seafood and Chowder House. To mark the special occasion, we shared a Captain's Platter.

Now that we had secured regular paychecks, there was something even more important I wanted to do. When we returned home from our delicious dinner, I sat down, looked over the list of loans friends had given me, and then drafted a schedule to pay them off—on a "first in, first out" basis. I also made the decision to add 10 percent simple interest to my payment for each loan. (With the high inflation rates of 1980, that rate seemed reasonable.)

I felt a deep sense of satisfaction in knowing that in the not-too-distant future, I would be able to pay off all of my debts. I remembered a French proverb that my father used to quote: *Les bons comptes font les bons amis* (Good accounts make good friends). Of course, I realized that, while paying off loans might help me to settle my financial obligations, I would always owe my friends an enormous debt of gratitude.

Catching Up

Once I started working, I was determined to succeed. Some things gnawed at me. One was the time I had lost in Vietnam. Against nearly everyone's advice, I had returned to Saigon in the fall of 1974, hoping to help build up my country. That had turned out to be a colossal mistake, and now I felt as if I had lost five years of my life. Meanwhile, my peers from Pacific and Berkeley had moved forward in their lives, establishing careers and, in many cases, starting families. Friends I had far surpassed academically during college were now in middle management or even executive positions, while I was starting from zero. Some of them were buying their second or third homes, they were purchasing multiple new cars, and I was virtually penniless. Though the events that had so dramatically changed my fate were largely beyond my control, it still troubled me that I had wasted so much time in the prime of my life.

Then there was the charity. Our friends were generous and open-hearted people who only wanted the best for Cathy and me. But it bothered me to accept their assistance. At first, it had been the donations of furniture and tableware. Later, we would go out socially with large groups and everyone would pay except Cathy and me—the others would split our share of the check. I had spent most of my academic career near the top of my class, and now my peers were paying my way. It didn't feel right.

That was why, once I finally did secure a job and a regular paycheck, I put most of my energy into work, even putting in long hours when nobody expected me to. I didn't want to spend the rest of my life behind my peers, at the receiving end of their largess. I wanted to prove myself professionally and catch up with them financially.

As I tried to build our savings, the one thing I did buy for myself, after I had collected a few paychecks, was a car, another used 1973 Volkswagen Beetle. It had its share of mechanical problems but ran well enough to get me from one place to another.

Most Saturdays and Sundays, I would drive to the office and put in a few hours of work. After all, I was new, and the best way to learn quickly and prove myself was to commit that extra time. I didn't mind doing so. What I didn't realize was that on most weekends, my boss's boss—John Shank, Johnstone's president and founder—drove past the office on his way to play golf at his country club.

One Monday, Mr. Shank called me into his office. "Tim, I noticed you're here most weekends," he said. "What are you doing here?"

I came up with some explanation, an important piece of work—an audit coming up, a tax-filing deadline, a pressing end-of-the-month closing.

"How much does it cost you in gas to get here on weekends?" Mr. Shank asked.

"Sir, please don't worry about that," I said. "It's part of my job."

The next day, he handed me a check for $100: gas money.

The truth was, I wasn't working only to get things done. I was also avoiding the uncomfortable feeling of being behind my friends professionally and financially, on the receiving end of their generosity and charity. I was determined to catch up.

Renewing Our Vows

By the time we got to Portland in 1979, Thuy and I had been married for more than four years. But we had no documentation to prove it. At the time of our wedding, in May 1975, the Communist government had had more urgent and important work to worry about than issuing marriage licenses. Sometimes I would jokingly confide in friends, "We don't have a marriage license—we're just living in sin!"

Our friend Jo Remensperger suggested that we ought to make it official: we should obtain an Oregon marriage license and take the opportunity to renew our wedding vows. Cathy and I both loved that idea. If something happened to one of us, the other person would not have to go through the hassle of proving we were husband and wife. Besides, a second wedding would be a good excuse for a party! Cathy and Jo immediately got to work planning the event. In fact, Jo was so excited for us that she nearly took over the party planning herself, until Jim, her husband, slowed her down. "Let them plan their own deal," he told her.

On May 29, 1981, Cathy and I went together to the Multnomah County Courthouse in downtown Portland, where a circuit court judge performed a brief ceremony, with Jim and Jo Remensperger signing the license as witnesses. That weekend, a few friends gathered at our apartment for a celebration, and everyone offered their congratulations.

"Did you marry for love or money?" one friend asked in jest.

"When we married the first time, Cathy did not have a lot of money, so I call that marrying for love," I replied. "This time, Cathy has a job that pays well, so it must be marrying for money." Then I added, "I'm looking forward to using that money to buy a lot of love!" Everybody laughed, except one person: Cathy was not amused.

Now that I had a solid income, I was committed to getting us on our feet financially. I had felt the humiliation of being turned down for a Sears credit card and not being able to rent an apartment without arranging for a friend to co-sign the lease. I also knew we shouldn't rent forever. As an accountant, I understood the tax advantages of homeownership, and I was ready to make that investment.

In December 1980, less than nine months after I'd landed my job at Johnstone, Cathy and I found a house for sale in northeast Portland, just half a mile from our apartment. At nine hundred square feet, it had two small bedrooms, one bathroom, a living room, an eat-in kitchen, and no garage. It wasn't fancy, but it would work for the two of us.

Of course, we needed to secure a mortgage, and I dreaded the prospect of facing rejection yet again. Fortunately, we had a friend who could help. Barbara, one of my Pacific classmates, was the manager of a savings and loan branch in Hillsboro, a suburb west of Portland. When I contacted her, she invited Cathy and me to visit her office and fill out an application. She offered to stay late one night, so after work, Cathy and I drove the twenty miles or so to Hillsboro. We filled out the application with the assistance of Barbara, who assured us that she would personally push it through. Sure enough, within a week or two we had our mortgage—and, soon after, our house.

We celebrated our new home in February 1981 by throwing a party to mark *Tet*, the Lunar New Year. It was the beginning of the Year of the Rooster, and we invited practically everyone we knew: work friends, college friends, new neighbors—even Mr. Shank, my boss's boss. Our home was hardly a mansion, but now, at last, we had our own little piece of America, and we were playing host and hostess. Less than a year and a half after we'd left the refugee camp, that was something to celebrate.

Still, even as Cathy and I settled into our new jobs, our new home, and our new routines, it was difficult to escape the past. At least once a month, I would have a terrible nightmare that took me back to the awful years of trying to escape the Communists. I dreamed of being stuck back in Saigon, speaking in Vietnamese with Communists, struggling with the difficulties and dangers of life in Communist Vietnam. I dreamed of escape attempts that always ended in failure, with my arrest or imprisonment. I dreamed about the night of my father's murder. Often I would wake up shaking and find it difficult to go back to sleep.

But over that first year in Oregon, the nightmares came less and less frequently. Then one night, I had a dream in which I was living in Portland and conversing in English with my American friends, enjoying myself and feeling happy and content. I had finally assimilated into American society—even in my dreams. I was no longer a prisoner of my painful past.

At work, however, I had a different kind of reminder of Vietnam—my Johnstone colleague Jerry Quilling. I noticed when I first met Jerry that he walked with a limp. He explained that he had served in the US Army as a tank commander in Vietnam. During the Tet Offensive, in 1968, he had been in the Saigon neighborhood of Cho Lon—only a mile from my high school—when a rocket-propelled grenade had struck his tank. He had been taken to the US Army's Third Field Hospital near Tan Son Nhut Air Base, just a few miles from my childhood home, where he was treated for a major injury to one of his heels. Later, he was awarded a Purple Heart.

I had relocated across the world and built a new life, and here in my own office was a man who had risked life and limb for the freedom of my native South Vietnam. I felt a deep sense of respect and gratitude for his sacrifice.

Should I Stay or Should I Go?

It turned out to be ironic that Myron had told me in that first interview that he worried I might use Johnstone as a stepping-stone. Instead, it was Myron who left Johnstone first, taking a position at a local investment company just a year after he had hired me.

When Myron broke the news to me, I felt concerned about my own position. He had been a supportive and considerate boss who had treated me well. In contrast, Mr. Shank, Johnstone's president, was tough, demanding, and direct, with a no-nonsense style of management. I worried that, with Myron gone, my future at Johnstone might be in jeopardy. But Myron told me not to worry—that he would look out for me at his new place of work. "As soon as I find a suitable position for you," he assured me, "I'll let you know."

True to his word, less than a year after his departure, Myron phoned me with an offer to come to work for him at the investment company—at a salary 50 percent higher than what I was earning at Johnstone! How could I turn it down? I told Myron I would need to give Johnstone two weeks' notice. "The position will be waiting for you," he told me.

Excited as I was about the new opportunity and salary, I felt apprehensive about breaking the news of my departure to Mr. Shank. Mr. Shank was very demanding and tough, but also fair and appreciative. We had worked well together and I had great respect for him. As a boss, he provided helpful critiques, and made me feel like an important and integral part of the organization.

To broach the topic when I sat down to break the news to Mr. Shank, I borrowed words from the biblical book of Ecclesiastes. "There is a time for everything and a season for every activity under the heavens," I said. "A time to be hired and a time to be fired, a time to say hello and a time to bid goodbye. I have appreciated the opportunity to work for you in the last year, but an opportunity has come up and I would like to give you two weeks' notice—"

Before I could finish, Mr. Shank cut me off. "Where are you *going*?" he asked.

"To work for Myron," I said, and explained that the position was in his new company's controller's department.

"How much are they offering you?" he asked.

I told him the salary I had been offered.

"I don't want you to leave," Mr. Shank said. "You've done a good job here and we work well together. I want you to stay, and I'll match the salary."

I felt conflicted. I was delighted by the counteroffer and by Mr. Shank's obvious desire to keep me at Johnstone, but I was unsure what to do. "I need a few days to think about it," I told him.

"Yes, think it over," Mr. Shank said. "Everybody here loves you, and you've already found a home here at Johnstone."

With that, I left his office. I was torn. I knew that Myron would make a terrific boss. And while Mr. Shank had a different style, I had worked well with him, too. Since Mr. Shank had agreed to match the salary, money was no longer a factor. I talked it over with Cathy. I asked my friends. Nobody could offer a convincing argument one way or the other.

In the meantime, I continued with my usual responsibilities at Johnstone. After one of our routine meetings, Mr. Shank brought up the subject again and offered me a compelling argument to stay: "Here at Johnstone, you run the show—and you're good at it," he said, and pointed out that I would be unlikely to find that kind of autonomy working for Myron, who himself had to report to a chief financial officer. "Over there, you'll get boxed in," Mr. Shank said. "Here, you are the boss of the finance department—you are the CFO."

At home that evening, I reviewed his words carefully in my mind. It was true that now I was running Johnstone's finance department. And Mr. Shank had told me that he thought I was doing it well. And had he mentioned the title CFO—chief financial officer—the pinnacle of a finance career? He had. But he had invoked it to describe my current *responsibilities*, not my official title.

I thought about how I had committed myself to working hard in order to catch up with my college peers professionally and financially after the four years I had wasted under the Communists. Now Mr. Shank had offered me a genuine opportunity to leap forward in that quest. It hadn't been a promise, but I knew that with hard work at Johnstone and under Mr.

Shank, I would eventually become CFO of the company.

The next morning, I walked into Mr. Shank's office. "Sir, I enjoy working for you, I love my work, and I would like to let you know about my decision," I told him. "I'm staying."

Mr. Shank walked over from behind his desk and gave me a firm handshake.

Questions and Answers

Now that I had committed to staying at Johnstone, I redoubled my efforts to succeed there. I worked hard, putting in additional time over the weekend to double-check and sometimes triple-check important reports. I realized that sometimes it would be impossible for me to outsmart the most intelligent people, but I knew for sure that I could outwork anyone.

I had always been an early riser. No matter what time I went to sleep, I was out of bed by five in the morning. Most days, I arrived at the office around seven, taking advantage of the quiet early hours to get things done. I would evaluate the day's tasks in terms of urgency and importance, assigning each project a value of high, medium, or low. One task might have a high urgency but low importance, while another might have both high urgency and high importance. I reshuffled my work priorities accordingly, delegated when I could, and otherwise tackled things myself.

I prided myself on managing Johnstone's accounting department, overseeing the production of financial statements and annual reports, disbursements, credit and collections, cash management, documentation and record keeping, payroll, investment, and banking. On a strategic level, I created financial plans, discussed financial strategies and risk management, and performed financial analysis, forecasting, and budgeting. I reported directly to Mr. Shank, who gave me the title of controller, but I also functioned as treasurer and chief financial officer. In addition, I managed the data processing (in today's parlance, information technology) department.

I had the feeling that Mr. Shank wanted to see if I was up to the job, and I appreciated the opportunity. I knew that if I rose to the challenge, a big promotion would come my way. I kept that thought to myself, worked hard, and put in the extra hours.

I also put particular effort into building a trusting relationship with Mr. Shank. My feeling was that as an entrepreneur, Mr. Shank ought to focus on the top and bottom lines, but it was my job to worry about the details. Once a month, I met with him to review the company's financial statements. Before those meetings, I made an effort to memorize as much of the material as I could, trying to anticipate any question Mr. Shank might ask. I tried to be as well prepared as the veterinarian who, despite having a very profitable practice, put himself through taxidermy school so he could promise pet owners, "Either way, you get your pet back."

In our meetings, I could usually answer Mr. Shank's questions from memory. Occasionally, I had to look at the financial report to find an answer. One time, though, Mr. Shank posed a question that I had not anticipated and could not answer.

"I don't know the answer," I admitted, "but I'll give it to you in twenty-four hours."

"How about making a guess?" Mr. Shank suggested.

"For you, sir, I'm not comfortable guessing," I replied. Others in the company were comfortable winging it, but I didn't want to take that risk with Mr. Shank.

As soon as our meeting broke up, I got to work digging for the answer to his question. I stayed up late that night working until I had worked out the details of my answer. The next day, exactly twenty-four hours after our meeting, Mr. Shank showed up at my office door. I was prepared with two identical stapled packets: one for him and one for me. I explained my answer to his question in detail. He listened patiently, then finally said, "Thank you!" and walked back to his office with the papers I had given him.

Another time, Mr. Shank asked me a question about a newly enacted law regarding the investment tax credit, which was based on acquisitions of certain business properties. Not prepared to give him my assessment, I again asked for twenty-four hours to do research. Fortunately, it was a Friday, so this time I had the entire weekend to do my homework.

Researching a new tax issue and the new tax law was neither simple nor easy (especially in those pre-internet days). That Saturday morning, I drove to the library of the law school at Lewis and Clark College, where a resourceful librarian helped me to find the answer. (Once again, a librarian came to my rescue!)

When Monday arrived, I gave Mr. Shank the answer.

"Yep, that's correct," he replied, not missing a beat.

"How do you know?" I asked.

"I already talked to Cliff," Mr. Shank said. Cliff was the partner at our

Big Eight independent auditing company. I was mystified. Why had Mr. Shank bothered to put me through all of that if he already had the answer?

For the moment, I let the question drop. But a month later, over a lunch with him, I told Mr. Shank that I had a question for him. "Were you trained as a lawyer?" I asked.

"Why do you ask?" he replied.

"You ask questions even when you already know the answers to them," I said.

Mr. Shank smiled. "I'm just keeping you guys on your toes."

I understood. He recognized by that time that I would always be honest with him. I would always say I did not know if indeed I didn't. Our business was constantly encountering new challenges, and Mr. Shank had wanted to test me to determine whether I was able to find solutions for unexpected problems.

Of course, I understood that corporate America was never meant to be a democracy. There had to be somebody at the top who earned a big paycheck to make the major decisions and take responsibility for them. I always appreciated it when my boss asked my opinion and then made his own decision, even if it was different from what mine would have been. And I automatically supported his position, even if it was different from mine.

Mr. Shank

No matter how closely I worked with Mr. Shank, he was still my boss. Once, we were out to lunch together when Mr. Shank asked that I call him by his first name.

"I can't do that," I told him. "In my culture, we don't call our grandparents, our uncles and aunts, or our teachers by their first names."

"Why not?" Mr. Shank asked.

"Because we show respect," I said. "I'll call you Mr. Shank. That's one thing you'll just have to accept." I don't know if he was ever comfortable with that habit of mine, but after that conversation, he let it go.

Mr. Shank rewarded my dedication in ways large and small. One way had to do with my car. The longer I owned my used Volkswagen, the more problems it seemed to have. Our modest home did not have a garage, so I parked it on the street, which, in Portland, meant that it was exposed to quite a bit of rain. One weekend evening in 1983, Cathy and I dressed up nicely to attend a fundraising dinner for my old acquaintance Congressman Les AuCoin. At a traffic signal I slammed on the brakes, and all of a sudden, a wave of water splashed from the front of the car, completely soaking Cathy, who had been wearing her fanciest dress and a new pair of shoes. Apparently the rainwater had been accumulating in the front compartment for a long time.

When I recounted the incident the next Monday morning for my co-workers, everyone had a good laugh, but the truth was, it was time for me to get a new car. As luck would have it, soon after that, Mr. Shank bought a new company car, a 1983 Buick Skylark, and sold me his three-year-old Skylark at a very good price. Since such matters were part of my responsibilities, I wrote up a purchase contract with a stated interest rate, monthly payments to the company, and no-penalty early payments. I enjoyed the car, and I know Cathy appreciated being able to dress up without worrying that she'd get soaked in the passenger seat!

My efforts to serve Mr. Shank and the company with loyalty and hard work paid off in larger ways, too. At the end of my first year working for him, Mr. Shank handed me a list of about a dozen employees and asked me to prepare bonus checks for them. I was delighted to discover that the list included my own name. When Mr. Shank later handed me my check, it was the first time I had ever received a cash bonus. I was so grateful that I wrote him a thank-you note. (He later told me he had rarely received such a note.)

In 1985, Mr. Shank gave me a major promotion, making me a corporate officer and giving me the title of vice president, finance. People took notice of that promotion far beyond the Johnstone offices. The business section of the *Oregonian* and the *Portland Business Journal* both ran an announcement about my new position along with my photograph. At the time, Portland's population was around 85 percent white, and certainly the ranks of its business executives were almost exclusively Caucasian. So it was newsworthy for a member of any minority group, let alone an Asian or a Vietnamese person—certainly a boat person—to achieve such a position.

The announcement attracted attention within the Vietnamese immigrant community as well. Many friends and acquaintances were surprised to see that I had reached such a level of success so quickly. Some of the Vietnamese people we knew had arrived in the United States long before our arrival in 1979 and had been in the workforce far longer than I had. They might not have realized that I had spent my college years in the United States and held a business degree from UC Berkeley.

The Art of Fitting In

The truth was that I didn't ascend so quickly at Johnstone through hard work alone. Three other factors helped me to distinguish myself in business, the same qualities that had helped me to succeed as a foreign student and that had helped me escape the Communists: I enjoyed connecting with all kinds of people, I was a careful observer of behavior, and I learned to adapt to new situations. Years earlier, when I had first set foot in the cafeteria at the University of Hawaii, I had been the one in our group to break the ice with the American students. At Pacific University, where foreign students and minority students tended to socialize mostly with people like themselves, I crossed boundaries. And after the fall of Saigon, when things had looked so bleak, I had managed to secure enough work to stay afloat.

At Johnstone, too, I connected socially with my co-workers, whose backgrounds couldn't have been more different from mine. And I observed the office culture and did my best to fit in. One thing I noticed was how important it was to keep up with the news and sports. Often Mr. Shank; Jerry Schultz, the vice president for merchandising; and others would bring up current events over lunch, so I wanted to be adequately informed. I always tried to watch the evening news on the major TV networks or PBS, and whenever I could, I tuned in to *60 Minutes* on CBS on Sundays.

For the same reason, I watched Seattle Seahawks football games and Portland Trail Blazers basketball games on TV. (I liked to remind friends that I had seen the Blazers' former star center, Bill Walton, during my college years when he was at UCLA.) Sometimes business associates invited me to dinner in their companies' suites in the Rose Garden (now the Moda Center) to watch the Blazers. This ultimate version of American business relationship-building in America reminded me of the time I'd presented the used motorcycle to the bank manager back in Communist Vietnam. What a difference an economic system makes!

Just as I was making efforts to observe carefully and learning to fit in, Cathy was doing the same. We both worked hard, not only at the typical tasks expected of us in our positions but also at the business of acclimating and assimilating. But as hard as we tried, there were inevitable mistakes along the way. When among friends, I always spoke in colloquial English—meaning that I tried to speak the way my peers spoke. That meant occasionally using colorful language if the situation called for it. Cathy was learning along with me, but she didn't always discern under which circumstances it was appropriate to use certain language. Once, speaking with some colleagues at work, she mentioned that someone was "pissed off." Her co-workers were surprised to hear that come out of her mouth. Hearing the story later, Dan Sullivan, her boss and the company's very kind controller, patiently and calmly set Cathy straight. "There are certain words," he explained, "that we don't use in this office." She learned her lesson.

What You Learn over Eighteen Holes

Another thing I had noticed was that many of the most successful people in business seemed to play golf. Mr. Shank was one of them, and when I asked him about it, he explained to me that golf was the best game a business executive could learn. "After eighteen holes, you know your business associate pretty well," he told me. "You know his character, whether he's accommodating, whether he's honest or a cheater, whether he can keep his score straight. Is he a patient person, or does he throw his clubs when he gets frustrated?"

At the time there were very few well-known Asian golfers; I had heard of just one Chinese and one Japanese pro. And country clubs weren't particularly popular among Asian Americans. But I decided to give golf a try. Following Mr. Shank's advice, I bought a used seven iron, half a dozen plastic balls, and a golf glove, and I began practicing my drive on the small patch of grass in our backyard. I reported to Mr. Shank that I had been practicing, and not long after that, he took me to lunch and presented me with a gift: my own set of clubs—all but the putter, which he said I ought to pick out on my own, since taste in putters was more individual. I was overwhelmed. And he had paid for the gift with his own money, not the company's.

Soon after that, I joined a semiprivate club where members paid an initial fee and monthly dues but didn't have an equity stake. The club wasn't fancy; it was a relatively inexpensive club for people who just wanted to play golf. I began playing with a group of men on Saturday mornings, and Cathy, as a member's spouse, played on Tuesdays with the women's group. We played together on Sundays. I once invited Mr. Shank as my guest, and though he didn't say it outright, I could tell that he felt the course wasn't as well maintained as the one at the private club he belonged to, Riverside Golf and Country Club.

A few years later, Mr. Shank invited me to join Riverside, which had one of the city's top courses. While there were plenty of Asian American golfers at my previous club, I understood that many members of minority groups still found it difficult to gain admission to prestigious golf clubs. Only half joking, I asked Mr. Shank, "Do you think your country club will admit a colored guy like me?"

He didn't like the question. "Don't talk like that," he said. "If they don't want you, then I don't want to belong there."

I applied, listing Mr. Shank as a sponsor, and I was admitted. Riverside was in a different league from my old club. Here, I would drive up and pop open my car's trunk, and a young man would run up and grab my clubs and clean them off for me. The service was excellent, the greens were fast, and the course was well manicured.

I got more serious about my game, too. "You don't need to hit the ball long," Mr. Shank had told me. "Just work on your short game." I followed that advice, focusing on improving my short game and my putting so much that if I could get the ball within a hundred yards of the green, I usually needed only two or three strokes to get it into the hole. My drive was straight and landed in the middle of the fairway, but it wasn't long. A co-worker I played with once remarked, "Tim hit his second shot from his own previous divot."

One of my golf buddies gave me the nickname "La Machine" for my skills on the green. I tried to maintain a handicap index between 18.0 and 20.0. Several business associates loved to have me in their foursomes when playing in a scramble tournament.

I noticed that most members of Riverside were executives or business owners. Most were affluent, accustomed to lives of privilege. As a newcomer to this group, I worked hard to observe their behavior and learn their etiquette. People weren't used to encountering someone who looked and sounded like me at a place like Riverside, but the game had a way of letting people traverse barriers, and I found that many of the members opened their arms and hearts to me.

Just as Mr. Shank had promised, golf also proved invaluable for business. Vendors with whom I worked began inviting me to their tournaments. On my business trips to Memphis, I played at the prestigious TPC Southwind Club and at the Colonial Country Club (where pro golfer Al Geiberger had earned the nickname "Mr. 59"). In Savannah, Georgia, I golfed at the Savannah Golf and Country Club, where my host, Billy Kehoe, a Johnstone member, pointed out Civil War-era trenches that still remained on the course. And a vendor invited me to play in Palm Springs at PGA West. What Mr. Shank had said proved true: after eighteen holes, I knew what kind of person I was doing business with, and then after a drink at the "nineteenth hole," I could finish a negotiation and seal a deal.

Some of my best times took place on the golf course. And playing golf certainly made me feel more at home as a business executive.

Back to School

Early in my time at Johnstone, I realized that I could be a more valuable employee there—or at any other business—if I had an advanced degree. It had been seven years since I graduated from Berkeley, and I suspected that it was important to be familiar with the latest developments and knowledge in the field. I explained to Mr. Shank that I wanted to pursue an MBA degree at Portland State University and asked if the company would help with the costs. He offered to cover the tuition if I turned in passing grades. That was fine with me—I intended to earn all A's and B's.

I enrolled in 1981, attending classes in the evening and taking only one course at a time because of my heavy workload at Johnstone. Even then, it wasn't easy. Occasionally I had to sit out a quarter because I was traveling extensively or dealing with an audit or fiscal year-end closing.

My favorite PSU professor was the associate dean of the MBA program, Steve Brenner, who had earned a doctorate in business administration from Harvard Business School. Dr. Brenner taught a class called Governmental Regulations and Responsibility. Many of my classmates didn't know what to expect from the class, but what we encountered was an instructor who offered a big-picture look at business and equipped us with the ability to look at issues from a thirty-thousand-foot vantage point rather than getting lost in the details. He was a demanding professor and a tough grader, but he also motivated students to work hard and engage with the material.

After the midterm exam, Dr. Brenner was so impressed with my writing and the way I had organized my answers (from outlines I had jotted in the margins) that he used my exam as an example for the other students. That led to a series of conversations with him, and I kept in touch after the class—and long after I finally earned my MBA in 1988. We met for lunch occasionally, and I invited him to Johnstone a few times to give talks about pertinent business issues. Sometimes Cathy and I had dinner with Steve and his wife, Sharon, and I even convinced him to join my golf club, Riverside, and acted as his sponsor. Mr. Shank had sponsored me many years earlier, and it was gratifying to be able to "pay it forward."

"I'll Have What He's Having"

While studying for my MBA gave me an academic grounding in business, I also learned a lot simply by paying attention—and sometimes gained lessons from other people's mistakes.

Once, Mr. Shank treated a group of managers to lunch to mark the departure of one of the managers. When the waitress asked one of my fellow managers, Henry, if he wanted a cocktail, he quickly replied, "Scotch and water."

Then she asked Mr. Shank, who shook his head. Everyone else followed Mr. Shank's lead and declined the cocktail. Later, I noticed that Henry wasn't enjoying his drink, and I made a mental note of it.

That weekend, Henry and I played a round of golf. Afterward, over a drink, Henry mentioned the lunch, which had obviously been bothering him.

"Did I bogey that?" he asked, smiling. I knew he was asking whether it had been a mistake to order a drink before Mr. Shank had opted not to order one.

"No, you didn't bogey," I replied. "You *double* bogeyed."

"That's the worst!" he said.

"Not really," I said. "You could have *triple* bogeyed!"

Henry asked what that would have meant.

"You could have ordered the twenty-five-year-old Chivas Regal!" I said with a grin.

"Maybe I should have," Henry shot back. I knew I had hit Henry's sweet spot; he was a scotch connoisseur.

A few weeks later, Mr. Shank took a group of us out to another restaurant for a Christmas lunch. This time, the cocktail waitress asked me for my drink order first. I hesitated a moment, then said, "Not for me!"

Mr. Shank jumped in. "Come on, Tim! Let's celebrate the holidays with a drink!"

"What are you going to have?" I asked. Mr. Shank ordered a margarita. I turned to the waitress. "I'll have what he's having!"

I had learned an important lesson: always take the lead from the leader—especially when the leader is paying the bill.

The Advantage of Being Underestimated

One advantage I realized long ago is that people underestimate me. In America, people place disproportionate value on appearance. I'm only five foot three and weigh about 105 pounds. I speak English with an accent. People who don't know me often assume I don't have much going for me. Perhaps they think I'm naive, or weak, or uninformed. They don't know I graduated from Cal Berkeley. They don't know that I survived seven bands of pirates, or that I endured months at a refugee camp and then rebuilt my life.

I have often used their underestimation to my advantage. I keep a low profile. I don't interject myself into the middle of things. I do my homework. I let them underestimate me.

Once, when Johnstone moved its offices to a new building, Mr. Shank asked me to oversee the acquisition of the new telephone system. I took the assignment seriously and read up on the latest features of such sophisticated systems in trade publications. I mastered the technical terms and specifications as well as I could.

When the team of salesmen was pitching us the system, Mr. Shank watched as I started throwing them technical jargon, asking things like, "How many RJ-11 jacks do we need?" I told the salesmen, "When you submit a proposal to us, you've got to sharpen your pencil!" To make my point, I even presented them with a gift: a pencil sharpener. I told them we would be taking bids from two other companies—and even shared the competitors' names.

Later, Mr. Shank asked me why I had divulged the names of the competitors.

I explained my two reasons. First, I felt that being honest would encourage them to trust me. Second, I had learned through my research that two of the companies were fierce competitors, and I felt sure that each company would go to great lengths to beat out the other for our business.

I also asked Mr. Shank to make it clear to the salesmen that I, not Mr. Shank, would make the ultimate call. Mr. Shank called all the salesmen, thanked them for the presentation, and added: "Tim Tran will make the final selection. There will be no appeal over his head." That further strengthened my negotiating position. I wanted them to understand that I was the person in charge, not just some third-world guy who was lucky to have landed a job.

Again and again in my career, I came face to face with vendors, bankers, executives, and others who underestimated my abilities and my toughness. And each time, I used their miscalculation to my advantage. I came to enjoy being underestimated, because eventually, the person ultimately came to recognize my ability and give me delayed but justified respect.

A Man with a Country

Five years after we arrived in the United States, Cathy and I applied for citizenship. The process wasn't complicated, but the result was profound. We each filled out an application of about twenty pages, providing details about our identities, backgrounds, political affiliations, and criminal records (we had none, of course). Not long after that, we received letters informing us that our applications had been approved. The letter instructed us to come to the federal courthouse in downtown Portland on a particular morning—May 22, 1986—for the swearing-in ceremony.

I didn't want to draw attention to myself, so when that morning came, I quietly slipped out of work and drove downtown, where I met Cathy. At the courthouse, Cathy and I joined a few dozen other new citizens in raising our right hands to take the oath of allegiance to the United States. A clerk gave each of us a certificate of naturalization, and together, Cathy and I walked out of the courthouse and into the spring morning in downtown Portland.

Everything was the same and everything was different. It had taken five years and four failed attempts to flee Vietnam. We had endured the treacherous passage across the Gulf of Thailand, barely escaping with our lives. We had made ourselves useful in Pulau Bidong and secured approval to settle in the United States. And now, finally, we were citizens of the United States of America. It felt like the ultimate accomplishment.

I was "a man without a country" no more.

I returned to a typical morning at the Johnstone office: I had phone messages waiting for me, a vendor was trying to track me down, and my colleague Sally was waiting to speak to me.

"I've been looking for you all morning!" she said. "Where *were* you?"

I replied quietly, "I had to go to the courthouse…" She looked at me, waiting for an explanation. I offered one: "…for the ceremony to become a US citizen."

Sally looked at me, stunned. "Why didn't you *tell* us?" she asked.

I explained to her that I had been focused on arriving at the ceremony on time—and I also didn't want to make a big deal about the occasion.

"Are you kidding?" she asked. "This *is* a big deal!"

The next day, Sally organized a surprise celebration party in my honor, complete with a cake and an American flag. Everyone offered their congratulations. My colleagues understood what a significant milestone this was for us, and for the first time in a long time, I felt like I was truly part of something much larger than myself.

Family Reunion

As soon as I became a naturalized US citizen, I applied to sponsor the immigration of my mother and my oldest sister Binh—the only members of my immediate family still in Vietnam—to the United States. At the time, the US government placed a high priority on reuniting families that had been torn apart by foreign strife, and I was optimistic that we could successfully bring them to America.

Mr. Shank, my boss, wrote a letter on my behalf confirming my position and salary. The goal was to assure the Immigration and Naturalization Service that I had the means to support my mother and sister.

After my mother and Binh applied to immigrate, the US consulate in Saigon called them in for an interview. The consulate also wanted evidence about the fate of my father, whose disappearance had never officially been declared a murder. My mother had to obtain a letter from the local police precinct. Since my father's case was never solved, the letter stated only that his fate had never been determined.

The process of sponsoring my mother and sister as US immigrants took five years. They finally arrived in Portland on February 3, 1989, nearly a decade after we had left Saigon. Stepping off the plane at Portland International Airport, my mother was excited to tell me about flying the last leg of the journey, from Seattle to Portland. "I looked down," she said, "and saw lots of white sand." After living her entire life in Vietnam, it was the first time my mother had set eyes on snow.

Binh adapted well to America, earning an associate degree at Portland Community College in computer programming and landing a good job. My mother, on the other hand, had a difficult adjustment. After a lifetime in the tropical climate of Vietnam, she had trouble getting used to Portland's cold, rainy climate. She missed her friends in Saigon. And because she didn't speak English, she felt isolated, unable to make new friends or even understand the dialogue when she watched TV. Binh got married in 1994 and gave birth to a son in 1995 and twin boys in 1998, and our mother became one of their primary caregivers, assuming a role that gave her some pleasure.

A Cemetery Desecrated

One evening in the late 1980s, I was watching a network news program when I caught a report from Vietnam. It focused on the Bien Hoa Military Cemetery, where I had once sought out the grave of my old friend Tung. The news was disturbing, revealing that the cemetery had been neglected, vandalized, defiled, and abandoned. I felt angry watching the tragic fate of this once-sacred place, South Vietnam's equivalent of Arlington National Cemetery. The large statute I remembered so vividly, *Thuong Tiec* (Sorrow Remembrance), had been destroyed. The news footage showed wandering cows munching on dry tufts of grass next to tilting tombstones that had been smashed and vandalized. Black moss was encroaching on the names of the dead. Some of the tombstones had been defaced and damaged; others were surrounded by tall weeds. Still others had been uprooted and were lying on the ground. One awful image revealed that someone had gouged out the eyes in a dead soldier's portrait etched on his tombstone.

I was appalled at the defacement and the desecration. It showed no respect for the dead, no reconciliation with the fraternal enemies. I could not help but wonder what had become of the grave of my high school classmate Tung. I recalled reading that in some American Civil War cemeteries, Union and Confederate soldiers were buried in adjacent graves. In fact, I had seen the Confederate memorial at Arlington National Cemetery. The comparison left me heartbroken.

Mr. Shank's Surprise

As a Johnstone corporate officer, I always attended the annual members' meeting. (Johnstone was organized as a cooperative, with the owner of each local branch considered a "member.") These were important gatherings where the corporate management team shared operational and financial reports and also distributed checks to members for that year's patronage dividends. Mr. Shank would personally present the reports, which the membership always received well. Mr. Shank had a good sense of humor and always offered a joke or two before launching into the reports.

One year, though, Mr. Shank sprang a surprise on me. Over breakfast just two hours before the meeting, he announced to Jerry Schultz, the vice president of merchandising, and me that he wanted to try a new approach this year. "I want the two of *you* to present the reports," he said.

Us? With just two hours' notice? Jerry and I were both completely caught off guard. Neither of us had anticipated Mr. Shank's request. And I, for one, felt completely unprepared.

"Why didn't you tell me last night?" Jerry asked.

Mr. Shank had an answer: "I didn't want you guys staying up all night worrying about your report."

With precious minutes ticking away, Jerry quickly excused himself and found a quiet corner to get to work writing out his report in longhand on a pad of paper.

As for me, what choice did I have? I set to work on my part of the presentation, the financial report. I wasn't worried about the content—I had been so immersed in the numbers in the months leading up to the meeting that I had memorized most of the material. But I did recognize that I had two significant challenges to overcome. First, most people dreaded the prospect of listening to an accountant—they just assumed that an accountant would be boring. And second, some people might find it difficult to understand me because of my accent. I remembered watching Henry Kissinger, the former secretary of state, deliver his famous remarks that "peace is at hand" in the early 1970s. I could barely understand his English through his thick German accent, but the more I listened, the more I understood. I wanted to sound more like the Israeli prime minister, Benjamin Netanyahu, who spoke like an American, but the truth was that I sounded like an immigrant from Vietnam. So I decided to launch my speech with a few funny stories that I would tell slowly to help the audience get used to the way I spoke. I also decided to steer clear of accounting jargon and present my report in simple, everyday English.

As we took our places at the head table, I sat next to Jerry and discreetly passed him two Tums to relieve heartburn. He promptly popped them into his mouth, and I started to chew two Tums myself. Before I knew it, the chairman of the board was calling the meeting to order and recognizing Mr. Shank to present the annual report. (To my surprise, not even the chairman knew about Mr. Shank's eleventh-hour change!) Mr. Shank stepped to the podium and announced that Jerry Schultz would be delivering the operations report and Tim Tran would be presenting the financial report. "Here's Jerry!"

Jerry stepped to the podium with a stack of handwritten notes and, speaking in calm voice, delivered a detailed, comprehensive report. At the end, the audience applauded with enthusiasm. I wasn't surprised. Jerry had a practically photographic memory, so he had easily assembled an impressive report, even with the short notice Mr. Shank had given us. "That was a home run!" I whispered to Jerry as he returned to his seat beside me.

Then Mr. Shank introduced me, and I stepped up. I opened with a story. "A successful and wealthy businessman summoned his attorney, his doctor, and his accountant to his deathbed," I began. "'Gentlemen, I have a favor to ask each of you. I'm going to give each of you an envelope containing ten thousand dollars in cash. After I die, I want each of you to put the cash envelope inside my open casket so that I have some spending money in the next life. Can you all promise me you will do that?' They all agreed. When the businessman finally died, the three of them all showed up at the funeral. As the mourners were filing past the casket, the three of them got in line. When they passed the coffin, each of them slipped an envelope next to the body, just as the businessman had instructed. But the attorney and the doctor both noticed that the accountant's envelope looked a lot thinner than theirs. 'Hey,' one of them said, 'why was your envelope so thin?' 'Oh, that's simple,' the accountant said. 'I wanted to make sure that nobody would steal the cash, so I replaced it with my personal check.'"

When the laughter finally subsided, I proceeded with the financial report. "I'm pleased to report that we had profit and not loss as a result of last fiscal year's operation. As a financial person, I don't like the word *loss*," I said. "*Loss* is a four-letter word and *profit* isn't."

I continued: "Let me address the profitability and liquidity of our company. *Profitability* is just a fancy term for the straightforward question, 'Did we make any money?' And *liquidity* is a fancy term for 'Do we have any money?' The answers to those questions are yes and yes."

I announced the annual patronage dividend. "We have money," I added, "so I'm confident that if you happen to drop the dividend checks you receive today, they will not bounce." I went on to explain other important information in the financial statements using simple language. As I spoke, I noticed some approving nods. When I finished, the audience offered a warm round of applause. As I sat down next to Jerry, we exchanged looks of satisfaction. We had risen to the challenge.

Calm, Cool, and Collected

Mr. Shank and I often had social lunches with colleagues, but when Mr. Shank had a serious business matter to bring up with me, he usually made it just the two of us. One day in the mid-1980s, at one of those one-on-one lunches, he brought up Jerry Schultz, the vice president for merchandising who'd given the operations report at the members' meeting.

"What do you think Jerry's strengths are?" he asked.

I thought about it a moment. "He's calm, cool, and collected," I said. It was true. I had seen Jerry in many situations, and those qualities always stood out.

"And what do you suppose are his weaknesses?" Mr. Shank asked.

I gave the same answer: "He's calm, cool, and collected."

"Goddammit, that's what I think, too!" he said. "If someone ran into his office yelling, 'Fire!' he would ask calmly, 'Has somebody called the fire department?'" We both laughed. Then Mr. Shank revealed why he had brought up the topic: he had been grooming Jerry to succeed him. "How do you think he'd perform as president?" he asked.

I wasn't surprised. I knew that Jerry had been the frontrunner—in fact, the only serious candidate—to succeed Mr. Shank. I offered my endorsement, telling Mr. Shank that with Jerry, the company would be in steady hands. Jerry had the experience and the logical mind to keep the company moving ahead. I also got along well with Jerry personally and knew that he appreciated my work. "He may not grow the business at the high rate you want," I told Mr. Shank, "but he won't run it off a cliff!"

"We Need More Towels"

As much as I have been able to assimilate into American society, like many people, I have occasionally encountered racism. More than once, when driving in city traffic, I've seen a random person lean out his car window and shout a racial epithet at me. I always coped by simply pretending I hadn't heard.

Sometimes the slurs were more anonymous. One morning in the late 1990s, I discovered that someone had spray-painted a swastika in black paint on the trunk of my white Buick Skylark as it sat in our driveway. I reported the incident to the local police precinct, and an officer showed up and apologized, but I never heard whether they found the perpetrator. I tried to remove the graffiti with paint thinner, but the chemicals started stripping the car's original paint, so I had to have a body shop repaint the car.

Then there was the morning I arrived at the locker room at Riverside, my golf club, and another member, seeing me pass, shouted at me: "Hey! We need more towels here! Hurry up!" Apparently, seeing an Asian man, he had assumed I was the locker room attendant. My golf buddy, angered, was preparing to confront the man when I raised a hand to discreetly signal him to keep quiet. "Yes, sir!" I said to the stranger. "Right away!"

Just then, a voice over the loudspeaker called our group to the first tee. As the two of us headed for the door, my friend smiled at me. "He'll be hopping mad waiting for his towels," he said.

"It's just a misunderstanding," I replied. "He'll figure it out soon enough."

While I occasionally encountered these kinds of slights and misunderstandings in my personal life, I rarely encountered racism in my business life. Most of my colleagues knew of my reputation as a tough negotiator who did his homework. Those who underestimated me paid the price. In all of my business dealings, though, I tried to be straightforward and honest: what you see is what you get. That approach, I believed, would pay off in the long run.

Colleagues and Friends

Over time, I built relationships with a wide array of business associates: bankers, independent auditors, investment brokers, equipment vendors, and service providers. I learned that it was worth forging these friendships outside the office, sharing a round of golf and a meal. Some associates invited me to play in golf tournaments or to watch professional tournaments in their hospitality tents.

One independent auditor who became a friend was Larry, an audit manager who worked at Coopers & Lybrand, a Big Eight CPA firm. Larry was a big man physically (I sometimes joked that Larry was so big that he had his own zip code) and a true professional who worked hard and played hard. No matter how busy he was, Larry was always pleasant and patient with clients. He also threw great parties. Cathy and I once dressed as Charlie Brown and Lucy at Larry's Halloween party, at which his wife dressed as a pregnant nun. They made sure everybody had a great time.

Another friend from Coopers & Lybrand was Monica, a tax manager. Monica was bright, beautiful, and blonde. What I loved most was her intellectual honesty: she wasn't afraid to admit that she didn't know or understand something. Once, over lunch with Monica and her colleague John, the conversation turned to personal problems: health challenges, financial difficulties, strained relationships.

"I only have two problems," I deadpanned. Monica seemed surprised. "Yes, I do," I insisted. "And the two problems are slow horses and fast women."

John broke into laughter, but Monica looked bewildered. "I understood the 'fast women' part," she said to John. "What does Tim mean by 'slow horses'?"

John explained: "Tim bet on slow horses at the racetrack and lost money!" Monica laughed.

That was just one of many wonderful moments with Monica, who remained a close friend to Cathy and me long after she left the accounting firm and moved to the Bay Area.

★ ★ ★ ★ ★

I also enjoyed getting to know people within the Johnstone organization. One was Bob Wieland, a branch owner and Johnstone board member who invited me to visit his ranch outside of Denver. It was my first time on a ranch, and I was impressed with almost everything: the stable of valuable racehorses; the oil well; and the extensive collection of ranch equipment, which included tractors, backhoe loaders, balers, combines, mowers, plows, and many more machines I did not recognize.

As a businessman, Bob worked hard and took good care of his customers and employees. And I especially appreciated that as a board member, he showed concerned for the corporate office employees and made sure that our compensation was competitive.

Once, in the late 1980s, Bob was looking for a new computer system for his many Johnstone stores, and he asked me to come along to a negotiation with a computer vendor. I did a great deal of research to prepare for the meeting, and at one point, when the saleswoman cut me off in midsentence, I waved her off, saying, "Hold your horses!" Out of the corner of my eye, I noticed Bob smiling. At the end of the negotiation, we reached terms that Bob was happy with, and I knew Bob always appreciated my hard work and tough negotiating.

Another of Johnstone's hundreds of branch owners was Oral Goble, who had left a comfortable Fortune 500 executive position to become an entrepreneur and ran Johnstone stores in Fort Lauderdale and West Palm Beach, Florida. I particularly enjoyed working with Oral in his early days and helping him navigate some of the challenges that came with the early stages of a start-up.

One of my closest Johnstone friends was Kim Cafferty, who managed a Johnstone store in San Jose, California. When a new owner took over that branch, Mr. Shank wanted to take care of Kim because he had been such a faithful employee, so he arranged for Kim to open a Johnstone branch in Omaha, Nebraska. He even assisted with the financing so that Kim could repay Mr. Shank with his profits. Kim turned out to be an excellent owner, paying his employees well, establishing a profit-sharing plan, and offering excellent retirement benefits. He expanded his business from one to three stores, and whenever I visited, I always noticed that Kim's employees were very positive. They knew they couldn't have found a better boss. It was a pleasure working with people like Kim, and his success was also a testament to Mr. Shank's enlightened management.

Fringe Benefits

Being a corporate officer and playing a decent game of golf occasionally earned me some remarkable fringe benefits. In 1994, a Johnstone member, Billy Kehoe, invited me to attend the Masters Golf Tournament in Augusta, Georgia. Attending the Masters is the dream of any golfer, and I felt privileged that Billy had extended the invitation. That April, I made the two-and-a-half-hour drive with Billy from his home in Savannah, Georgia, to Augusta. There, I felt like I was in golf heaven: the fairways were immaculate, the rhododendrons were in full bloom, and the golf was supreme. I witnessed Tiger Woods become the youngest winner ever and set the records for the widest winning margin and the lowest winning score.

Twice I was invited to play in LPGA Pro-Am golf tournaments, once with professional golfer Dawn Coe-Jones and another time with Liselotte Neumann. Each time, I felt nervous, particularly at the first tee, where hundreds of fans were looking on. I prayed that I would avoid the embarrassment of a fat shot (the driver hitting the ground before striking the ball). Fortunately, each time I managed to drive the ball straight up the fairway.

On another corporate golf outing, I had the opportunity to play with professional golfer Tom Weiskopf, who proved to be both funny and pleasant. In fact, every professional golfer I encountered had great people skills: they knew how to tell jokes and relate to people. They made everyone around them feel comfortable. Another highlight was getting lessons from Dr. Bob Rotella, a golfer and psychologist and the author of *Golf Is a Game of Confidence*.

Each time I had these experiences on the golf course, I felt fortunate to get a glimpse of how the other half lives and plays.

Besides golf outings and lifelong friendships, my position at Johnstone came with another nice reward: occasionally I got some good press. The local newspaper, the *Oregonian*, occasionally mentioned my promotions or other noteworthy career developments in their business sections, and the *Portland Business Journal* also noted some of my career highlights in print. One of my greatest thrills came in 1991, when *CFO* magazine—a national publication for and about senior financial executives—did a cover story about me.

At the time, my favorite banker and golf buddy was Dave Perry, who was then a vice president at First Interstate Bank. When he learned that the magazine wanted to take some photos for the article, he offered his country club, Columbia Edgewater, as the location for the photo shoot.

I had read *CFO* for a number of years, always admiring the prominent Fortune 500 executives who typically appeared on the cover. So it was both humbling and thrilling to see on the magazine's cover a photograph of me in a red sweater on the course at Columbia Edgewater beside the headline: "*American Dreamer: Tim Tran's 10-Year Journey from Boat to Boardroom.*" The article inside even included a photograph of the Pulau Bidong refugee camp.

After the article ran, I heard from people all around the country, many of whom knew me but had had no idea what I'd been through to get to my position. It was gratifying to share some of my life story, and I hoped it would inspire others and show what was possible with hard work and some luck.

Funny or Not Funny?

I have always loved to tell jokes to put people at ease. Most of my friends and business associates know that I pride myself on my sense of humor, so over the years, they came to expect jokes from me.

Once, after I delivered the financial report at a Johnstone annual members' meeting, a store owner posed a question about why I had recommended bank borrowing for the first time in Johnstone's history to support growth.

I explained that an optimum combination of debt and equity financing was less expensive than equity financing alone. And the right combination would allow us to pay more dividends to the members and still have the cash necessary to support our company's growth.

"At what interest rate are we borrowing?" he asked.

When I revealed the rate, I noticed many audience members nodding their heads in approval. Obviously, they were impressed that I'd managed to secure such a favorable interest rate. At that point, I decided to inject a bit of humor. "I would like to add that interest rates fluctuate," I said. "Sometimes they fluc down, other times they fluc *up*!" The audience burst into laughter.

As much as I enjoyed such moments, I also came to understand that, while most people enjoyed my sense of humor, not everyone did. Once, a female employee at Johnstone complained that she didn't appreciate a joke I had told. Of course, I accepted responsibility and apologized. I always wanted to use humor to connect with people and put them at ease, and when someone felt offended, it was important to express regret and hope to move on.

Switching Gears

As much as I enjoyed my work, it came with its share of stress. That manifested itself in some serious health challenges. In 1992 I started experiencing an unusual physical sensation: I began hearing the sound of my own heartbeats, loudly, in my left ear. Figuring that something was amiss with my ear, I made an appointment with an ear, nose, and throat specialist. The physician couldn't pinpoint the problem, but he scheduled exploratory surgery for me and then left for a European vacation. In the meantime, the sound continued, and I began to suffer from double vision. I consulted an ophthalmologist, who sent me to a neurologist.

That doctor did offer a diagnosis: I didn't have an ear problem; I was suffering from a leak in a blood vessel in my brain. The doctor admitted me to the hospital immediately and performed a complex, delicate surgery, finally stopping the leakage—and putting an end to the mysterious sound in my head. Thank goodness I hadn't decided to wait for the ENT doctor to return from his vacation!

Six years later, I had another serious health scare. I was at work when I felt a sharp pain in my right arm, and my upper arm suddenly ballooned to twice its size. I nearly lost consciousness. Sheila, my administrative assistant, called 911, and Jerry Schultz, by then my boss and Johnstone's president, directed traffic. An ambulance transported me to Legacy Emanuel Medical Center's trauma center, where I regained consciousness but kept fading in and out. The doctor diagnosed me with a spontaneous rupture of the brachial artery. Ultimately, the doctors were able to save my life, but the loss of blood caused so much nerve damage that I lost some of the use of my right hand. My physician later explained that the combination of a weak spot in the artery and high blood pressure had caused the ailment.

I was forty-eight years old. I felt grateful to be alive, but I was also concerned about my health. Although I was eager to return to my routine, my physicians advised me that staying in a stressful, high-stakes job could be harmful to my health. I loved the work, but being responsible for the financial welfare of a large business made stress inevitable. Finally, I decided to heed my doctors' advice, and in 2002, after twenty-three wonderful years, I retired from Johnstone.

In December 2002, at a hotel in Vancouver, Washington, Johnstone held a celebration—a roast, to be exact—to mark my retirement. It followed another retirement event the company had hosted for me in Minneapolis. After the health struggles of the previous few years, it warmed my heart to be surrounded by so many people who had meant so much to me: colleagues, co-workers, board members, friends, and relatives. Cathy and I sat at a table with my mother, several of my siblings, and their spouses, and the room was filled with people I had known for decades. Even my college friends Jim Remensperger and Joe Haber made it.

Mr. Shank, who couldn't attend because of his own health challenges, had recorded a moving video message thanking me for my service. "You've worked hard and put your heart and soul into it," he said. "We are all grateful for your service."

Jerry Schultz, the president who succeeded Mr. Shank, had recorded his own message, praising my "integrity and character" but also, in the spirit of the roast, ribbing me about my reputation for frugality. "Since you'll be letting go of your purse strings," he said, "we can look forward to the economy starting to move again."

Jerry Quilling, my friend and a Purple Heart recipient, skillfully served as master of ceremonies with humor and his own gentle teasing.

When it was my turn, I thanked everyone for coming and took a moment to single out Jim and Joe and thank them for our great time together in college. I also recounted receiving the telegram from Jim's parents in Saigon—a ray of hope just before one of the darkest moments of my life, the day of the fall of Saigon.

I thanked Mr. Shank, and I praised Jerry Schultz for his photographic memory, and for always being calm, cool, and collected. Jerry, I said, was a firm believer in the fundamental principle of democracy: "one man, one vote." "Jerry is the one man," I said, "and he gets the one vote!" The audience responded with plenty of laughter.

I shared a bit of tongue-in-cheek wisdom I had picked up along the way:

"Early to bed, early to rise. Work like hell and advertise!" And I candidly re-counted the difficult decision that had faced me following my health strug-gles, which had forced me to choose between the career I loved and my own health. Summing up that painful choice, I quoted a line from Robert Frost's "The Road Not Taken": I was *"sorry I could not travel both."*

As difficult as that decision had been, I couldn't help but be moved and gratified that night. Looking out at the room full of people who had given me so much, I felt grateful for my career, for my family, for my friends, and for my life.

Back to the Classroom

My retirement was anything but sedentary. A year before I left Johnstone, I had begun a new chapter, teaching business classes at the University of Phoenix, and I pursued teaching with great enthusiasm. Standing up in front of students reminded me of my early teaching days as an Upward Bound instructor for my friends Paul Hebb and Bobbi Nickels.

Just as I had back then, I tried to use humor to get my students' attention. I always introduced myself by telling the students that although I had a business degree from Berkeley, my teaching philosophy was very different from what I had experienced at Berkeley.

"At Berkeley, they taught using the Afghan Burka Method," I liked to tell the students. The students would look puzzled. I made sure they understood what a burka was—a garment that some Muslim women wear that covers everything from head to toe. "At Berkeley," I said, "like the burka covering every inch of the body, the professor *covers everything* in the lecture, from the introduction of the textbook to the last footnote."

Then I explained that I called my teaching approach the French Bikini Method: "Like the French bikini, I only cover the important and essential parts. For the rest of the material, you can read it on your own. You can't cover less than the French bikini, or you'll be arrested for indecent exposure!"

That always got the students' attention.

I tried to treat my students—especially the graduate students in my evening classes—like colleagues. And when it was appropriate, I also shared with them the practical aspects of how business executives make decisions. Most of these students had full-time jobs and were paying to put themselves through school at night. That required a great deal of effort and sacrifice, and I wanted to recognize their efforts by teaching them as well as I could.

While the subject I taught was finance, I also made an effort to share wisdom about surviving corporate life and dealing with high-ranking executives. Once, after a student gave a class presentation that went on far too long, I seized the opportunity to teach a lesson about the importance of brevity.

"If you were a top corporate executive," I asked the students, "what would be the most important factor in your day-to-day management of the business?"

A few students raised their hands and offered answers: Money? Respect? Loyalty? Honesty?

"You each have a valid point," I told them, "but in my personal experience, what I value most is *time*." I explained that busy executives always wish they had more time. I told them that when they made a presentation to a top executive, they should keep it short and to the point. "Once you get your points across, say thank you and leave," I said. "When you go on too long, you can get into trouble."

To make the point, I told them a story.

A few years ago, when our local economy went through a downturn, one young man lost his job. He was so desperate to get protein to feed his hungry children that he resorted to shooting seagulls. Unfortunately, the game warden caught him.

"You can't shoot seagulls," he said. "It's illegal!"

"But they're not an endangered species, are they?" the young man asked.

The warden explained that seagulls were protected wildlife. He started writing a citation, then stopped and asked, "Why are you shooting them, anyway?"

The man explained that he'd lost his job and needed to feed his family.

"I'll let you go this time, but don't do it again," the warden said.

The man thanked the warden. "My kids love any kind of meat I can give them," he explained. "They love seagull—barbecued, stewed, or fried!"

This made the warden curious. "What does seagull taste like?" he asked. "Chicken?"

"Not at all," the man said. "Kind of halfway between bald eagle and northern spotted owl!"

That young man should have heeded my advice and stopped talking while he was ahead!

While I was the teacher, I also learned from the students about their own fields of specialty. One of my favorite students was Tom, whom I taught in the University of Phoenix's MBA program. Tom, a friendly, intelligent, and positive student, worked in marketing for a big coffee retailer. Tom had excellent leadership skills, and his classmates looked to him to make decisions on team projects.

I also taught in the MBA program at Marylhurst University, where I met Wayne, a remarkable student. Wayne, was a marketing vice president for a dental-equipment manufacturer. He was honest, focused, and passionate about learning. Wayne had attained a top executive position in his company even without an MBA, but he loved to learn about finance. He once told me that my finance class had helped him understand the intricate relationship between his department and the company's finances.

While the students appreciated my efforts, not everyone recognized me. Once I showed up for the first session of a new class that I was to teach in the MBA program. As I stepped off the elevator, a university staffer offered a warm greeting: "Welcome to a new term. What class are you taking this term?" she asked, mistaking me for a student.

Not missing a beat, I played along: "I'm taking the corporate finance class from Professor Tran."

"Okay," she said, "right this way."

I kept on: "I heard from other students that Professor Tran's course is a difficult one and he's a tough professor," I said.

"From what I know, he sets the bar high for his class, but he's also fair," she said. The staffer led me into a half-full classroom and pointed me to an empty chair. "Professor Tran will be coming in shortly," she said. "Have a great term!"

Almost immediately, I heard laughter from the back of the room. Turning around, I spotted two students who had taken my finance management course. They greeted me warmly: "Good evening, Professor Tran!"

My true identity had been revealed. I said good evening to my former students and thanked the staff person, who made a quick exit.

★ ★ ★ ★ ★

I loved the students, and they returned my affection. In fact, in 2004, graduate students at the University of Phoenix voted me "Faculty of the Year."

At the awards luncheon, I was seated next to another instructor, Raul, who I noticed spoke English with an accent.

"Where are you from?" I asked.

"Cuba," he said.

I told Raul I was from Vietnam. We struck up a conversation and soon realized that our stories were remarkably similar. Like me, he had been one of the top high school students in his country. Like me, he had earned a scholarship to study at a foreign university—in his case, in Moscow, the Soviet capital. Like me, he'd been obligated to return to his native country after he completed his studies. Just as I'd had to return to Saigon, Raul had been required to return to Havana.

That was where the similarities ended. I had gone back to Saigon and worked for Shell. Raul's flight from Moscow had had a stopover in Montreal, and he'd stepped off the plane and become a defector, asking for asylum in Canada. Later, he'd immigrated to the United States, where, like me, he'd worked in business before retiring and starting a second career as an adjunct professor.

The parallels in our life stories were remarkable. I looked at Raul. He looked at me.

"We are both products of the Cold War," I said. Raul nodded. The truth was, the scholarships we'd each received were part of the efforts by the superpowers to extend their influence in developing countries. Indeed, both of us were products of the Cold War as well as its beneficiaries.

And now here we were, both of us in the land of opportunity, sharing what we had learned along the way with students at the university.

Only in America.

Lessons from My Travels

My love of learning took me not only into the classroom but also on the road. I have always loved to travel, particularly to visit presidential libraries and national parks. Ever since Mr. Hoat taught me about the United States back at Chu Van An High School, I have been fascinated by US presidents. As an adult, I have continued to learn about American history, reading countless presidential biographies and memoirs.

I feel a particular debt to the series of presidents whose actions directly affected me. President Eisenhower, who made the US the first country to recognize South Vietnam, supported the mass migration from North to South Vietnam, which I was a part of at age four. President Kennedy sent military advisers to help build the South Vietnamese army so it could stand up to insurgents from the North. President Johnson sent some five hundred thousand troops to stop the advances of the Communist army—without that buildup, the North Vietnamese might well have been victorious many years earlier. President Nixon was a firm anti-Communist but had to placate anti-war activists and follow his "peace with honor." South Vietnam fell under President Ford's watch, but I can hardly blame him: US public opinion was overwhelmingly against the war. He did sign the special order that lifted the quota on refugees from Vietnam, allowing hundreds of thousands of Vietnamese refugees to enter the United States. And President Carter allowed the flow of refugees to continue, a decision that let me become an American.

The more I travel to presidential libraries, those shrines to American leaders and history, the more I realize that the past isn't really very distant from our lives. Once, on a business trip to Texas, I rented a car and drove to the LBJ Presidential Library in Austin. Touring the archives and looking through the exhibits focused on Vietnam, I felt like I was watching a rerun of an old movie.

From there, I took the ninety-minute drive from the library to Stonewall, Texas, President Johnson's birthplace, where he is buried along with other members of his family. After getting out of the car, I walked along a path and paused directly in front of LBJ's resting place. I bowed my head and stood in silence for a long minute. I closed my eyes and remembered that warm morning on the road in Saigon when then Vice President Johnson had ridden by in his motorcade and waved at me, one of the hundreds of smiling children on the streets that morning holding South Vietnamese and American flags.

When I lifted my head, there was a man beside me.

"I saw you standing there, looking at the tomb and bowing your head," he said. "What were you thinking about?"

I told him that I was Vietnamese and that I had seen President Johnson when he visited Vietnam in 1961 as vice president. "I owe him a great debt for keeping South Vietnam free from Communism for many, many years," I said. "I'm here to pay my respects."

The man shook my hand. "Thank you for sharing that," he said. "We loved LBJ, too."

Another time, I was playing golf with a colleague in Rancho Mirage, California, when a ball I hit veered off the fairway and landed in the yard of a neighboring home. I ambled over and started to extend my ball-retrieving device when a man in a dark suit emerged and approached me.

"Sir," he said, "I need you to step away from the property."

Perplexed, I asked if he would toss me my ball, and he did. When we finished the round, I told my host what had happened—that I had encountered a man in a suit who wouldn't let me retrieve my own ball. The host asked me where we had been on the course when the man had appeared, and I told him.

"Oh," he said, "that was probably President Ford's residence."

If only I had known, I would have asked the man in the suit to pass on my thanks to President Ford for raising the quota and allowing the Vietnamese refugees into the country. Without President Ford's efforts, I would have had a far more difficult time returning to the United States.

Another president who played a significant role in the Vietnam War was Richard Nixon, so I was delighted when, on another occasion, my colleague Bob Pritchard gave me a pair of tickets for the Richard Nixon Library and Museum in Yorba Linda, California. Cathy and I visited after spending the night at the home of my Berkeley classmate Jim McWalters. The Watergate exhibit there brought me back to those many hours sitting with friends and watching on a small black-and-white TV as senators Sam Irving, Howard Baker, and others grilled the witnesses.

In all of my travels, two museums left the greatest impression. One was the National Civil Rights Museum, in Memphis. I traveled to Memphis frequently for business, and on one of my earliest trips, I was in a taxi on the way to the airport when I mentioned to the driver, who happened to be African American, that I remembered hearing when I was a high school student in Saigon that Dr. Martin Luther King Jr. had been killed in Memphis. I asked if he could drive by the Lorraine Motel, the site of the assassination. He agreed, and I saw the motel, which at that time was a boarded-up, run-down building. We got out of the car and he pointed out where Dr. King had been standing when he was shot. I told him about the tremendous sadness I felt that day even though I was living in a different country halfway around the world.

Years later, I was back in Memphis and had the opportunity to visit the Lorraine Motel again. By then it had been transformed into the National Civil Rights Museum, an outstanding institution documenting and explaining the history of the civil rights movement. I learned about Dr. King, Jesse Jackson, Congressman John Lewis, and so many others. Being there brought to mind stories my teacher Mr. Hoat had told us decades earlier about South Vietnamese military officers who had been training on US bases in the South and couldn't venture off their military bases for meals because restaurants discriminated against people of color, including Asians. Of course, I also thought of Tony and Cliff, my friends at Pacific University, who had been my first African American friends and had taught me so much about the experience of African Americans. Being there felt like a tribute to those important people in my life. Leaving the National Civil Rights Museum, I felt inspired by the success of the civil rights movement in changing America from a segregated nation to one with more opportunities and equality for all. Still, we need to do more since other challenges still remain. But we shall overcome!

I had a similar experience the time I took a day during a trip to Washington, DC, to visit the United States Holocaust Memorial Museum. I found it difficult and painful but important to spend those hours learning about how the Nazis murdered six million Jews and so many others. Something I'd read in the past struck me while I was there, a quote from the theologian Abraham Joshua Heschel: "The question about Auschwitz is not where was God, but where was man?" I was also moved to see a full-size railcar, the kind usually used for cattle, similar to those in which Nazis forcibly transported Jews to death camps.

I had endured my own horrendous struggles. In my years living under Communism, I had seen how cruel human beings could be to each other. In escaping the Communist regime, I had been packed onto a boat in awful conditions and had faced pirates who were intent on taking advantage of people in the most desperate circumstances. All the while, I had been aware of what was going on nearby in Cambodia, where Pol Pot's regime murdered between 1.5 million and 2 million people from 1975 to 1979 in the killing fields. What I had come to learn was that terrible things keep happening. Humans have the capacity to do great harm, to wreak horrific destruction. But in the midst of the most appalling situations, there are also heroes like Dr. King, Mother Teresa, and Nelson Mandela, who help people survive against all odds. History keeps repeating itself, but humanity manages to emerge in the darkest places.

As a corporate officer, I didn't have much spare time on business trips, but one morning on a different visit to Washington, DC, I woke up early, dressed in suit and tie, and asked the bellhop to hail me a cab.

"To the Vietnam Memorial," I told him. He drove me to a spot on the National Mall, and I stepped out and asked the driver to wait for me. "I'll just be a few minutes," I said. He nodded, and I looked across the Mall and spotted the memorial, that V-shaped cut in the earth lined with black granite slabs bearing the names of more than fifty-eight thousand American service members who had given their lives. I approached the first panel, where the two sides of the memorial met. There, fifteen rows from the top, I found the name I was looking for: Kenneth N. Good, my friend Jim's uncle, who had died in the Battle of Ap Bac, the same battle where my own Uncle Bac had fought on the same side.

At that early hour, I was one of the few people at the memorial. I stood quietly and said a prayer thanking Captain Good for making the ultimate sacrifice in defense of South Vietnam's freedom. Then I walked back toward the street and found my cab. The driver sped me back to my hotel, just in time for my breakfast meeting.

The Past Comes Back in Surprising Ways

In 1998, I was on a business trip to Memphis, Tennessee, when I picked up a copy of *USA Today* and saw a front-page picture with a familiar face. Taking a closer look, I realized that it was my beloved high school teacher, Mr. Hoat! The article explained that he had endured repeated arrests and the Communist government had imprisoned him multiple times in re-education camps because of his status as an intellectual, his American education, and his demands for democracy and free elections. After a concerted international effort, the Vietnamese government had released Mr. Hoat from prison and expelled him from the country. The US granted him asylum and he settled near Washington, DC

Not long after that, Roger, my fraternity brother from Pacific University, sent me a copy of the alumni magazine from Catholic University of America, where he had attended law school. The cover story was on Catholic University's scholar in residence: Mr. Hoat! Roger remembered my talking about Mr. Hoat. What a small world.

Several years later, a Portland friend who had also known Mr. Hoat told me that Mr. Hoat would be coming to town. He invited me to join them at a Vietnamese restaurant. We recognized each other immediately, though he certainly looked older and weaker, with his thinning, gray hair. He couldn't believe it had been more than three decades since we had seen each other in Saigon.

Over bowls of *pho*, the Vietnamese noodle soup, we reminisced and caught up. I congratulated him for winning many awards, including the CPJ International Press Freedom Award and the Robert F. Kennedy Human Rights Award. Mr. Hoat asked me about my many attempts to escape Communist Vietnam. With humility, I told him that I, too, had endured painful experiences, but I had not been arrested or imprisoned, as he had. It felt so good to re-connect with this important figure from my youth.

★ ★ ★ ★ ★

My past came back in other ways, too. While the nightmares I suffered in my first months back in the United States eventually subsided, I still sometimes wake up in the middle of the night, and my mind often goes to those terrible last moments with my father. Anything can trigger a reaction: a violent scene in a movie or television show, a particular sound, a news report of a terrorist stabbing. Suddenly I am back there, on the river, in the darkness.

Then there are people I had hoped I had left behind. One Sunday in 2016, I was driving with Cathy when her cell phone rang. I heard only her end of the conversation, in Vietnamese. Someone from out of town was planning a visit to Portland. The person would be staying with relatives. Cathy shared our home address, then hung up.

"Who was that?" I asked.

"Nam's friend Phat. He's going to be in Portland."

Phat. Cathy's brother's friend. The one whose uncle had promised us a place on a boat out of Vietnam. The one who had told us to meet him in the restaurant—and then never showed up. The one who, four decades earlier, had helped swindle me out of a precious tael of gold.

"You gave him our address?" I asked, incredulous.

Somehow, Cathy didn't remember what Phat had done to us. She had moved on, but I hadn't forgotten.

The next day, Monday, Cathy was at work and I was home, preparing for a class I would be teaching that evening, when the doorbell rang. I opened the front door to find Phat standing on the other side of the screen door. His face looked the same, just four decades older. I left the screen door closed between Phat and me.

"Hello," he said.

I hesitated. "You had an uncle you once introduced me to," I said. "How's he doing?"

"He's dead," Phat said flatly. I could see his mind working, thinking back a few decades.

"Do you remember that you and he cheated me out of a tael of gold?" I asked.

Phat didn't answer. Was it possible that he had actually forgotten the entire incident, how he'd told us to be at the restaurant near the highway to Vung Tau and had left us waiting, desperate, our hopes shattered? After all, if he remembered, why would he come to my house? Maybe he had simply planned a trip to Portland and figured he would say hello to his old friend's sister. But *I* remembered. And in that moment, it all came flooding back—my desperate efforts to escape from Saigon. The pilot and the trip to Rach Gia. The Filipino and the phony papers. The night my father was murdered and Cathy and I nearly drowned. I looked at Phat, this phantom from my past, standing in my doorway in the suburbs.

"Why are you here? You cheated me when I was desperate," I said. He was silent. "You're not welcome in my home," I said. "Goodbye."

I watched Phat turn around, walk back to the street, and get into a car that then pulled away. And I thought about how the past is at once so far away and so very close.

Some occasions bring my new life and old lives together. Some of my dearest memories from my youth are of the annual Tet celebrations (with the notable exception of the 1968 Tet Offensive). In our new lives in Oregon, Cathy and I developed a custom of holding a Lunar New Year party each year, inviting friends, colleagues, and neighbors over for Vietnamese food. On the fiftieth anniversary of the Tet Offensive, the party included a special person: my Johnstone colleague Jerry Quilling. In the midst of the celebration, I announced that I wished to honor Jerry, a veteran tank commander and Purple Heart recipient who had suffered a major injury half a century ago in my hometown of Saigon. Moved by Jerry's sacrifice, every guest shook his hand and signed a thank-you card for him.

Part Eight

Giving Back

A Lifetime of Libraries

At nearly every important moment on my journey through life, there has been a library.

As a teenager, I discovered the Abraham Lincoln Library in Saigon, where I perused *Time* and *Life* magazines and taught myself English as I made use of the side-by-side translations and enjoyed the air-conditioning and chilled water.

When Cathy and I learned that USAID would be sending us to Pacific University, one of my first stops was the map room of one of the Georgetown University libraries, where a librarian helped me thumb through an atlas and locate Forest Grove, Oregon.

At Pacific University, the library was where I struggled through *Goodbye, Columbus*, dictionary in hand, and where I would escape to (and occasionally nap) when the social life of the dorm became too distracting. Just outside the library, Cathy noticed my smile in a moment that ultimately led to our love and marriage.

At Berkeley, where I lived most of the time in a tiny boardinghouse room, Moffitt Library served as the comfortable spot where I could spread out and study.

When I was desperate to flee Saigon after the Communists took over, it was a library worker from the Abraham Lincoln Library who snuck me a map from a *National Geographic* magazine to help chart the route from Rach Gia to Malaysia. (Though the pilot made off with that map, studying it gave me insight that served us on our journey across the Gulf of Thailand.)

At the Pulau Bidong refugee camp, desperate for reading material, I asked virtually every visiting English speaker to leave books or magazines and gradually helped to build up a library in the least likely of places.

When I settled back in Portland, my first job—tutoring for Upward Bound—was at Multnomah County's Central Library, which was also where I perused the *Oregonian*'s want ads and spent months reading back issues of *Time* to catch up on the five years of news I had missed. (Back then, I was often stumped by *Jeopardy* questions in the "late 1970s" category.)

When I needed to research a tax issue for my job at Johnstone, I sometimes visited the library at Lewis and Clark College's law school.

And on my travels for Johnstone and since retirement, I have savored the opportunity to visit nearly every presidential library, honoring these important men whose actions had such a profound impact and gaining a new perspective on history.

Perhaps it is because libraries have figured so prominently in my life that when I wanted to find a way to give back, I did so through a library.

I have learned that when you reach a certain age, you find yourself attending more and more funerals. In recent years, Cathy and I have done so all too often. One thing I have never seen is a U-Haul truck following the hearse to the cemetery. In other words, no matter how much wealth you accumulate in life, you can't take it with you.

With that in mind, a few years ago Cathy and I began discussing how to give away a good portion of our estate. We considered various organizations that were important to both of us, and one institution emerged as the most significant to the lives we have built: Pacific University. Pacific was where we met, where we formed many dear and life-long friendships, where our American college educations began. Pacific was where I became a teacher for Upward Bound, and "Pacific University, Oregon" was the address my sister Thao wrote on the envelope she sent to Paul Hebb from the Wake Island refugee center in 1975.

Cathy and I decided that we wanted our legacy to be a library at Pacific University. Pacific already had a library, of course, but we arranged to create an endowment that would support the library's operations for many years to come.

On the Friday of Pacific's homecoming weekend in October 2017, a crowd gathered for the dedication of the Tim & Cathy Tran Library.

I also made one request of the university that was just as important to me as any other part of the library. I asked that the library include plaques in areas honoring three other people: Professor George Evans, my English professor; his wife Donna, who had extended such hospitality to us as students; and, of course, Bobbi Nickels, whose generosity and caring had proved so transformative for our family in so many ways. My father taught me always to express gratitude and try to repay debts. When the university agreed to my requests, I felt an overwhelming sense of satisfaction.

That morning, Bobbi was in the audience, as were Professor Evans and Donna. So were a number of my Pacific classmates, some of whom I hadn't seen in four decades. Looking out across the campus that day, I couldn't help but think back on that day in June 1970 when I first set foot in Forest Grove and everyone wanted to show me around.

Standing at a podium, I recounted how Cathy and I had begun our college education at Pacific with Professor Evans's American literature class. Looking at my easygoing professor, I couldn't resist injecting some humor: "When we first met him, Dr. Evans had long, dark hair. Yes, it's true. He was a hippie at that time. I'm a little concerned that his hair now is thinner and gray, he is a little older and slower, and his memory is not as sharp as it used to be. Don't you worry! Just remember, old professors never die, they just lose their faculties." The audience burst into laughter.

On a more serious note, I recalled returning from Forest Grove to Saigon full of hopes and dreams and then seeing them dashed, and how Bobbi had worked so tirelessly trying to get us out.

"An old proverb says a journey of a thousand miles begins with a single step," I said. "I took that first step escaping Communism in 1979. And where and when will the final step be? My answer: I just took the final step right here, in front of this library, this beautiful building. To me, personally, coming here today and attending this dedication is the completion of a long journey of thirty-eight years and more than ten thousand miles. I'm glad it ended right here."

That day, I felt proud and nostalgic and grateful all at once. Even standing there in front of all of those people and celebrating our gift, it was difficult to remember just how far I had come.

That's why I had made one more donation to Pacific. Besides the plaques bearing Cathy's and my names and the special plaques honoring Professor Evans, Donna, and Bobbi, I left another item to be displayed in the library, something one might not expect to see in a library.

It was the handmade stove I'd been given by Big Fat Eight.

It was important to me that the stove be displayed at the library because it reminds me of my roots, my time as a penniless, homeless refugee—a man without a country. The stove signifies one of the lowest moments of my life. But even within that awful period, there were pleasures.

To this day, when I wake up every morning, the first thing I do is make myself a cup of coffee. In Saigon, too, I started each day with a cup of coffee or tea. Even on Pulau Bidong, I enjoyed a cup of tea in the morning, thanks to the kindness of my friend Big Fat Eight. Those quiet mornings were momentary pleasures in the midst of a difficult period. The stove reminds me of those lovely, shared moments.

It also inspires humility. Many successful people forget where they came from. They lose track of their past. I kept the stove, crafted from discarded food-ration cans, as a reminder over the years that no matter how high I rose in the corporate world, no matter how comfortable a lifestyle I achieved, I should always remember my darkest days.

I hope that when students look at that curious artifact, they'll be reminded that you cannot separate yourself from your past. It's always a part of you. Your story is what made you who and what you are. I'm proud to leave a legacy with two parts: The first is the Tim & Cathy Tran Library. The second is this story.

DEDICATED OCTOBER 2017

TIM & CATHY TRAN LIBRARY

Tim (Khiem) and Cathy (Thuy) Tran, citizens of South Vietnam,
were awarded scholarships to attend college in America. One of
the requirements of the scholarship was they had to return to their
home country, bringing their new knowledge and skills with them.
They enrolled at Pacific University in 1970, where the faculty and
the library became our gift to them, the gift of free inquiry.

Honoring their earlier commitments, they returned to South Vietnam
after graduation in 1974, and after only a few months, saw their
country overrun by communist forces. Suspected of American
sympathies, they found life becoming more difficult and dangerous.
They had to escape, and finally they did in 1979 on a small,
overloaded boat that was attacked by sea pirates in the gulf of
Thailand. Surviving months in a chaotic Malaysian refugee camp,
they finally arrived in their new home in Oregon.

After years of outstanding success in the business world,
Tim and Cathy decided to repay the gift they received so many years
before. In the spirit of giving that animates both of their lives,
they chose Pacific's Library as the recipient of their gratitude.
It was a fitting conclusion to the inspiring story of these
two Americans' giving back to their adopted country.

— WRITTEN BY GEORGE EVANS —

Text of the plaque written by Dr. George Evans that now hangs inside main entrance of the Tim & Cathy Tran Library.

IN HONOR OF DR. GEORGE & DONNA EVANS

Professor Emeritus George Evans taught
language and literature at Pacific University
when Khiem "Tim" '74 and Thuy "Cathy" Tran '74
arrived as students. He and his wife, Donna,
opened their hearts and home to the
young students and later became close friends
as the Trans resettled in the United States.

This section of the Tran Library is dedicated to
the refuge, support and opportunity that the
Evanses helped make possible and honors
their legacy at Pacific University.

An area of the Tim & Cathy Tran Library was dedicated in 2017 to Dr. George and Donna Evans in recognition of their friendship and support. A plaque with this text hangs in the area.

IN HONOR OF ROBERTA "BOBBI" NICKELS '70

As an administrator of Pacific University's
Upward Bound, Bobbi Nickels '70 worked with
Khiem "Tim" Tran '74 when he was a math teacher
for Upward Bound. Later, as Director of Upward Bound,
Bobbi was a dedicated advocate for both
Tim and Thuy "Cathy" Tran '74 as they attempted to
escape communist South Vietnam. She opened her
home to the Tran family and was there to welcome them
when they resettled in the United States.

This section of the Tran Library is dedicated to
the refuge, support and opportunity that
Ms. Nickels helped make possible and honors
her legacy at Pacific University.

Another area of the Tim & Cathy Tran Library was dedicated in honor of Bobbi Nickels, with the above plaque to recognize her support of our family.

Epilogue

In July 2017, our family gathered at a spot on the Oregon coast to remember my mother, who had died a year earlier at the age of ninety-one in a memory-care facility in Oregon.

My mother was the calmest person I knew. She lived through decades of political turmoil, and when the rest of us were panicking, she kept her cool. She made shrewd decisions. In the days leading up to the fall of Saigon, she didn't panic; she began stockpiling food—rice, dried meat, anything that would keep. She knew the war against the Communists might be drawn out, and we would always need to eat.

While the rest of us worked desperately to flee the country, she was content to stay. She had seen so much in her life that she didn't fear what might come. Her work selling PX goods on the gray market helped her to develop a shrewd aptitude for judging people and evaluating options with a cool head. When my own judgment was clouded, she was able to see with a clarity that saved my life and the lives of our entire family.

After all of that, it was difficult to watch her in her final years as she lost her independence, her intellect, her capacities, and, eventually, her identity. Once, near the end, Cathy was visiting and Mom asked, "When is my husband coming?" She had forgotten that my father had been gone for many, many years.

That July Sunday, we spread some of her ashes in the waves of the Pacific, and I imagined her soul finding its way across the ocean and back to Ho Doi, her village on the northern coast of Vietnam, the place where she grew up and met my father. And I hoped she had found some peace.

Of course, giving my mother that fitting tribute brought to mind my father, who never received a proper memorial.

It was my father, who was largely self-educated, who instilled in me the value of education and hard work. Before I ever went to school, he drilled me in reading and writing and math. I was ahead of my classmates from the beginning because my father saw some potential in me and gave me advanced homework to do, even when my teachers didn't. Without that push, I would never have become the student I was, would never have earned the scholarship to study in America, would never have created the life I have achieved.

My father also inspired my work ethic, which served me all the way through school and my career. "If you start something, finish it," he would say, "and do it well." At Pacific, sometimes I would hear classmates talk about their more challenging classes. "All I want to do is get a C in the class—I just need to pass," they would say. That was never an option for me. I worked as hard as possible and always did my best.

Finally, my father gave me a moral compass and told me to be honest in everything I do. "Your standing in society depends on how much people trust you," he would tell me. I lived through painful and difficult times, when society was breaking down and, in their desperation, people made moral compromises. But I always remembered my father's words, and I never betrayed my integrity.

Vietnamese fathers were not generally known for their warmth and emotional openness. Even when I left to spend four years in America, my father didn't come to the airport to see me off. That morning, he simply urged me to study hard, get good grades, and write home. No hugs, no kisses.

Sometimes I wonder what my father would have thought about the life I have managed to build in America. I think he would have approved. He would have been proud of what I have accomplished, but he would never have said so. If he were here today to see my life, he might have a tiny smile on his face, not a big grin. He would approve, but he wouldn't come out and say so. That wasn't his way.

As I look back on my life, it's clear that fate had a hand at every turn. I benefited from parents who pushed me from an early age to succeed. I was lucky to earn a scholarship to America and to be sent to, of all places, Pacific University in Forest Grove, Oregon. I had to move across the world to meet my future wife, Cathy. It felt miraculous to secure a place on the boat from Rach Gia, and even more so to survive the perilous journey. Fate landed me in a refugee camp where my skills were needed, and fate had me turn down one job offer and accept another, which led to meeting my mentor, Mr. John M. Shank, and to a fulfilling and rewarding career.

Of course, if fate had a role in the high points, then clearly it also played a hand in the more difficult moments: when the bus driver gave up on reaching the airport on April 29, 1975; the four failed escapes; the murder of my father.

Believing in fate can lessen pain. It can also keep our heads from getting too big by reminding us that we don't control everything.

In Vietnamese Confucian philosophy, fate comprises two factors. The first is the individual's own actions. The second is an invisible force that propels a person into a particular situation. All of my efforts—my studies, my preparation, my research, my social skills—contributed to my successful career. But all along, I also benefited from something else, an invisible force that I attribute to the spirit of my father. I feel his presence in much of what I do.

I don't think my father could have imagined what I have been able to experience in my life. I have traveled America and the world. Cathy and I have visited most of America's national parks and presidential libraries. We've made multiple trips to Europe. We've gone on a three-week Amazon cruise and have been to a dozen Caribbean countries. We've taken a bus tour around the British Isles. We've been to St. Petersburg, Russia, to the Scandinavian countries, to Western Europe, and to Australia.

My favorite trips have been to the national parks: Acadia, Arches, Yellowstone, Yosemite, Bryce Canyon, Grand Canyon, Sequoia, Great Smoky Mountains, Everglades, and many more. Cathy sometimes complains that I'm not careful to look where I'm walking—I'm too busy gazing at the animals, the views, the incredible natural wonders. Together we have seen things we couldn't have dreamed of: geysers gushing from the ground, thousand-year-old trees, huge stone arches. After the ups and downs of my life, I cherish the peace and quiet, the opportunity to be away from civilization, to be in nature.

With all of my travels, there is one place I have no desire to go: Vietnam. Returning to Vietnam would bring back too many painful memories of the worst period of my life. Of course, everyone prefers to remember the pleasant and forget what is painful. But the painful parts will always be a part of me.

I cannot imagine standing in front of my old house, where Cathy and I lived right after our simple marriage ceremony, and being reminded that some Communist official seized it after we left everything intact to escape to Rach Gia in 1979.

I cannot imagine standing outside and looking into my parents' home, which was confiscated by Communist authorities after my mother and Binh emigrated to the US.

My heart would sink if I stood in front of the beautiful building formerly known as Cong Ty Shell Viet Nam, where I started my promising career only to have the Communist regime unceremoniously fire me in 1976 because I had earned a college degree in America.

I would feel a tremendous sense of sadness if I went to the Mekong Delta, remembering my wife Cathy's uncle, the intellectual and gentle Dr. Tao, who hanged himself after suffering for years in the re-education camps and encountering more mistreatment when he returned home.

My heart would hurt terribly if I stood on the banks of the Saigon River, looking at the body of water that has held the remains of my father since he was murdered in 1977.

It would pain me to visit the Bien Hoa Military Cemetery and see that what had once been a sacred resting place for South Vietnamese soldiers has been damaged and neglected.

No, I don't want to visit Vietnam. My home is America. My country is the United States of America.

I do sometimes wonder what my fate would have been if I hadn't managed to escape Vietnam. I probably would have served some jail time for my efforts to flee, or for being suspected of being a CIA agent, or just for having an American college degree. But they couldn't have held me forever; I was not a dissident or a democratic activist, nor was I involved in any attempt to overthrow the Communist regime. Just as Soviet Jews during the Cold War wanted to emigrate to America or Israel, I simply wanted to get out of Communist Vietnam and move to the United States. *I just wanted to get the hell out.*

Had I failed to escape Vietnam, I would probably have built a modest career teaching English or working as a tour guide for English-speaking tourists. Maybe I'd have a website advertising my services and my Cal Berkeley degree. I would take visiting international tourists to Vietnam's attractions: the tunnels of Cu Chi; the former Presidential Palace, where a North Vietnamese tank crashed the gate in April 1975; the Imperial City of Hue, the Mekong Delta, the resort city of Nha Trang, and other sites.

I would support myself on cash tips, trading dollars or euros on the black market to increase my income. And I would ask every tourist if they had brought along any books that they didn't want to haul back home. With all of those volumes, I could build my own library.

I'm grateful that that wasn't my fate, that I made it to America, the land of opportunity, that I built a modestly successful career and a successful life, that I have many dear friends, and that I have had the opportunity to give back.

I hope people will remember me as an American, a naturalized citizen of the United States of America who, through hard work and determination, overcame most of the difficulties and hardships that were thrown my way, who attained some modest success and had the opportunity to give back. I will be forever grateful to the country that I adopted and that adopted me, and to all of the people who helped me along the way, including my professors, college friends, my mentors, and my business associates. Fate has truly blessed me.

I do have one regret. I have managed to repay the financial debts I owed my friends. But I have not found a way to repay the tremendous debt of gratitude I owe America. I have often heard people say, "It's great to serve your country!" I would love to have the opportunity to serve my country, the United States of America, because I feel so fortunate to have a great country to serve.

Acronyms

AID	Agency for International Development
ARVN	Army of the Republic of Vietnam
AWOL	Absent without leave
CFO	Chief Financial Officer
CIA	Central Intelligence Agency
CIA	Certified Internal Auditor
MAAGV	Military Assistance Advisory Group—Vietnam
MACV	Military Assistance Command—Vietnam
POW	Prisoner of War
PX	Post exchange, a retail store on US military bases
UNHCR	United Nations High Commission for Refugees, the UN refugee agency
USAID	United States Agency for International Development
USIS	United States Information Service
TOEFL	Test of English as a Foreign Language
VAA	Vietnamese American Association

Chronology

This listing includes some events not directly related to the story for the sake of historical context. It starts with the founding of the Nguyen dynasty in 1802 and ends with the re-establishment of diplomatic relations between the Socialist Republic of Vietnam and the United States in 1995. Entries for the period that is the focus of this book, 1954-1979, include more details than other entries.

1802

- Emperor Gia Long unifies Vietnam and establishes the Nguyen dynasty.

1859-1861

- French forces capture Saigon and begin the colonization of Indochina (Vietnam, Cambodia, and Laos).

1890

- Ho Chi Minh is born in Nghe An Province in central Vietnam.

1911

- Ho Chi Minh leaves Vietnam aboard a steamer, where he spent three years traveling the world as a cook. He then settled in London from 1915-17, moved to France in 1917, and left there for Moscow at the end of 1923.

1924

- Ho leaves Moscow for Canton, China, a Communist stronghold.

1930

- Ho forms the Indochinese Communist party.

1940

- France falls to Germany in World War II.
- Japan forces occupy Indochina.

1941

- Ho returns to Vietnam from China and forms the Viet Minh to fight both the French and the Japanese for Vietnam's independence.

1945

- Ho declares the independence of Vietnam as Democratic Republic of Vietnam, Emperor Bao Dai abdicates.
- Japanese forces replace the French administration.
- Japan surrenders after the US drops atomic bombs in August.
- Nationalist Chinese forces enter northern Vietnam, as agreed upon by Allied forces during the Potsdam Conference in order to disarm the Japanese.
- British forces land in southern Vietnam for the same purpose.
- French soldiers arrive in southern Vietnam to retake control of Vietnam, Laos, and Cambodia as agreed upon at the Potsdam Conference.

1946

- French negotiate with China to replace Chinese troops in northern Vietnam.
- French troops land in Hai Phong and re-establish their control of northern Vietnam.
- Viet Minh forces attack French forces in Hanoi.
- Ho and Viet Minh forces withdraw from Hanoi and start guerrilla warfare against the French. The First Indochina War begins.

1947

- Emperor Bao Dai, then living in exile in Hong Kong, offers to negotiate with France to achieve Vietnam's independence.

1949-1950

- Bao Dai reaches an agreement with France recognizing Vietnam as a state in the French Union.
- Mao Zedong and the People's Liberation Army achieve complete victory over Chiang Kai Shek's Nationalist forces.
- With help from Chinese forces under the new Communist leader, Viet Minh forces drive the French from the border region to establish their base and begin to receive large amounts of weapons from China. Viet Minh forces transform from a guerrilla force into a conventional army.
- Ho's Democratic Republic of Vietnam (DRV) is recognized by the Soviet Union and China.
- Bao Dai's State of Vietnam is recognized by the United States and Britain.
- The US Defense Attaché Office (DAO) is established in Saigon.
- President Truman sends the Military Assistance Advisory Group (MAAG) as well as assistance in the form of military equipment and finance to help the French.

1951

- Ho Chi Minh establishes the Lao Dong (Workers) Party to replace the Communist Party.

1952

- Dwight Eisenhower is elected President of the United States.

1953

- Soviet leader Joseph Stalin dies.

- Armistice agreement is agreed to, putting an end to the Korean War, in which 2.5 million people died.
- French forces occupy Dien Bien Phu.
- Viet Minh forces prepare for the battle of Dien Bien Phu.

1954

- The Viet Minh forces defeat the French at Dien Bien Phu.
- Geneva Conference on Indochina starts.
- France grants independence to Laos and Cambodia as part of the Geneva Accords.
- Geneva Accords divides Vietnam at the 17th parallel, pending a nation-wide election to be held in 1956. North Vietnam is controlled by Ho Chi Minh and the Communists. South Vietnam is under the control of the nationalists. The United States and South Vietnam (or State of Vietnam, to be later known as the Republic of Vietnam) do not directly sign onto or accept the agreement.
- Ngo Dinh Diem is appointed as prime minister of the Republic of Vietnam by Bao Dai, who lives in Paris and remains South Vietnam's Chief of State.
- About 900,000 refugees flee from North to South Vietnam with help from the US Navy and the French Navy. About 52,000 Communists regroup and move from South to North Vietnam.

1955

- The United States provides economic and military aid for South Vietnam. President Eisenhower deploys the Military Assistance Advisory Group (MAAG) to train South Vietnam troops. This is considered the official beginning of American involvement in the Vietnam War.
- Ho Chi Minh accepts aid from the Soviet Union and China.
- Ngo Dinh Diem refuses to hold a nationwide election.
- Diem overthrows Bao Dai in a referendum, becoming President of the Republic of Vietnam.
- North Vietnam launches a land reform campaign, actually an "anti-landlord" campaign.

1956

- President Diem begins repression of suspected Communists and political dissidents.
- The last French troops leave Vietnam.

1958

- Communist guerrillas begin attacks on South Vietnam's rural hamlet and village officials.

1959

- North Vietnam begins infiltrating fighters and weapons into South Vietnam via the Ho Chi Minh trail.

1960

- John F. Kennedy is elected president of the United States.
- Coup attempt against President Diem by South Vietnamese paratroopers fails.
- National Liberation Front (NLF, aka Viet Cong) was formed.

1961

- US Vice President Lyndon Johnson visits South Vietnam.
- US President Kennedy sends US Special Forces personnel to Vietnam to train South Vietnamese—to become known as the Army of the Republic of Vietnam, or ARVN.
- President Kennedy increases military aid and the number of advisors to South Vietnam.

1962

- Military Assistance Command for Vietnam (MACV) is formed to replace MAAG.

- Vietnam Air Force (VNAF) officers fail in their attempted assassination of Diem by bombing the presidential palace.
- International Agreement on the Neutrality of Laos is signed in Geneva.
- US planes begin spraying herbicides and defoliants (Agent Orange) in South Vietnam (codename Operation Ranch Hand) to destroy forests and crops used by the North Vietnamese and the Viet Cong.

1963

- Viet Cong guerrillas win a major battle against American-equipped ARVN forces at Ap Bac.
- South Vietnamese ARVN shoot at Buddhist demonstrators in Hue. The anti-Diem Buddhist crisis begins with demonstrations in major cities. Buddhist monk Thich Quang Duc burns himself to death in protest.
- General Duong Van "Big" Minh leads a successful coup against Diem, killing Diem and his brother Nhu.
- President Kennedy is assassinated. Lyndon Johnson becomes president.
- The number of US military personnel in South Vietnam reaches 17,000.

1964

- Numerous coups are attempted by South Vietnamese generals. Numerous governments form and fall over the next year. South Vietnam enters a politically unstable period.
- North Vietnamese patrol boats attack the destroyer USS Maddox in the Gulf of Tonkin in August. In retaliation, American aircraft start bombing North Vietnam.
- US Congress passes the Gulf of Tonkin resolution, giving President Johnson special powers to act in Southeast Asia.
- Lyndon Johnson is elected president.

1965

- The first sustained US bombing of North Vietnam occurs under Operation Rolling Thunder.
- General Nguyen Khanh takes control of the government of South Vietnam.

- US sends its first combat troops to Vietnam: US Marines land on China Beach to defend Da Nang.
- Major General Nguyen Van Thieu becomes chief of state and Air Vice-Marshal Nguyen Cao Ky takes over as prime minister.
- American combat troops in Vietnam reach almost 200,000.

1966

- US bombing of North Vietnam increases, with higher intensity.
- American combat troops in Vietnam reach almost 400,000.

1967

- Nguyen Van Thieu is elected president and Nguyen Cao Ky is elected vice president of South Vietnam.
- American combat troops in Vietnam reach almost 500,000 by year end.
- Anti-war demonstrations ramp up in the US.

1968

- North Vietnamese and Viet Cong forces attack South Vietnam cities and towns in the Tet Offensive.
- North Vietnamese and American begin peace talk in Paris.
- President Johnson announces that he will not seek re-election.
- Martin Luther King is assassinated.
- Richard Nixon wins the Republican nomination for president.
- Hubert Humphrey wins the Democratic nomination for president.
- Richard Nixon is elected president of the US.
- Anti-war protests strengthen in the US and Europe.

1969

- Peace talks in Paris expand to include the South Vietnamese and the Viet Cong.
- US begins to withdraw combat troops from Vietnam.
- Henry Kissinger, Nixon's national security advisor, has secret meetings

with North Vietnamese's Le Duc Tho in Paris.
- Ho Chi Minh dies in Hanoi.
- Massive anti-war demonstrations take place in Washington D.C. and other cities.
- US continues to withdraw combat troops from Vietnam—reduced by some 115,000 men by the end of the year.

1970

- American and South Vietnamese forces attack Communist bases in Cambodia, prompting large anti-war demonstrations across the US.
- American troop levels in Vietnam reduce to 280,000 by year end.

1971

- South Vietnamese troops begin incursions into Laos to cut off the Ho Chi Minh supply trails.
- Kissinger goes to Beijing to prepare for Nixon's visit to China.
- Nguyen Van Thieu runs unopposed and is re-elected president of South Vietnam.
- American troop levels in Vietnam reduce to just under 160,000 by year end.

1972

- President Nixon visits China.
- North Vietnamese troops open a major offensive called the Easter or Eastertide Offensive (US) or Red Fiery Summer Offensive (South Vietnam).
- Kissinger goes to Moscow to prepare for Nixon's visit to the Soviet Union.
- Nixon visits the Soviet Union.
- The Watergate scandal begins with several burglars arrested in the Watergate complex in Washington, D.C.
- Kissinger and Le Duc Tho reach a peace agreement to end the war. Kissinger declares "peace is at hand."

- President Thieu opposes the draft peace agreement and refuses to sign.
- Nixon is re-elected president in a landslide.
- Kissinger and Le Duc Tho resume negotiations, but they soon break down.
- Nixon orders the Christmas bombing of Hanoi and Hai Phong.

1973

- Kissinger and Le Duc Tho resume talks, reaching a final agreement.
- A cease-fire agreement is formally signed by the US, North Vietnam, South Vietnam and the Viet Cong in Paris.
- All American troops leave South Vietnam and all American POWs are released in Hanoi.
- Kissinger is named US Secretary of State.
- Gerald Ford becomes US vice president, replacing Spiro Agnew, who resigned.

1974

- Chinese naval forces attack South Vietnamese garrison and naval ships at the Paracel Islands in January. Chinese forces occupy the islands.
- US House Judiciary Committee starts impeachment hearings for President Nixon and votes to recommend impeaching him.
- North Vietnam begins building up their forces in South Vietnam in preparation for a major offensive the following year.
- Nixon resigns and Ford becomes president.

1975

- Communist forces capture Phuoc Long province north of Saigon in January to test the US reaction; there is no response from the Americans.
- Communist forces capture Ban Me Thuot province in the central highland in March, again with no response from the US.
- President Thieu orders South Vietnamese forces and civilians to evacuate from the highland provinces to more defensible positions in the coastal areas and the south.
- Hue, the imperial capital, and Da Nang, the second-largest city in South

Vietnam, fall to the Communists in March.

- The Khmer Rouge in Cambodia achieve total victory by capturing Phnom Penh in April, establishing Democratic Kampuchea. Pol Pot becomes prime minister.
- Communist forces sweep through the northern provinces of South Vietnam virtually unopposed in their push toward Saigon.
- President Thieu resigns and leaves for Taiwan. Vice president Tran Van Huong becomes president.
- The Battle of Xuan Loc, the last major battle of the Vietnam War, is fought in April. After two weeks of fighting, North Vietnamese forces capture Xuan Loc and their gateway to Saigon is wide open.
- President Ford declares that the Vietnam War is "finished" as far as the US is concerned.
- By late April, Saigon is encircled by North Vietnamese soldiers. Huong resigns and is succeeded by General Duong Van Minh late April.
- Americans and South Vietnamese refugees are evacuated from Saigon by helicopters.
- Communist forces enter the presidential palace in Saigon, and President Duong Van Minh surrenders. The last Americans—10 marines—leave Saigon. The war ends with Communist victory on April 30, 1975.
- America imposes economic and trade embargoes on Communist Vietnam.
- *May*: The Communist government orders hundreds of thousands of former South Vietnamese military personnel, government bureaucrats, and civilians, including teachers, to present themselves and register.
- *June*: The Communist government orders former South Vietnamese military personnel and government bureaucrats to report for re-education: (a) enlisted men and non-commissioned officers to attend three days of re-education from June 11 to June 13; (b) officers with ranks of captain and below to attend 10 days of re-education beginning on June 23; (c) officers with rank of major and above, including generals, to attend one month of re-education beginning June 23.
- *June*: Hundreds of thousands of enlisted men and non-commission officers participate in a three-day re-education course and are then released. This leads the former ARVN (Army of the Republic of Vietnam) officers to believe that they will also be released after their 10-day or one-month of re-education.

- *June*: Former South Vietnamese officers report for re-education as required. They and their families anticipate that they will return home after 10 days or a month, depending on their rank. Ten days and a month go by and no one receives any news about these officers. The truth is that high ranking officers were sent to prison camps in the north, and others were sent to remote prison camps in the south. Some are finally released after three years. Some spend ten years or more in the prison camps.
- *August*: The Communist government closes private banks.
- *September*: The Communist government declares South Vietnamese Treasury Notes and Bills null and void.
- *September*: The Communist government launches Operation "X-2" to arrest Chinese merchants in Saigon and confiscate their property, including cash, gold, foreign currencies, and diamonds.
- *September*: The Communist government declares South Vietnamese monetary unit, the piasters, null and void, requiring everyone to exchange old piasters for new Communist currencies subject to a set limitation under code name "X-3."

1976

- Jimmy Carter is elected president.
- The Communist government arrests writers, authors, poets, composers, former newspapermen, film directors, producers, intellectuals, religious leaders, and others.
- The Communist government intensifies their anti-ethnic Chinese activities in Saigon, arresting more Chinese merchants and confiscating their property.
- *July 2*: Vietnam is officially unified and renamed Socialist Republic of Vietnam, with its capital in Hanoi.
- Saigon is renamed Ho Chi Minh City.
- The Lao Dong (Workers) Party changes its name to the Communist Party of Vietnam (CPV).
- The National Liberation Front (NLF aka Viet Cong) is dissolved.
- Hanoi forces more than 600,000 Saigon residents into internal exile by relocating to "new economic zones" set up in undeveloped thick jungle areas to clear land and increase agricultural output.

- Vietnam's economy collapses, inflation reaches triple figures, and there are severe shortages of food and basic necessities.
- Vietnam adopts the Five-Year Economic Plan, modelled after the Soviet planned economy with goals of developing heavy industries and collectivization of agriculture.
- Tension between Vietnam and Cambodia increases as border skirmishes occur regularly.
- Tension between Vietnam and China increases.

1977

- Small-scale fighting between Vietnam and Cambodia continues along their border.
- Socialist Republic of Vietnam is admitted to the United Nations.

1978

- Vuot bien (crossing the border) reaches its highest level: over a million ethnic Chinese and Vietnamese escape by boat to Southeast Asian countries.
- *March*: A wave of nationalization of private businesses is implemented in a "private business reform," suspending all private enterprise activities; this is mainly aimed at ethnic Chinese, who own a majority of private businesses.
- *May*: China accuses the government of Vietnam of oppression, mistreatment, expelling and discrimination against the ethnic Chinese minority in Vietnam.
- *June*: The Communist Party of Vietnam, suspecting the ethnic Chinese population in Saigon of spying for China, plans to (a) force ethnic Chinese to move from Saigon to "new economic zones" or (b) allow them to flee the country by boat (the "semi-official" way) and collect their gold or foreign currencies and take over their houses and property under "Plan 2." Plan 2 also allows the ethnic Chinese to purchase or build boats for the purpose of leaving Vietnam without being subject to arrest.
- *June*: Vietnam becomes increasingly aligned with the Soviet Union by joining the Council for Mutual Economic Assistance (Comecon) and signing a Friendship Pact, a military alliance, at the displeasure of China.

- Vietnam and the Communist Khmer Rouge engage in serious border skirmishes.
- Chinese-Vietnamese relations deteriorate rapidly. Trade between China and Vietnam ceases.
- Soviet Union and Vietnam sign a mutual defense treaty.
- *December*: Vietnam launches a full-scale armed invasion of Cambodia, overthrowing Pol Pot's Khmer Rouge and creating the new People's Republic of Kampuchea.

1979

- Chinese leader Deng Xiaoping declares "Vietnam is a hooligan; we must teach them a lesson."
- *February*: China invades northern Vietnam, capturing several cities near the border provinces.
- *March*: Chinese troops withdraw from Vietnam, after declaring victory. Vietnam also claimed victory.

1981

- Vietnam remains one of the poorest countries economically in the world. It becomes clear that the Second Five-Year Plan has not achieved its goals.

1982

- At the 5th National Congress of the Communist Party of Vietnam, CPV admits shortcomings and errors in achieving its economic and social goals set in 1976 due to lack of party discipline and corruption.
- Also at the meeting, Vietnam adopts the Third Five-Year Economic Plan, which shows a move toward more market reforms and away from rigid central planning.

1985

- Vietnam faces multiple difficulties: It is internationally isolated, economically devastated, and facing worldwide condemnation for its occupation of Cambodia.

1986

- Le Duan, General Secretary of the CPV, dies.
- Nguyen Van Linh becomes General Secretary of the CPV and institutes economic reform called "Doi Moi" (renovation), which shifts from a highly centralized command economy to a "socialist-oriented market economy," disbands agricultural collectives, encourages private businesses, and promotes foreign investment and foreign-owned enterprises. The government also invested in education and infrastructure.

1989

- *September*: Vietnam withdraws its forces from Cambodia.

1991

- Vietnam re-establishes diplomatic and economic relations with most Western nations.
- Vietnam re-establishes diplomatic ties with China.

1994

- The US lifts its economic embargo against Vietnam.

1995

- Vietnam and the US normalize diplomatic relations.